The Politically Incorrect Guide® to the Presidents
Part 1: from Washington to Taft

Be sure to check out

The Politically Incorrect Guides® to...

American History
Thomas Woods
9780895260475

The Bible
Robert J. Hutchinson
9781596985209

The British Empire
H. W. Crocker III
9781596986299

Capitalism
Robert P. Murphy
9781596985049

Catholicism
John Zmirak
9781621575863

The Civil War
H. W. Crocker III
9781596985490

The Constitution
Kevin R. C. Gutzman
9781596985056

Darwinism and Intelligent Design
Jonathan Wells
9781596980136

English and American Literature
Elizabeth Kantor
9781596980112

The Founding Fathers
Brion McClanahan
9781596980921

Global Warming
Christopher C. Horner
9781596985018

The Great Depression and the New Deal
Robert Murphy
9781596980969

Hunting
Frank Miniter
9781596985216

Islam (And the Crusades)
Robert Spencer
9780895260130

Jihad
William Kilpatrick
9781621575771

The Middle East
Martin Sieff
9781596980518

The Presidents, Part 2
Steven F. Hayward
9781621575795

Real American Heroes
Brion McClanahan
9781596983205

Science
Tom Bethell
9780895260314

The Sixties
Jonathan Leaf
9781596985728

Socialism
Kevin D. Williamson
9781596986497

The South (And Why It Will Rise Again)
Clint Johnson
9781596985001

The Vietnam War
Phillip Jennings
9781596985674

Western Civilization
Anthony Esolen
9781596980594

Women, Sex, and Feminism
Carrie L. Lukas
9781596980037

The **Politically Incorrect Guide®** to
The Presidents

PART 1: from Washingon to Taft

Larry Schweikart

REGNERY
PUBLISHING

A Division of Salem Media Group

Regnery® is a registered trademark of Salem Communications Holding Corporation

Cataloging-in-Publication data on file with the Library of Congress

ISBN 978-1-62157-524-5

Published in the United States by
Regnery Publishing
A Division of Salem Media Group
300 New Jersey Ave NW
Washington, DC 20001
www.Regnery.com

Manufactured in the United States of America

10 9 8 7 6 5 4 3 2 1

Books are available in quantity for promotional or premium use. For information on discounts and terms, please visit our website: www.Regnery.com.

Distributed to the trade by
Perseus Distribution
www.perseusdistribution.com

To Jeff Head, Freeper and Friend

Contents

What Did the Founders Have in Mind?

"The executive Power shall be vested in a President of the United States of America. He shall hold his Office during the Term of four Years.... The President shall be Commander in Chief of the Army and Navy of the United States, and of the Militia of the several States.... He shall from time to time give to the Congress Information of the State of the Union, and recommend to their Consideration...."
—United States Constitution, Article II, Sections 1, 2, and 3

What does it mean to be the president of the United States? We know, of course, what the office has become over time. Head of American public relations. Advocate for his political party. Singular voice of the most powerful nation in the world. Quasi-royalty in a nation that has shunned aristocracy and titles. Top dog, big cheese, head honcho.

Asking modern Americans who the president is, or what the president does, would elicit responses from the astute to the utterly inane. Very few answers would contain the terms "chief executive," "commander in chief," or "head of state." These are terms from long ago, in a galaxy far away from the experiences of mass media and pop culture in twenty-first-century America.

Before the Devolution

No one in particular is to blame for the evolution—some might say, the devolution—of the presidency into the hashtag-issuing, saxophone- and basketball-playing, golfing, jogging-suit-wearing, executive-order-issuing equivalent of a Hollywood movie studio or a Fortune 500 company. Like most changes in American politics, this transformation has occurred slowly, a step at a time, and seldom with any formal discussion, let alone the approval of either Congress or the American people as a whole. Rather, as the old saying goes, silence gives consent. The modern presidents are no more to blame for the relentless aggrandizement of executive power than are the Congresses and courts that meekly handed ever more control to them or the people themselves who timidly stood by as their ability to control their circumstances diminished.

But what was the presidency before this transformation—as it unfolded from 1789 until 1912? With a few exceptions, we would find a much different office, occupied by a set of men who, even in the worst of cases, had a view of their powers and responsibilities that is very different from the office as it exists today. It goes without saying that attitudes have changed, and it is not within the scope of this book to argue whether the expansion of federal executive power changed the attitudes or whether the transformed views of what was acceptable paved the way for the inhabitants of the most important office in the world to take more control. What there is no debate about, on Left or Right, is that the position filled by George Washington, James K. Polk, Rutherford B. Hayes, and even William Howard Taft shared little with the presidential office of those who came later, particularly after the Great Depression and World War II. Whether that growth was entirely, or even mostly (as Robert Higgs argues in *Crisis and Leviathan*), the result of crises, there is little doubt that crises do present almost irresistible opportunities for governments to grow, and specifically for presidents to use their powers in new and (often perversely) imaginative ways. Rahm Emanuel, former chief of staff to President Barack Obama, notoriously said, "You never want a serious crisis to go to waste. And what I mean by that [is] it's an opportunity to do things you think you could not do before."

Who thinks like that? Many politicians today, perhaps. But for well over a hundred years from the time the nation was founded, no president viewed his office in terms of "doing things he could not do before." Quite the contrary, before the twentieth century not even the worst presidents ever deliberately attempted to pervert or alter the parameters and restrictions of their constitutionally defined powers. For all the accusations of his critics, Abraham Lincoln

A Book You're Not Supposed to Read

Crisis and Leviathan: Critical Episodes in the Growth of American Government, 25th Anniversary Edition, by Robert Higgs (Oakland, CA: The Independent Institute, 2012).

constantly fretted about whether what he was doing during the Civil War was permitted constitutionally. He frequently admitted he didn't know, saying that it was up to the people to interpret his actions as either within or outside of the Constitution through elections. His opponents raged that the people could not judge—that it was up to either the Supreme Court (in the case of *ex parte Merryman*) or Congress to determine what was constitutional. Of course, in the twenty-first century, when the U.S. Supreme Court under Chief Justice John Roberts ruled "Obamacare" constitutional, critics of the president's policies made just the opposite argument, insisting that the Court did *not* have the right of judicial review.

Given that the modern presidency has become far more than the Founders ever expected or intended, and that its influence has been vastly expanded beyond its official powers, it is a fascinating fact that in almost any poll or survey of the "best" or "most important" presidents, two of the top three or four are always George Washington and Abraham Lincoln, while Thomas Jefferson, Andrew Jackson, and Theodore Roosevelt often appear in the top ten. If conservatives are asked to list the best presidents, Grover Cleveland, Martin Van Buren, and William McKinley often join them. Despite the presentist tendency to list the more recent chief executives, reverence, respect, and disproportionate preference for those who held the position more than

★ ★ ★

Not the Be-All and End-All

Except to become United Nations secretary general or chief justice of the United States Supreme Court, it is inconceivable today that a former president of the United States would take a step down to become a senator, a member of Congress, or a governor. Yet John Quincy Adams gladly served in Congress for eighteen years (1830–1848) after his single presidential term, while Andrew Johnson, having filled out the assassinated Abraham Lincoln's second term, briefly held a U.S. Senate seat from March to July 1875. To them, the presidency was not the be-all and end-all of their political lives.

a hundred years ago remain. Why would that be, if the modern presidency is "what the people want"? Perhaps the reason is that despite their inclination to—as Steven Hayward put it in *The Politically Incorrect Guide® to the Presidents from Wilson to Obama*—see the president as "some kind of miracle worker," the public still has an appreciation for the concept of limited and restrained powers—even if it doesn't always want to see those limits in action.

The sobering fact is that since at least World War II neither Congresses nor Supreme Courts have proven themselves worthy adversaries in the checks-and-balance system. This is not to blame Congress and the Court, but to acknowledge that nature abhors a vacuum, especially in leadership. The reality is that as technology has made the world smaller, the reaction time to changes in international situations (here I refuse to employ the term crisis to characterize daily events) necessarily means that smaller groups, such as a president and his staff, make the decisions. While House and Senate members debate and talk, presidents can act through a number of constitutionally delegated powers and through an elastic interpretation of Article II, Section 3, namely that "he shall take Care that the Laws be faithfully executed...." The more laws, the more "execution" is needed, and the wider the latitude in executing them. So with each new law Congress passed, it was unwittingly expanding the power of the presidency.

As British historian Paul Johnson has noted, "almost by accident...America got a very strong presidency—or, rather, an office which any particular president could make strong if he chose." By virtue of the separate election of the president by all the people (even if direct democracy is mitigated by the Electoral College), which made the presidency different from all parliamentary and ministerial forms of government, the office had from the beginning a special moral legitimacy. And then unlike congressmen and senators, who could only introduce bills or vote, a president could *act*, effectively defying or at least preempting the judgment of the legislative and judicial branches. Given his veto power, as well, the president even at the outset had as much power as many European kings at the time.

Yet virtually no one recognized that fact at first, largely because the earliest presidents—George Washington, John Adams, Thomas Jefferson, James Madison, and James Monroe—all came from the Whig tradition in which the legislature was the true voice of the people and should be elevated in national affairs. Over time, however, three events would reshape the office. None of them had anything to do with Robert Higgs's "crises"—certainly nothing to do with war. In fact, between 1789 and 1912, the United States fought four major wars, of which only the Civil War "grew" the government. And even then, the presidency remained rather limited. For example, while in 1808 Thomas Jefferson answered the White House door himself and ran the government with only a secretary, by 1862 Abraham Lincoln had only two secretaries and a very small domestic staff. Instead of crises generating massive changes in the scope of government power and the nature of the presidency, three peacetime developments expanded the office—all long before the first of the truly "big government" modern presidents, Woodrow Wilson, settled into the office in 1913.

How to Expand the Presidency in Three Easy Steps

The first "non-crisis" factor that greatly changed the nature of the presidency and simultaneously paved the way for *automatically* expanding government—regardless of a president's personal predilections—appeared in 1824 with the birth of the Second American Party System. A nitpicker might argue that there was a crisis involved, though it was not a war, but rather a piece of legislation, the Missouri Compromise. Many saw this bill as a political earthquake. An aging Thomas Jefferson said news of the Compromise awakened him like a "fire bell in the night" and the "[death] knell of the Union." Congressman Martin Van Buren, deeply engaged in a political battle with the forces of DeWitt Clinton in New York, feared that the debate over slavery in Missouri would seep into his home state and generate "inflammatory assaults on the institution of slavery" that could in turn erupt into a civil war. Seeing that the Missouri bill itself was out of his hands, Van Buren steeled himself to achieve a momentous change in the political elections process by which he might exert control and prevent dissension.

Van Buren's solution failed to prevent a war over slavery. It also saddled the United States with a two-party system in which both parties were forced to grow government with each election to gain power. But politically the scheme of the "Little Magician" was nothing less than brilliant. Here is how it worked: to Van Buren, the central objective was to prevent slavery from tearing apart the Union. And like many politicians today who "reach across the aisle," Van Buren was willing to keep the peace at virtually any cost. Rather than *abolish* slavery, he wanted to *protect* it by dousing any sparks of emancipation that might be ignited in the halls of the legislature by his fire-retardant. His fire extinguisher was government jobs, then called "patronage" or "the Spoils System." Van Buren recognized that there would be many people—perhaps a majority—who wanted to abolish slavery, but that the minority of Southerners would literally fight to keep it. How to convince anti-slave Northerners to go along with the "peculiar institution"? Bribe them. The new party that Van Buren organized, the Democratic Party, would reward supporters for election victories with party, state government, and ultimately national government jobs. While the bribes were not direct, they were very effective. The largest government institution of the day, second only to the U.S. Army, was the Post Office, which, by the 1830s, had nearly nine thousand employees. The position of every postmaster and mail carrier was a political job, to be awarded by the party boss in every town that the victorious Democrats had carried. But the political plums extended to every office and function in government—customs collection, Indian agents, special ministers, sheriffs, customs agents, judges. If there was a party or government job, it was going to go to the person most effective at getting out the vote in the election, not the most qualified.

> ### A Book You're Not Supposed to Read
>
> *Martin Van Buren and the Making of the Democratic Party* by Robert V. Remini (New York: Columbia University Press, 1959). Remini, a Democrat who adored Andrew Jackson, seemingly failed to understand that he had written a book showing that the Democratic Party was founded entirely on the principle of protecting and perpetuating slavery.

It was inevitable that *all* governments, including county, state, and federal, would grow under Van Buren's new political party system. At first, however, the rate of expansion remained small. Quickly more jobs had to be created, especially when the Whigs, a rival party to the Democrats, appeared on the scene in the 1830s. Now there was competition for patronage—the power to give away jobs—in every election. Measurements of the growth of government, both in total numbers and per capita, show a steady and inexorable rise after 1828—the first election in which Van Buren's new party system was put to the test. This growth was not a result of the victory of "big government" ideology over "small government"—such discussions were never heard before the twentieth century. The simple fact was that, to get elected, you had to promise people jobs, a reward for their service.

As the government grew, the power of the man in charge of its administration grew too. But Van Buren's impact on the presidency didn't end there.

An Article You're Not Supposed to Read

"The Missouri Crisis, Slavery, and the Politics of Jacksonianism," by Richard H. Brown, in Stanley N. Kurtz and Stanley I. Kutler, eds., *New Perspectives on the American Past, vol. 1, 1607–1877* (Boston: Little, Brown, 1969), 241–55.

He rightly surmised that no slaveholder from a Deep South state could be elected president after James Monroe. (Of the first six presidents, four had come from Virginia—and no elected president has since come from that state.) In this assessment, Van Buren was astute. (Tennessee, Kentucky, Indiana, Ohio, Michigan, and points further west were at the time considered the West, not the South or the North. Later, Texas would as often as not be viewed as a Western rather than a Southern state. By that definition of the South, no president was elected from that region again until Jimmy Carter in 1976.) But Van Buren also believed that no vocal anti-slave advocate could be elected to the presidency. His system for winning elections, therefore, was for the Democrats to run a Westerner (like Van Buren's first winning choice, Andrew Jackson from Tennessee), or a "Northern man of Southern principles," that is to say, a Northerner who would acquiesce in the perpetuation of slavery.

How effective was Van Buren's system? *No pro-slave Southerner or anti-slave Northerner was elected for thirty years*, until finally, in a four-way contest, Abraham Lincoln (a Northern man of *Northern* principles) was elected. And, just as Van Buren had foreseen, the South fought rather than be governed by someone who held and practiced anti-slavery values.

Lincoln's presidency in fact proved the point that Van Buren's system grew government. By 1860, the president had vast appointment powers, with Lincoln himself spending countless days signing letters for political appointees. Moreover, those appointees—from postmasters, who could allow abolitionist materials to pass through the mail, to customs inspectors, who could allow free men of color to disembark in Southern ports—threatened to overturn the slave system. Federal marshals and judges would be even more threatening to the perpetuation of slavery in the South. Hence, the very edifice that Van Buren had erected to *prevent* a war played a central role in *causing* it. (Van Buren, it must be remembered, had worked his way into dominance of New York politics and from there forged the alliance with Virginia pols to create the "Albany-Richmond Axis" that put the power to select candidates, more or less, in his hands.) And no office had gained more power than the presidency, thanks in large part to Van Buren's first selection to run for president from the new Democratic Party, Andrew Jackson, who wielded presidential power like Thor wields his hammer.

A second development, closely tied to the creation of the Democratic Party and the Spoils System, changed the presidency even more profoundly. In 1880, James Garfield was elected president largely on a platform of reforming the patronage system that was swamping the government with job-seekers. When he was assassinated in 1881 by a disaffected job-seeker, the impetus for reform led to the passage of the Pendleton Civil Service Reform Act in 1883, which established the Civil Service Commission to administer tests for government employment.

As with most "reforms," it made things worse. Whereas before the Pendleton Act, politicians (especially those running for the presidency) could promise limited numbers of jobs to party insiders who could whip up the vote, they suddenly found themselves without as many positions to reward supporters. But instead of stopping the entire practice of promising bribes for support, presidential candidates merely raised their sights. They began to embrace whole government programs that rewarded entire groups of voters—veterans benefits for the Grand Army of the Republic, tariffs for businesses, inflation for borrowers, and, eventually (in our own time) government-mandated health insurance via "Obamacare." The Pendleton Act fundamentally moved electioneering from the courting of small groups of individuals into broad promises to large blocs of voters. By the election of 1896, the two major candidates were promising either "hard money"—that is, maintaining the gold standard to help businesses—or "free and unlimited silver"—that is, inflation to bail out debtors and farmers. Hard money won, but it didn't change the essential character of the political system, in which the way to get elected was to woo "interest groups," not individuals.

What was the impact on the size of government and the power of the presidency? To use a modern term, ginormous. Before Pendleton, government grew inexorably with each election, but only a little. Once the few thousand "spoils" appointees were mollified, there was no reason to promise anything else. After Pendleton, though, the numbers of jobs each presidential candidate had to give away through one program or another soared exponentially, and worse, to ensure that the candidate won, he had to promise far more than his opponent! Entire programs were tossed to the voters, from veterans' pensions to increases in military production geared more to paying off constituents than to the actual needs of national security. Grover Cleveland, one of the few to buck this system, implemented a full review of every pensioner and notoriously vetoed a seed corn bill—a pure giveaway to Texas farmers—on the grounds that such handouts were not authorized by the Constitution. But they only accelerated—seventy years later, Lyndon Johnson would create a blizzard of new giveaways in the "Great Society" and the "War on Poverty," all with the secondary purpose of securing millions of new welfare clients as Democrat voters.

Ironically, Van Buren himself had thought of the presidency as smaller and weaker than the Congress because, again, he intended that the national government had to be weak to keep it from acting on slavery, and with party discipline, Congress would never address the issue. But because the president was the *only* national candidate, it was inevitable that the powers of the office would balloon far more than the Little Magician could have imagined. By the late twentieth century, the presidents' State of the Union messages had become little more than shopping lists for goodies that the president intended to provide (and, one should note, on average the speeches got a lot longer).

A third factor—again, unrelated to any war or other crisis—vastly expanded the office of the presidency in still a different way: the adoption of the Seventeenth Amendment in May 1913, establishing direct election of U.S. senators by the people of each state. At first glance, one might wonder how this change for *senators* affected the presidency; in fact, this seemingly innocent change significantly altered the checks and balances established by the Constitution as originally written and ratified, tilting power further toward the inhabitant of the Oval Office.

On the surface, the direct election of senators seemed merely an extension of "democracy" to "the people"; in reality, it nearly ended the key role of state power as a separate check and balance on the expansion of federal power. It transformed the Senate from a body that resisted federal intrusion into issues of states' rights into one that had no check and balance function at all within the context of federalism. It also accelerated and deepened partisan divides because, from that point on, senators no longer had common ground in protecting their institutional power, which they derived from the states, against the encroachment of federal—and especially presidential—power. The senators were now just cogs in the party structure, which flourished by increasing a party's power and influence within government, even at the expense of state authority. Consequently, senators frequently became little more than glorified cheerleaders for the president when he was of their party, as opposed to watchdogs of the rights of their own states.

There you have it: in three powerful institutional changes, the presidency became an office that depended heavily on handouts to voters, then those handouts were geometrically expanded to entire groups as opposed to individuals, then a major check on the power of presidents disappeared.

That is not to say that other profound transformations did not occur within the presidency in its first one-hundred-plus years, but even the wartime powers employed by Abraham Lincoln dissipated after the conflict; not until World War I would a president wield such broad authority.

Then there was the media. Prior to 1860—again, thanks to Van Buren—the press was *entirely* partisan. That is, newspapers existed only to act as propaganda outlets for the Democratic Party (and later the Whig Party as well). Van Buren went so far as to subsidize the papers (none could make a profit off sales) and even selected the editors. One editor essentially said his positions were whatever Andrew Jackson's positions were that day! But over time the media became independent of the party structure, and congressmen and senators had little hope of countering its power—only a president could withstand the power of the media. By the late twentieth century, being able to "deal" with the media became an essential prerequisite for any presidential candidate. Ronald Reagan and Bill Clinton, in particular, were heralded for their ability to go over the heads of the media to the American people. This had only started to become a problem for presidents by the late 1800s. Even then, most presidents were not intimidated by the entire press corps, let alone a single paper.

Finally, as parties developed, by the late 1800s the president had become not just the head of the American state but also the head of his party. He was expected to be the "front man" of the party, to represent it to the American people, and to exemplify its platform and ambitions. The Whig presidents were some of the first to experience the difficulties of this role, as their party was a coalition of disparate and irreconcilable groups. And Abraham Lincoln had to deal with the recalcitrant "Radical" Republicans. But not until Reconstruction, when the wars between the "Spoilsmen" who wanted to continue the practice of presidential patronage, and the "Reformers" who wanted to end it erupted, did presidents find themselves immersed in interparty politics. This problem came to a head in 1912 with the reelection

★ ★ ★

Head of State, Head of Government

The American presidency differs from almost all other chief executive offices in the world because it combines a political position (the head of a major party) with the diplomatic duties of the head of state with the functional executive duties of the head of government. In England and Israel, in contrast, the prime minister is almost always the head of the party—holding his or her position because the party has selected him or her—but not the head of state. In England, the head of state is still technically the king or queen, while in Israel it is the elected president rather than the prime minister. (Then, too, in America, presidents are frequently of a different party than from houses of Congress and even, on occasion, a majority of the Supreme Court.) As a result, in the United States it is difficult to oppose the government without specifically also opposing the president, and vice versa, while in England, opposition to the prime minister who leads the ruling party in Parliament and is the head of government can be waved off with a hearty "God Save the Queen!"

campaign of Republican William Howard Taft, whose party was split because Teddy Roosevelt, the previous occupant of the White House, who did not view Taft as "progressive enough," ran against him as the Progressive Party candidate, and threw the election to Democrat Woodrow Wilson. Such conflicts had not torn a major political party asunder before 1912, and even then the Republicans recovered after Wilson's presidency.

So what was the presidency? What should it be? What did the Founders have in mind? Few modern historians even ask these question, let alone attempt to answer them. To the modernists, with their lapdog apologies for bigger and bigger government, the attitude is more often than not, "Who cares what the Founders had in mind?" Arthur Schlesinger Jr., in his celebrations of the Franklin D. Roosevelt presidency, could not contain himself in describing the new and wondrous uses of presidential power that had been employed in the New Deal. Only when Richard Nixon began to use that same power against his political enemies did Schlesinger write of the

★ ★ ★

An Exemplary President

Grover Cleveland was the last president to take seriously the question of *whether* an action belonged within the authority of the president, and few people know who he was.

dangers of the "imperial presidency." Court historians gleefully wrote of "Camelot" and the quasi-royal era of John F. Kennedy. I have reviewed over twenty mainstream modern history textbooks that rarely, if ever, discuss the limitations the Constitution places on the presidency, let alone whether or not such limitations are desirable. Often presidential power is subsumed into a much broader and thoroughly pervasive rubric of "government" power, and it is assumed that only government can accomplish certain tasks. For example, most of those twenty textbooks either directly state or imply that federal government subsidies for the transcontinental railroads—something that early presidents would have considered "internal improvements" outside the scope of the federal government powers enumerated in the Constitution—were essential.

Certainly by the time of Theodore Roosevelt and William Howard Taft, presidents rarely asked any longer if it was desirable that the president take action when action needed to be taken. The default position was "Of course!"

In the first century after the founding of the United States, the presidency was different. It is important to realize that, with the exception of James Madison, early presidents saw the office as apart from party and failed to consider the long-term implications of the "spoils system" because it didn't really exist yet.

One thing that will stand out to the reader is how many presidents expressed relief at leaving the job. Some pined for release before their second term was over. Almost all could not wait to get out of the office, and several left before the next president was sworn in. But there are other, more uplifting and inspiring elements to their stories.

By and large, the reader will find that most of the first twenty-six presidents took their constitutional duties seriously. They questioned the propriety of taking any given action—not just whether it was a good idea in the abstract. They may not have always succeeded, but the inhabitants of the White House tried to be faithful to serving the American people, to providing sound oversight of the nation's fiscal

★ ★ ★

A Bully President

Despite some bad policies (see chapter twenty-five), no American can hate Teddy Roosevelt, for he wanted Americanism and the fruits of its bounty made available to all.

affairs, and above all to placing America's national interests above everything else. None—*not one*—ever apologized for anything America did. Every one of them saw the nation as the best hope for all on earth, and they understood that even when the U.S. made mistakes, those errors were driven in large part by the motivation to improve the lives of all.

CHAPTER 1

George Washington, 1789–1797

"…of my election to the Presidency…it has no enticing charms, and no fascinating allurements for me."
—*George Washington*

President Washington's Constitutional Grade: N/A (not applicable)

How does one grade the coach who wrote the playbook? The Constitution is so extremely vague on what a president may do, and it gives him so few explicit powers, that the yardstick became George Washington himself. And he knew it. He approached his tenure in office with a full understanding that from then on—at least for a very long time—his administration would become the model for what was and was not accepted. "I walk on untrodden ground," he wrote as he took office. "There is scarcely any part of my conduct which may not hereafter be drawn into precedent."

America dodged a bullet in having George Washington as its first chief executive. Like other Founders, including James Madison, James Monroe, and Alexander Hamilton, Washington was a military man. Unlike the others—many lawyers and planters—he was a military man first and foremost. As such, he came into office with a deep appreciation for following orders and battle plans and a respect for the chain of command. During the Revolution, his focus on victory had enabled him to sweep aside the petty power grabs and rivalries of Charles Lee and others, while at the same time subjecting him to regular (if often unsatisfying) appeals to the Continental Congress

Did you know?

★ Though he is often thought of as being old when he assumed the presidency, Washington was thirteen years Ronald Reagan's junior and only ten years older than Bill Clinton and Barack Obama

★ Some of Washington's most famous addresses were written by his Treasury secretary and friend Alexander Hamilton

★ Washington selected his cabinet as much for their regional and political differences as for their expertise

★ ★ ★

You're In the Army Now

All but four of the first twenty-six U.S. presidents had been in the military or in the militia, though Madison held a rank without actually serving, Jefferson never saw combat as the commander of the Albemarle County Militia, James Buchanan was a private, and William Howard Taft was the honorary commander of the Connecticut Home Guard.

for money. He understood right out of the gate how the separation of powers worked, how to delegate, and when to make the final decisions. His military training—far better than the experience of any lawyer or merchant—instilled in him a sense of line and staff command (though they wouldn't be formally invented for another fifteen years, by the Prussians). Other Founders who were steeped in law, the legislature, or the executive, including John Adams, James Madison, Alexander Hamilton, and Thomas Jefferson, might have applied legal reasoning to every subject (as in fact Hamilton and Edmund Randolph, Washington's attorney general, did on multiple occasions) or ideological passion (as Jefferson did), sweeping aside the spirit of the laws put in place to contain both.

As a planter, Washington also had an understanding of commerce and could therefore analyze and assess laws and edicts for their impact, if not on the "common man," at least on the person who was not inside the halls of government. Many are aware that Washington did not particularly want the job of president, but felt it his duty to serve. On the eve of his retirement in 1788, he wrote to Alexander Hamilton, "I tell you, that it is my great and sole desire to live and die, in peace and retirement on my own farm." Washington thus possessed something utterly rare and nearly extinct in modern politicians, namely, a life outside of politics.

A Man Who Didn't Need the Job

That life he lived apart from government shaped his views on the presidency. Washington had strongly supported the Constitution in his words and in his letters. Having presided over the Constitutional Convention, he found the finished document quite satisfactory and saw no need for additional amendments. He saw no need for term limits, either, arguing to Jefferson, "There cannot, in my judgment, be the least danger that the President will by any practicable intrigue ever be able to continue himself one moment in office, much less perpetuate himself in it; but in the last stage of corrupted morals and political depravity...." Therefore, he added, "I can see no propriety in precluding ourselves from the services of any man, who on some great emergency be deemed, universally, most capable of serving the Public." We frequently, and correctly, attribute to the Founders great foresight, but Washington at least did not envision the rise of the "career politician."

★ ★ ★

Not Hungry for Power

When reelected, George Washington angrily described his forthcoming second term as four more years of "slavery." Can anyone conceive of *any* modern politician with such views?

His lack of prescience on that subject was almost certainly due to the universal nature of all government in his day, not just the presidency. Colonial and later state legislatures met, then adjourned, as men (always men at that time) got on with their lives, their businesses, and their families. Yet Washington's attitude is still somewhat puzzling, given the dire warnings, from both his own Federalist allies such as Alexander Hamilton and his political opponents under the banner of Thomas Jefferson, that the lust for power was intoxicating.

Unlike Presidents Bill Clinton and Barack Obama, whose narcissism seemed to know no bounds, Washington was a profoundly humble man. In his First Inaugural Address, he characterized himself to the Congress (of all groups!) as "one, who, inheriting inferior endowments from nature, and unpractised in the duties of civil administration, ought to be peculiarly conscious of his own deficiencies." If Washington's judgment proved poor,

★ ★ ★
A Stack of Bibles

It has become a ritual for the president to swear the oath to protect and defend the Constitution on a Bible, yet at the first Inauguration it seems that no one remembered to actually *bring* one. So Robert Livingston, the highest-ranking judicial figure in New York, who was to administer the oath, sent for the Bible of the local Masonic lodge, where he was Grand Master, to be delivered. Secretary of the Senate Samuel Otis was to hold the Bible, on a red satin cushion. A short man, Otis pondered how best to present it to the 6′4″ Washington, who reached his hand down. After Washington said "So help me God," Otis slightly raised the cushion. Washington, a bit surprised, instead of raising his hand pushed it down, then dramatically bent over to kiss the Bible. "Long Live George Washington, President of the United States!" came the cheer, as the general bowed to the crowd.

he asked that his "errors" would be mitigated by a consideration of his motivations. And since he was unanimously elected, and few people are willing to admit they have made a mistake, he probably wouldn't have been blamed even if he had exhibited any such "errors."

A Christian Believer and a Whig President

Washington believed that everything was tied together in subservience to God's will, and in his first official act he offered "supplications to that Almighty Being who rules over the universe; who presides in the councils of nations; and whose providential aid can supply every human defect...." Modern revisionists have attempted to define Washington as a "deist," lumping him in with other Founders whom they also erroneously give the same label. For the record, a deist was someone who did not believe in a God Who takes part in daily human affairs. Hence, anyone who prayed for guidance, wisdom, and most of all intervention can in no way legitimately be called a deist. Of all the Founders, perhaps only Thomas Jefferson fits that definition. Benjamin Franklin, who came close, nevertheless called for prayer at the Constitutional Convention at a particularly dicey time. But Washington was a devout and practicing Christian. As a vestryman, he took regular oaths in the name of Jesus Christ (and we know his propensity for honesty). He regularly prayed in the name of Jesus, prayed for remission of sins, and in a dozen other ways proved himself beyond all doubt to be a Christian.

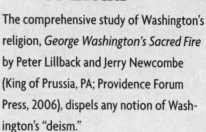

A Book You're Not Supposed to Read

The comprehensive study of Washington's religion, *George Washington's Sacred Fire* by Peter Lillback and Jerry Newcombe (King of Prussia, PA; Providence Forum Press, 2006), dispels any notion of Washington's "deism."

Washington's faith in God constituted one of the pillars of his presidency, but equally important was his intellectual and practical commitment to what was known as the "Whig" style of government. Named for the English Whigs, for whom Parliament constituted the true voice of the people and hence the locus of legitimacy for the government, Whiggery elevated legislatures above governors in America and prime ministers in England. By Washington's presidency, Whig beliefs were a given among the Founders and the drafters of the Constitution. Hence, *all* revenue bills were to originate in the House of Representatives, the Senate was to have "advise and consent" powers over executive appointments, and the power to declare war rested with the two houses of Congress. But beyond the mere letter of the Constitution, Washington intended to employ Whig principles in his every action. He showed enormous deference to the Congress as the representatives of the people.

On the other hand, Washington expected deference and dignified treatment in return. When he submitted an Indian treaty to the Senate, that body asked him to appear in person to discuss some of the articles. Washington good-naturedly agreed to appear, only to be greeted with skepticism and a decision to submit the treaty to a committee. "This defeats every purpose of my coming here," he furiously exclaimed, and vowed to never again submit to a personal grilling, setting a precedent for all future presidents. On one occasion, during a 1789 visit to Massachusetts with John Adams to meet with Governor John Hancock, Washington was kept waiting in his

★ ★ ★

Not Getting Rich off Government Service

In a move that would shock most modern politicians, Washington did not want any pay while in office, and sought only to be reimbursed for his expenses. Pecuniary remuneration for the presidency, he said, must "be limited to such actual expenditures as the public good may be thought to require." But Congress insisted he take the salary of $25,000 as required by the law. Washington soon found that in New York—then much as today—prices were abnormally high and his salary barely covered all his expenses for the required entertaining and other extras expected of a president.

hotel room for Hancock's arrival and greeting. As the higher-ranking official, Washington insisted that Hancock come to him. Yet…nothing. A note finally arrived saying the governor was too ill to come to see Washington. Perceiving a slight, Washington sent back a note saying that Hancock was then obviously too ill to receive the president at his quarters. Washington and Adams dined together that night, alone at the inn. The next day another note arrived from the governor asking if the president had any time in the afternoon. Washington coldly responded that he had an hour. Hancock showed up in thirty minutes—looking deathly ill, wrapped up and bloated with gout. In fact, he had been quite sick. From that point on, according to the authors of *Washington's Circle*, Washington "dropped his curt manner" and talked to Hancock as a friend. Nevertheless, the precedent had been set.

Creating the Nation's First Cabinet

In one of his first unofficial acts that soon became a formal part of every presidency, Washington began to meet in his house near Wall Street with his vice president John Adams, as well as Alexander Hamilton, Henry Knox, and Thomas Jefferson. This was a re-creation of Washington's formation of a command staff for the Continental Army in 1776. He submitted Hamilton's name to Congress for approval as the secretary of the Treasury on September 11, 1789, and the Senate unanimously approved the confirmation. Knox was confirmed shortly thereafter as secretary of War, followed by Edmund Randolph as attorney general and Thomas Jefferson as secretary of State. Together, these five men represented Massachusetts and New England, New York, and Virginia—the main power hubs of the new nation. In Jefferson and Randolph, Washington had two strong states' rights advocates, while Hamilton was a centralizer. Adams brought a moral, even pious voice. The group was made up of anything but "yes men"; Washington indeed chose them for their willingness to disagree with him as well as for regional and political balance.

Even if the cabinet, as it was called after 1793, had no official standing in the Constitution, and even if it represented Washington's taking the first step in expanding the power and influence of the office of the president, it is worth noting that, as Paul Johnson points out, he "employed more people on his Mount Vernon estate than the whole of the central executive of his government." The men he chose, and the departments they headed, accurately represented Washington's priorities in his new administration—namely, securing the nation militarily, diplomatically, and financially, and ensuring that the laws be enforced. In his administration, cabinet meetings did not occur at any particular interval—and would not, in fact, until Jefferson began to hold weekly meetings.

The new president found that as "head of state" he was obliged to, well, deal with people. Congress had outlined the positions in the various government departments in 1789, but left the staffing of said positions to Washington and his secretaries. Washington immediately set another precedent by insisting that he alone had final say over his employees, that Congress did not have refusal power over the lower-level appointees (as they do over the secretaries of the departments, whose presidential appointments have to be confirmed by the Senate). Ultimately, John Adams broke a Senate tie in favor of Washington's position. That meant, however, that Washington was deluged with requests for appointments, which he sought

★ ★ ★

Puttin' on the Ritz

In addition to meeting with job applicants, Washington found that another set of presidential duties involved schmoozing. He was, after all, America's "First Citizen," and people wanted to see him, talk with him, and merely be around him. Washington consulted on protocol with Hamilton, Jefferson, Madison, and Adams, piecing together a social strategy that worked as follows:

On Tuesday afternoons, he would hold an informal meeting or party, called a "levee," for men, who assembled in a room. When he was introduced, Washington would arrive in formal dress (he never met *anyone* in a presidential public setting, even unexpected dinner visitors, without wearing formal attire!) and bearing a ceremonial sword. Each man would be announced, Washington and the guest would ceremonially bow (the general did not like shaking hands), and then the men would begin to form a semicircle around Washington, who would position himself with his back to the fireplace. From 3:15 to 4:00, the president would "work the circle," speaking briefly with each man, and spending time with them until he knew each face and name well.

Friday evenings from 7:00 to 10:00 were reserved for "Martha's levee," a mixed company event with tea, ice cream, cookies, and other light refreshments. Abigail Adams was given a special seat of honor to Martha's right. The following week, Mrs. Washington would visit each of the attendees at their home. Washington, always at home with the ladies, was described as a "gallant charmer."

Formal dinners, mostly for the benefit of foreign dignitaries, were graced with copious amounts of food, including chickens, bacon, turkeys, ducks, fish, lobsters, crabs, eggs, cheese, bread, vegetables, melons, fruits, honey, and plenty of Madeira, Claret, Sherry, Champagne, and other liquor. Dinners contained several courses, and innumerable toasts, which foreigners found peculiar. When the ladies retired to their own room, Washington might even tell a story or two, engaging a rapt audience. All of these gatherings set important precedents that signaled that the president of the United States was the leader of all the people, all of the time.

to make first on the basis of competence, but then second with an eye toward sectional balance. Finally, Washington insisted that qualified veterans always have priority. The commander in chief who had won the

Revolution was still keenly interested in the military, but it stayed small during his tenure.

In for a Penny

The young nation needed a solid financial foundation that would enable it to borrow money, if necessary. And that required paying off the United States' existing debts. Here Hamilton proved a brilliant appointment. Ron Chernow's masterful biography of Hamilton shows that after Hamilton stepped down from his position as secretary of the Treasury, his rival, the new president Thomas Jefferson, launched a dirt-digging investigation by his own secretary of the Treasury, Albert Gallatin. When Jefferson asked, "Well, Gallatin, what have you found?" Gallatin answered, "I have found the most perfect system ever formed. Any change that should be made in it would injure it. Hamilton made no blunders, committed no frauds. He did nothing wrong." Gallatin remarked, "I think Mr. Jefferson was disappointed."

So what was the "perfect system" that Hamilton had devised? As Washington intended, his Treasury secretary created a structure that enabled the government to pay off its debts and establish itself on a sound financial footing. Jefferson, ironically, would be the main beneficiary of Hamilton's work; it was in the Jefferson administration that the national debt was finally liquidated—including all the debts that the states had incurred during the Revolution. In the "Report on Public Credit" that he presented to the House of Representatives on January 14, 1790, Hamilton recommended a risky step—namely, that the United States government would assume all the debts of the states as well as those of the Articles of Confederation Congress. That was a radical position for him to take, but one that solidified the principle that the United States was a nation, not merely a confederation of states. Then Hamilton persuaded Congress to create a "sinking fund" to pay

A Book You're Not Supposed to Read

Alexander Hamilton by Ron Chernow (New York: Penguin, 2004).

off the debt gradually. Washington endorsed Hamilton's approach, and even Jefferson, who took the view that "the earth belongs in usufruct to the living," could not object to Hamilton's sinking fund. Washington's wise selection of Hamilton for the Treasury Department bequeathed to the nation a solvent, stable, and vibrant financial structure that was the envy of Britain and France. It worked so effectively to establish America's credit that, by the time of his Second Inaugural, Washington could announce a loan of three million florins from Holland.

The Jeffersonians did strongly resist Hamilton's bill for the assumption of the states' debt until Washington personally intervened. (One story, recounted by historian Joseph Ellis, is that Washington directed the principals on both sides to meet at a dinner party and not come out until they had arrived at a compromise over the funding and assumption bill. Another implausible version has Hamilton and Jefferson in a rowboat with Washington, who parked

★ ★ ★

Pomp and Circumstance

While it was tame in comparison to the pageantry of the European monarchies, Washington's travel involved a level of fanfare and spectacle. He made only two major trips as president, one in the North and one in the South, but in each case he was transported in his white coach specially built by the Clarke Brothers of Philadelphia, accompanied by his aide de camp and a valet, with two footmen and a mounted squadron of dragoons in tow. He also brought along five of his private horses and a baggage wagon. Arrival in major towns would be heralded by a trumpet blast ("Hail to the Chief" was not played regularly until the administration of John Tyler in 1842), and in each his visit culminated in a formal dinner that would include at least a dozen toasts, with a speech for every toast. The people, most of whom had never seen the American president, loved it.

★ ★ ★

The Original Rock-and-Roller?

Our typical picture of Washington is the man with the grim face, the wig, and the prim and proper manner.

In fact, he loved to dance—except at state functions, of which he hated every element. His secretary noted that "the President wishes to command his own time, which these [official balls and celebrations] always forbid in a greater or lesser degree, and they are to him fatiguing and oftentimes painful. He wishes not to exclude himself from the sight or conversation of his fellow citizens, but their eagerness to show their affection frequently imposes a heavy tax on him." Nevertheless, for the sake of precedent Washington submitted graciously—as he did to all indignities he underwent for the good of the country—to parades, balls, and speeches.

But when he did engage in smaller family events and parties, Washington was something of a rock-and-roller. His love of dancing is attested by the fact that surviving music sheets from the Mount Vernon estate include not only the expected minuets and Mozart pieces but also numerous Scots-Irish folk tunes—the rock and roll of the day. It would not be unrealistic to think that Washington, who could not sing at all, danced a mean jig to these 1700s versions of "Johnny B. Goode" and "I Want to Hold Your Hand." Long before Bill Clinton played a saxophone on *The Arsenio Hall Show*, George Washington knew how to rock.

---

them in a lake until they came to an agreement.) Washington wanted the bill, and he threw his influence behind it. Even though the compromise to move the nation's capital to Virginia had already been reached in theory, the bank agreement seemed to solidify in both parties' minds that, in fact, it would be a reality.

Critics may claim that Washington had nothing to do with Hamilton's financial achievements—just as sports fans sometimes say that coaches aren't responsible for the success of their players on the field. Yet somehow great coaches always seem to have great players, and Washington had Hamilton—partly because the younger man reflected his views, preferences, and priorities. In the same way as a coach is important for the tone he sets and his presence on the sidelines, Washington brought stability and confidence everywhere he went. Part of that stability and confidence stemmed from another precedent he set by speaking directly to the people (as far as the technology of the day would allow)—such as in his proclamation making Thursday, November 26, a day of Thanksgiving in the first year of his presidency.

More Precedents

Probably no more important decision involving precedent—though it was one of the least commented-upon—was the first president's treatment of the position of vice president. Washington knew that the Continental Army had had only one ultimate decision-maker, and every ship has only one captain. John Adams was thus consigned to a near-invisible role, not incorporated into Washington's inner circle, even if he was officially a cabinet member. Even though his own vice president agreed with him on almost everything, Washington understood that having a "co-presidency"—an idea that would be proposed nearly two hundred years later when ex-president Gerald Ford was being touted as a vice presidential pick at the Republican convention that nominated Ronald Reagan—could prove destructive. And within a few years, the situation would change radically, when the election of 1796 put a Federalist (Adams) into the presidency and a man hostile to Federalist positions (Jefferson) into the vice presidency.

Washington anticipated that the deluge of people seeking political appointments would cause "distress...ten thousand embarrassments, perplexities, and troubles to which I must again be exposed." And Washington was spared the *real* deluge of political job-seekers that would swell in the period following the creation of the Democratic Party and its concomitant rewards system for political supporters. He had a tremendous insight into the mischief that government power offered.

Additionally, Washington clearly saw that the new Supreme Court and the federal judiciary would soon become a critically important arm of the government and thus the selection of the chief justice would be a key early decision. Washington's choice, John Jay, was a safe one: Jay had ardently argued for the new federal structure as one of the authors of *The Federalist Papers*, and could be counted on to support Federalist policies on the court.

A Book You're Not Supposed to Read

A History of the American People by Paul Johnson (New York: HarperCollins, 1997).

Hamilton introduced Washington's agenda in Congress through subsequent reports, including the "Report on a National Bank" (1790) in which he recommended the establishment of a four-fifths privately-owned national bank (called the Bank of the United States) that would eventually be able to lend money to the government. The bank was to have precisely the same structure and purpose for which the Bank of England and the Bank of France were, or would be, created.

In both the case of the assumption of debts and the creation of the national bank (later ruled constitutional by Chief Justice John Marshall, one of John Adams's appointees), Washington was hardly interested in "growing government." Rather, these were common sense, practical steps for tackling the financial challenges facing a new nation. But growth was inherent in government: Hamilton already had thirty-five clerks taking in revenues and keeping books in the Treasury, while Jefferson at the State Department made do with five.

Rejecting America's First Business Bailout

The nation faced an early potential financial crisis in 1791 when a New York banker, William Duer, went belly up. Duer approached Hamilton about getting a bailout. Here was an early precedent. Would the government routinely save businessmen who made poor decisions—especially when there might be a contagion effect to other stable businesses (in this case, banks)? Hamilton, with Washington's blessing, wisely told Duer there would be no government bailout. Behind the scenes, however, he met with other prominent New York bankers to encourage them to help each other out if a panic showed its face. But it would be up to them—those in the free market—to handle the problem, not the government. Duer failed, and the New York bankers supported each other.

Hamilton presented a third proposal to Congress that year, the "Report on Manufactures" (1791), which addressed another of Washington's early concerns, specifically the equipping of an American military. Hamilton's critics have condemned his system of subsidies and tariffs as either latent mercantilism or pre-pubescent Keynesianism. The fact is, neither Washington nor Hamilton had any intention of picking winners and losers in business. Rather they were concerned with the dangers of lacking a national industrial base, particularly in iron and textiles (for muskets, cannon, and uniforms). Since the Revolution the United States had used a private "contract system," whereby the government would put in orders with private suppliers for weapons, powder, and so forth. Washington and Hamilton did not want to rely on Europeans to provide weapons…that might be needed against Europeans. Therefore Congress created a national armory at Springfield, Massachusetts, and a second at Harpers Ferry, Virginia. Washington's concern was to ensure an industrial base so that the United States would not be unprepared in time of war.

The United States Army, when Washington handed it over to Henry Knox, was little more than eight hundred men and officers. Washington concluded that a separate department of the Navy was not needed, since there were no ships. In accordance with his established habit of delegation, Washington left it to Congress to provide for the details of the Army, and in

★ ★ ★

Regulars vs. Militia

While a general, Washington had groused about the effectiveness of militia and, despite claims made in *The Patriot*, went out of his way to train an effective regular army that, in the words of the hero of that movie, Benjamin Martin (played by Mel Gibson) could "go toe to toe with Redcoats in open field." The efforts of such European drill masters as Friedrich von Steuben, Kazimierz Pulaski, and Tadeusz Kosciuszko paid off. But in the new American Republic, many feared a standing army. Washington bowed to popular senti-ment, but insisted the militias be well trained. Congress responded with a militia law in 1792 calling for the enrollment of military-aged men, their organization into divisions, regiments, and so on, and stipulating what they personally provide in the way of equipment for the field. While it was somewhat effective as a show of force in the Whiskey Rebellion, in major combat operations against the British in the War of 1812 the militia more often than not lived down to Washington's expectations.

1794 Congress established the appropriate offices to ensure that the military had the needed supplies.

"First in War…"

Confrontations with the Indians bore out Washington's warnings about untrained militias. Opening the Northwest Territory inevitably put whites and Indians into conflict. Many tribes had no sense of personal land ownership. Washington knew that he couldn't control the migration of thousands of citizens into newly-opening lands in the west, and that they would clash with Indians there. The orderly settlement envisioned by the Articles of Confederation Congress under the Land Ordinance of 1785, with its nice, neat little boxes of sections and townships was being upset by the reality of settlers running willy-nilly into Ohio and Indiana and staking out their claims. America's "Common Law" tradition came down on the side of having the law follow what the people practiced and allowed them to file claims for deeds. The Indians responded with war.

The American campaign into the Northwest Territory in June 1790 under General Josiah Harmar and Territory Governor Arthur St. Clair, with some fifteen hundred men, proved a failure. A second campaign, with nearly fourteen hundred men, again led by St. Clair, was also a disaster. Finally General "Mad Anthony" Wayne with a large body of regulars reinforced by large numbers of militia crushed the Indians at the Battle of Fallen Timbers in 1794. Once again, Washington's instincts about the necessity of organizing a regular army proved to be on the money.

Yet when it came to the Indian tribes, Washington's first tendency—beginning in the Revolution—was to talk rather than fight. He sought out alliances with any tribes he could, receiving support from the Passamaquoddy of Maine, for example. In June 1789, War Secretary Henry Knox laid out the first Indian policy of the new administration, revising the accepted notion that Americans would take all Indian territories east of the Mississippi. Although the logical home of Indian policy would have been the State Department, Washington concluded that the secretary of War, who had been dealing with the Indians for years and who seemed to have a vision, should have authority over the tribes as well. Unfortunately, Knox suggested that the tribes be viewed as "foreign nations," and not as subjects of a particular state. That meant that ultimately only the federal government would have a say over the Indians. While that arrangement was respectful of their heritage, it was badly flawed in terms of assimilating them into American society.

Instead of war, the United States began—on Knox's recommendation and with Washington's approval—negotiating a series of treaties, each of which contained a provision for supplying a type of "foreign aid" to tribes in the form of agricultural implements. Imbedded in this strategy was the understanding that private property rights were key, and that Indians who didn't have any concept of private property were inevitably going to come into conflict with whites who moved into their hunting lands. Washington viewed the treaties as binding on all parties in perpetuity. When in 1790 Seneca leaders traveled to Philadelphia to complain to Washington about incursions into Indian lands, they asked him flat out, "Does this promise [treaty] bind you?" Washington gave them an unequivocal affirmative answer and provided annual restitution of $250 to the chief. Had Washington been immortal, it is unlikely that any promises to any tribe would ever have been broken—or, at least, had a treaty been violated, the issue would have been rectified in favor of the Indians. But having done as much as he possibly could do, with as much honor as anyone could bring to the table, inevitably Washington had to hand this policy—like all others—off to lesser men. But he had set another crucial precedent by labeling the Indian tribes "foreign nations" and moving all negotiations with them under the auspices of the executive branch's treaty-making powers.

In the only incident in which a sitting U.S. president personally commanded troops in the field, Washington initially led forces out to disperse the "Whiskey Rebels" in 1794 when Pennsylvania protesters refused to pay the excise tax on whiskey imposed in Hamilton's fiscal plans. Washington rode at the head of an army of thirteen thousand Virginia, Maryland, New Jersey, and Pennsylvania militia before handing command off to Henry "Light-Horse Harry" Lee in the south while Alexander Hamilton rode alone essentially in command of the northern wing, and the insurrection collapsed in the face of Washington's army. Washington expressed pleasure that "my fellow citizens understand the true principles of government and liberty," but he had helped them understand by making the case for national action. The large army so intimidated the rebels that they did not have the will to fight, and even Republican foes believed it was better for Americans to unite than to risk anarchy. A grand jury indicted twenty-four of the rebels for treason, only ten stood trial, and only two

★ ★ ★
A Rebellious People

Beginning even before the Revolution, Americans had staged a number of rebellions and insurrections against authority, including Bacon's Rebellion (1676), Leisler's Rebellion (1689), the Paxton Boys' raids (1764), the Stamp Act riots (1765), the Boston Tea Party (1773), and Shays' Rebellion (1786). Washington's care in applying force to quell the Whiskey Rebellion—sending in the troops only after numerous emissaries of peace were dispatched, and treating the defeated rebels with mercy—shows his understanding of the need to let Americans govern themselves as much as possible and intervene only when their behavior poses a threat to the order of all.

were convicted and sentenced to death. Washington pardoned both men.

A more prickly issue was the rise of the "Democratic Societies" in the West and in Republican areas of the country, which Washington blamed in part for the Whiskey Rebellion. He lit into these groups hard in his Sixth Annual Address (what we would call the State of the Union), with the result being that the presidency (as it inevitably would) became a partisan office as well as a political one. Jefferson had warned that any attacks on opponents by the president would make him the head of a party instead of the head of the nation. In fact, of course, Washington and all successive presidents have been both.

A Fight between Our Friends

In foreign affairs, Washington had to face numerous thorny issues with the rise of the revolutionary French Republic as soon as he took office. He issued a generic and somewhat pro-French statement: "We surely cannot deny to any nation that right whereon our own government is founded, that every nation may govern itself according to whatever form it pleases...." In his measured approach, Washington stood well apart from his two hot-headed cabinet members Jefferson and Hamilton, who were ardently pro– and anti–French Revolution, respectively. The president thought it quite possible for the United States to steer clear of the coming European conflicts. And there is no doubt he expected conflict there, writing "All our late accounts from Europe hold up the expectations of a general war in that quartor."

Of course, the United States did have merchant ships, and did wish to trade in Europe. That posed the most immediate risk of drawing America into war, because inevitably American ships would encounter foreign warships of one nation or another. Then there was the treaty with France that had been in place since the American Revolution: Did it still bind the two countries together? Already French privateers were raiding British shipping and coming to America to sell their goods and re-outfit. Once England and other European nations fearful of the revolution spreading invaded France and set off a series of wars that would last over twenty years, the status of the treaty between France and the United States had to be addressed.

And Congress was not in session when the decision needed to be made about what kind of statement should be put out—one affirming America's commitment to France, or one declaring the United States' neutrality. Everything about the situation, including especially the decision on whether or not to involve Congress, would set a constitutional precedent. To make matters worse, Washington's cabinet was split between Hamilton and Knox (and the less influential Adams) arguing the case for England, and Jefferson and Randolph pleading the case for France. Washington convened his cabinet to explore a list of thirteen questions he had drafted, including what to do with the French privateers, whether or not to call Congress into session, and if not, what of the "advice and consent" of the Senate? The Constitution had granted Congress the power to declare war, but what about declaring neutrality? Did that also require Congress, or could a president do it on his own? And if neutrality was desired, how far could government go to ensure it?

Jefferson, presented with a hanging curveball, agreed with Washington that although only Congress had the authority to declare war, currently a state of peace existed and that a president could perpetuate peace without additional legislative authority. The next prickly issue—whether or not to officially acknowledge the new French government—was kicked down the road. The cabinet agreed that under international law treaties did not automatically renew when governments changed and for the time being Edmond Genet, the minister sent by the Revolutionary government, would be recognized without conditions pending a review by the attorney general. Finally, in a unanimous vote, Washington's cabinet recommended that he not call Congress into special session. The ensuing Proclamation of Neutrality in April 1971 urged, but did not require, citizens to "avoid all acts…which may…tend to contravene" neutrality and warned that any Americans who abetted hostilities at sea would receive no protection from the United States. Washington had straddled the issue in a way that made it difficult for either Britain or France to complain: the U.S. recognized Ambassador Edmond-Charles Genet as an official representative of the French Republic, but that did not automatically render a judgment on the previously existing treaty with France.

Presidential scholars have argued that by issuing a Declaration of Neutrality, Washington expanded the power of the presidency. He had, after all, made policy when Congress was not in session. But Jefferson's position on the issue is more tenable: by simply maintaining the status quo, Washington had not really acted, and therefore had not changed the constitutional parameters of the presidency. As Washington recognized, there would be times when an immediate decision that might involve the survival of the nation would be demanded before the constitutional requirements could be met. While that was not yet put to the test in the way it would be with Thomas Jefferson's purchase of Louisiana or Abraham Lincoln's numerous wartime decisions after 1861, Washington had settled it in his mind that when such an emergency occurred he would have to act on his own best judgment and then submit his decision to the people for their verdict. This relationship of trust demanded regular explanations to the House and Senate via reports and statements, including proposals of what the president wanted to do—as the Constitution requires: "He [the president] shall from time to time give to Congress information of the State of the Union and recommend to their Consideration such measures as he shall judge necessary and expedient." These communications would eventually develop into what we know as the president's annual "State of the Union" address.

There remained only one issue in regard to neutrality: enforcement. Since America had no large standing army, how could any aspect of the Neutrality Proclamation be enforced? For example, if shippers insisted on dealing with France or receiving booty from privateers, only the customs agents could in any way police that activity, something that raised the specter of an imperial president using the customs service for political ends (much as FDR used the Internal Revenue Service to punish enemies in the 1930s). Randolph came up with a compromise that pleased everyone, including the president. Customs collectors would merely report violations of neutrality to federal attorneys, who would notify him as attorney general. In a series of clever, fully constitutional moves, Washington had ensured America's neutrality, refrained from establishing a federal spy network, and found a way to act decisively in a crisis that demanded executive action without substantially expanding the power of the presidency.

But it didn't take Genet long to wear out his welcome. Obnoxious and ill-mannered, the French "diplomat" went behind Washington's back to gin up support for France. Even his strongest advocate, Jefferson, grew exasperated: "Never in my opinion was so calamitous an appointment made.... [Genet is] hotheaded, all imagination, no judgment, passionate, disrespectful and even indecent towards [President Washington]." John Adams wrote of "ten thousand people" drunk on terror assembled in the streets of Philadelphia, and brought up his chest of guns to defend his house. Genet was also raising money on American soil for privateers, which proved the final straw. The *Little Sarah* affair, in which Genet was again involved, nearly brought on a new constitutional crisis. The French minister sought to outfit a captured British ship (in the American port of Philadelphia) with cannon as a privateer in support of the French Republic. Washington allowed Jefferson to request a ruling from the U.S. Supreme Court on what acts were permissible under neutrality. Chief Justice Jay followed the Constitution to the letter, replying that "the lines of separation" between the different branches of the federal government made it unsuitable for the Court to give extralegal advice to any branch, or to clarify law before it was made. Jay softened his refusal to rule by praising Washington's judgment and his "usual prudence, decision, and firmness…." So the issue was thrown back into Washington's lap, and the president convened his cabinet and came up with a number of basic rules concerning belligerents. Even the determination of what America's territorial limits were at sea involved political and military consequences: the line of sight, argued for by Jefferson, was twenty miles, but the distance most cannon could fire was three. Washington opted for the lower number so as to not provoke the British.

Washington had had enough and demanded France recall Genet, which it did.

"Damn John Jay and Damn John Jay's Treaty"

Washington wished to strengthen ties to Great Britain and sent John Jay to negotiate several thorny issues remaining after the Revolutionary War. In Jay's Treaty, as it was called, the British abandoned their forts around the Great Lakes, agreed to a readjustment of the Canadian border, opened the West Indies to American trade, and guaranteed payment of some debts held over from 1783. Though highly favorable to the United States, Jay's Treaty was reviled by the Jeffersonians, who wanted to have closer ties with France, not England. A common phrase of the day was "Damn John Jay and

Damn John Jay's Treaty." Jay said he could ride from Boston to Philadelphia by the light of his burning effigies. Washington, brushing off the criticism—they weren't *his* effigies, after all—signed the treaty in 1794.

The Jay Treaty brought into focus a number of constitutional issues, especially when strong opposition arose in the House, where the Jeffersonians dominated. House members demanded some of the correspondence and papers associated with Jay's negotiations. Washington, once again consulting the Constitution and discussing the issue with his cabinet, concluded that it would be a violation of the spirit of the Constitution for one branch of the government to yield to another in that fashion. Moreover, he rightly argued that since representatives were elected to mere two-year terms and treaties were by their nature of extremely long tenure, the Constitution had correctly given the executive branch the authority to negotiate them, then present the product of the negotiations to the Senate, with its six-year terms, for review. House members balked at the payment of funds to Great Britain under some of the treaty provisions, claiming that by virtue of their "power of the purse," they had a role in treaty-making as well. But Washington found this unpersuasive and pointed out there was nothing in the Constitution to justify it. Ultimately he presented the ratified treaty and dared the House to withhold the money for the enabling provisions. The House did not. Washington had set at least two precedents, one involving "executive privilege" (though Washington never called it that) and another involving how treaties were implemented.

The following year Thomas Pinckney negotiated a similarly beneficial treaty with Spain, settling America's southern border. It was a remarkable achievement, as Pinckney's Treaty of San Lorenzo opened the Mississippi to American shipping, got a concession that American goods deposited in New Orleans for export could be stored with no Spanish tax, acknowledged the American claim in Florida to the thirty-first parallel—and, additionally, Spain agreed to restrain her Indian allies on the frontiers. Together, the Jay

★ ★ ★
An Exemplary President

Washington's Second Inaugural Address was only an astonishing 137 words, or two short paragraphs. He referred to himself only six times.

and Pinkney treaties eliminated problems posed by Europeans on all American frontiers, expanded trade, and cleared the way for future growth. Both agreements were achieved because Washington trusted his agents and because the president, Jay, and Pinckney all shared a belief in American exceptionalism that foresaw a great and growing nation.

To counter the entrenchment of the Canada-based Hudson's Bay Company in fur trading areas, in 1795 Washington sanctioned the creation of federal fur trading posts all through the Old Northwest. These were put out of business by 1819 by John Jacob Astor and his non-subsidized American trading company, illustrating that, even facing competition from government subsidies, the private sector is superior in most endeavors.

Washington had been reelected with a unanimous electoral vote—his two closest rivals, John Adams and George Clinton, together could not equal his 132 electoral votes—and had seen Hamilton's financial plan begin to take effect. As he began his fifth year in office, Washington emphasized to Congress the need for improving the nation's military arts through the foundation of a school that would eventually, in 1802, become West Point.

America's First Reelection

Jefferson had left his position as secretary of State in 1793, in what was probably the administration's greatest setback. Lyndon Johnson would later say of a political opponent: "It's better to have him inside the tent pissing out than outside pissing in." With Jefferson, having him "inside the tent" was particularly important because he was the de facto leader of the opposition. As long as Jefferson served in Washington's administration, it provided the general with a certain amount of political Kev-lar™. Once out of the cabinet, Jefferson would turn loose his minions in the press and back rooms to attack Washington—despite the fact that Jefferson had received more support from the president than had his hated rival Hamilton during the first term. James Flexner, the most thorough and the finest of all the Washington biographers, was engaging in sheer speculation

when he wondered if the aging Washington feared being left with a much younger advisor (Hamilton) who lacked a counterweight in genius (Jefferson).

One cannot fully appreciate the difficulty of Washington's position without recognizing that the Hamiltonians, on the one hand, were absolutely sure that the Republicans sought a French-style Jacobin revolution at home, while the Jeffersonians were every bit as certain that the Federalists were focused on establishing a monarchy. Washington thought each camp insanely excessive, and his good sense occasionally opened him to severe criticism. On the other hand, even when Washington went out of his way to be conciliatory—especially to Jefferson's cabal—his overtures were received as either insincere or manipulative. In short, Washington quickly learned there was no pleasing either group.

In the hands of any modern politician, Washington's Seventh Annual Message to Congress, presented at a time of incredible vitriol and personal attacks associated with the pro-British Federalists and the Francophile Republicans, would likely have contained one zinger after another, laying of blame on his critics and political enemies. Instead, Washington stunned the members by ignoring the issues dividing the legislators and instead praising them. "Fellow citizens," he said, "I have never met you at any period when more than at present the situation of our public affairs has afforded just cause for mutual congratulation; and for inviting you to join with me in profound gratitude to the Author of all good for the numerous and extraordinary blessings we enjoy." He then recounted all the successes the young nation had seen, including Wayne's defeat of the Indians and new treaties, including the renewal of treaties with the Mediterranean beys to reduce piracy and Pinckney's treaty. And then, when he got to Jay's Treaty, he noted that only a single condition remained under debate. Washington outflanked the Jeffersonians by claiming to have extinguished all causes of discord "which have heretofore menaced our tranquility." His statements were broad enough that no side could accuse him of supporting the other. He mentioned the Whiskey Rebellion, celebrating the return of quiet and order and noting that he had pardoned the convicted rebels. He ended by urging congress to attend to coastal fortifications and improve the Army, the Navy, and the militias. Since he identified no enemy, who could oppose him? It was a tour de force, unthinkable for later hyper-political presidents such as Obama or even Jimmy Carter. There was nothing to condemn, everything to praise, and Washington thus entered his final year with even his opponents again marveling at his willingness to put the nation first.

Farewell

Washington's Farewell Address, written in draft form by Hamilton but with alterations in style to fit Washington, criticized parties (which "fostered geographic schisms and foreign intrigues"), while accepting that "popular factions" were inevitable. (This of course, was Madison's view—that they were not only inevitable but necessary. "Let faction check faction," he had argued, "ambition check ambition.") The most important part of the address, on foreign relations, observed that America was "detached and distant" from Europe. Why should America "entangle our peace and prosperity" in European ambitions, the president asked. Of the existing treaties and political connections with Europe and others, "So far as we have already formed engagements, let them be fulfilled with perfect good faith. Here let us stop." Washington urged harmony and liberal trade with all nations, and urged that America "steer clear of permanent alliances...." Many readers, especially of the libertarian bent, stop there and claim Washington was an isolationist. But he went on to say, "Our detached and distant situation invites and enables us to pursue a different course. If we remain one people under an efficient government, the period is not far off when we may defy material injury from external annoyance; when we may take such an attitude as will cause the neutrality, *we may at any time resolve upon, to be scrupulously respected; when belligerent nations, under the impossibility of making acquisitions upon us, will not lightly hazard the giving us provocation; when we may choose peace or war*, as our interest, guided by justice, shall counsel [emphasis added]."

Washington had said something similar in a December 22, 1795, letter to Gouverneur Morris, but with a revealing condition: "Nothing short of self-respect and that justice which is essential to national character ought to involve us in the war; for sure I am *if this country is preserved in tranquility twenty years longer*, it may bid defiance in a just cause to any power whatsoever." A draft version of the Farewell Address also mentioned the twenty-year period. Washington saw that in twenty years the nation would be much different. In that time he expected the military, economic, and commercial strength of the nation to reach a point where the United States could tell any nation anywhere to buzz off. But America needed time to become strong. Washington recommended neutrality out of an awareness of America's military weakness and vulnerability; he was not celebrating neutrality for neutrality's sake.

Washington set one final critical precedent. Urged to run for yet another term—which all historians agree he would have won—Washington considered all the possibilities, some of them extremely unpleasant. He was not in the best of health. What if he were to die in office? His vice president,

John Adams, would automatically assume the presidency without an election. Washington thought it critical that there be an election for the next president. Unlike Europe, with its hereditary monarchies, the United States should demonstrate the concept of "rotation in office." It had to be shown that men could resist the lure of power and submit their ambitions to the law and the will of the people. The rival Jeffersonians might win in the Electoral College, but that possibility had to be risked so that the Constitution's scheme for the transfer of power could be tested. France had already shown she could not handle the transition peaceably; the revolution had disintegrated into the Reign of Terror. So stepping down would, in Washington biographer James Flexner's words, "be the consummating precedent [Washington] would leave to his people, the final governmental achievement he would leave to the world."

Yet Washington considered himself a failure. The nation he left to John Adams (as it turned out) was not a unified band of brothers, cheerfully embodying republican precepts, but a divided citizenry personified by the two ministers who had left his administration, Thomas Jefferson and Alexander Hamilton.

Washington had learned that the new federal city would be named after him. He gave a series of balls and parties for the diplomats and the military corps; then, on his last birthday in office, he attended a ball in his honor, joined by twelve thousand guests. Upon being announced, Washington was greeted by such deafening applause that Martha Washington wept. Washington himself could scarcely speak, being so overcome with gratitude.

By the time he handed over the levers of power to John Adams at the inauguration, Washington had come to realize that the man now taking the oath of office was his most loyal and consistent supporter. Washington stood in a black coat to one side of the dais. As Adams walked in, there was not a dry eye in the house—but the tears were not for him. Following Adams's speech, the new president enjoyed applause, then walked down the aisle, leaving Jefferson and Washington standing behind. Vice President Jefferson waited for Washington to precede him, but the general gestured for Jefferson to go ahead. When Jefferson hesitated, Washington gestured a second time, more forcefully. Thus George Washington, private citizen, was the last one to leave the dais and exit the building. The crowds that had cheered Adams turned to see "the Indispensable Man" standing in the doorway, and in a final mark of honor roared with "a sound like thunder."

The Indispensable Man

It is safe to say that George Washington was the greatest of all presidents. In everything he did, he was aware of the precedents he was setting. And the example he set for his successors was one of sterling integrity, ambition under superb control, and respect for the Constitution in every decision he made. That alone would have elevated him to the top. His treatment of Indians was, even from the perspective of the twenty-first century, enlightened: dealing with the tribes as independent nations, while it proved impracticable over time, constituted an ingenious *modus vivendi* until the nation had both the military force and the humanitarian urge to find other solutions. The almost immediate onset of a Franco-British conflict at the beginning of the very first administration under the new Constitution would have destroyed almost any other president in 1791. But by roping all the hotheads on each side—Hamilton, Madison, Jefferson—together as members of his administration, or at least close advisors to it, Washington bought precious time for the young nation to find its feet. By his bold endorsement of Hamilton's fiscal policies, Washington ensured the United States a quick ascent to prosperity, which always makes difficult political choices easier and heated tempers cooler.

Flexner argues that it was essential Washington serve the second term. Had he not, infighting and tensions might have ended the experiment in democracy right at the start. But it was also essential that Washington serve *only* two terms, even if his health had permitted more, for by stepping down so soon Washington set the precedent of rotation in office. His appreciation for the fact that America needed stability but not permanence in its chief executive, and his decision to run for a second term but step down after two was his greatest service to his country. As one looks forward a mere fifty years, to the popular but thuggish Andrew Jackson, whose petty "war" on the Bank of the United States, unconstitutional removal of the Cherokee, and infantile feuds stained his otherwise successful record, Washington seems even more impressive for always rising above such nonsense to be "First in war, first in peace, and first in the hearts of his countrymen."

Washington and the Constitution

It would be glib to say that Washington could have done whatever he wanted in interpreting the Constitution for the office of the presidency. After all, what precedent was there? That makes it all the more impressive that he deliberately and meticulously sought out the real meaning of the Constitution before he acted. When it came to policies, Washington took the defense of the United States and its security as the overarching duty of the president. Hamilton's protective tariffs were at least as much oriented toward ensuring a foundation for arming and equipping an army as for the protection American businesses for its own sake. The Proclamation of Neutrality proved constitutional genius: Washington acted quickly when speed was of the essence, but rather than taking a position that might have gotten the United

States into a war with two Old World superpowers, he merely perpetuated the status quo with both France and England. Contrary to the views of many libertarians, Washington was not an isolationist who wished to avoid all foreign treaties in perpetuity. He merely sought to keep the United States out of any European wars for a period of about twenty years, until the growth of the American population, national defense network, economy, and military would ensure that the young republic could survive such an encounter. The War of 1812 proved Washington correct: the United States was just powerful enough by then to fend off a powerful British Empire.

Finally, by serving two terms, Washington provided the stability essential to the new nation while at the same time setting the precedent of rotation in office. Even if John Adams was of his party, the election that put Adams in the presidency was fair and open, and the people had spoken.

While no constitutional grade is truly appropriate for the "guy who wrote the book," if he had to be given a grade, Washington would receive an A+, as well as the perpetual thanks of his countrymen.

CHAPTER 2

John Adams, 1797–1801

"Our Constitution was made only for a moral and religious people. It is wholly inadequate
to the government of any other."

—*John Adams*

President Adams's Constitutional Grade: B–

Other than Alexander Hamilton, whose enemies *really* hated him, John Adams was likely the most unpopular of all the Founders. By his frequent moralizing, he constantly reminded others of their inadequacies. Lacking Washington's history as commander of the army, Adams could not attract men by his sheer aura alone. Certainly Adams was ambitious—who among the Founders was not?—but thirst for office did not consume him as it did Hamilton or Aaron Burr.

No one could surpass Washington, with his "first in war, first in peace, first in the hearts of his countrymen" appeal (those words are from the eulogy written for the general by Henry "Light-Horse Harry" Lee). But few knew constitutional government as well as Adams. Adams took part in what were arguably the two most important elections ever in the nation's history, once as a winner, once as a loser. His victory in 1796 meant that for the first time in modern history a large nation turned over its governance to an entirely new man as the result of free elections, and his loss in 1800 meant that that same nation could entrust not only different people with

Did you know?

★ John Adams successfully defended British soldiers against murder charges in the Boston Massacre

★ Abigail Adams was an early advocate for racial integration in education

★ Adams was so eager to get out of Washington, D.C., after Jefferson was elected to replace him that he left town before his successor's inauguration

the office, but people of vastly different ideas and ideologies. Such broad faith in the political system did not exist anywhere else in the world.

Crowning Achievement

The presidency was a job Adams had hoped to gain from the moment the Constitutional Convention designed it. He felt intellectually superior to Washington and resented the general's popularity. Washington, of course, knew what the job entailed after eight years, and his manner of handing over the reins of power to his successor caused Adams to sense that the job wasn't what it was cracked up to be. Writing to his wife Abigail Adams, John said he "thought" he "heard [Washington] think," "I am fairly out and you are fairly in. See which of us will be the happiest." It could have been Adams's own conscience speaking to him. Just four years later, after losing the election of 1800 to his frenemy Jefferson, Adams hopped in a carriage and left Washington before the Virginian could even take the oath of office. Perhaps as he left town, Adams was reminded of Washington's yearning to spend his final days on his farm. By any account, his swift departure is yet another example of the fact that most of the Founders considered their life in government as a short period of service, not a career.

Adams, who had been a lawyer at the time of the Revolution (he had successfully defended the British soldiers accused of murder in the "Boston Massacre"), had, ironically, actually been in government in one way or another since that time. Having served as the ambassador to England under the Articles of Confederation and then for eight years as Washington's vice president, when Adams was elected president he was finally ready to come into his own. His self-acknowledged intellectual and moral superiority notwithstanding, Adams had watched and learned from Washington and remained constantly supportive. "I am heir apparent," he told Abigail in 1796.

★ ★ ★

A Woman's Touch

Two of the most influential women of the early Republic were close friends: Abigail Adams and Mercy Otis Warren. Mercy Otis Warren was the daughter of Colonel James Otis, a descendant of Edward Doty, a *Mayflower* passenger, and the wife of James Warren, president of the Massachusetts Provincial Congress. She studied informally with her brothers when they were being tutored for Harvard College. The Warren home was the scene of Sons of Liberty meetings and "correspondent" to Sam Adams, John Hancock, and Patrick Henry in the "Committees of Correspondence." After the Revolution, Warren published poetry, plays of a political and satirical nature, and then, in 1799, *Observations on the New Constitution*. That Anti-Federalist work warned that the threats to individual liberty in the new government framework were great. "There is no security in the proffered system," she wrote, "either for the rights of conscience or the liberty of the Press." In a phrase that must resonate with modern Americans, who have seen Congress become little more than a rubber stamp of the executive branch, she argued that in the proposed Constitution "The Executive and the Legislative are so dangerously blended as to give just cause of alarm...." Warren also warned against allowing the Constitution to go into effect on ratification by only nine states—rather than unanimously—expressed misgivings about a standing army, and (how's this for prescience) predicted that the six-year term for a senator would in reality be "an appointment for life." Warren's insights are worth consideration even in the twenty-first century.

Abigail Adams, of course, tended to follow her husband's Federalist views more closely—they were both supporters of the new Constitution. But she became John Adams's most effective and ardent critic as well as his biggest supporter. She despised the different cabals jockeying for political influence and particularly distrusted Hamilton ("I have seen the devil in his eyes," she said, "his wicked eyes. The very devil is in them. They are lasciviousness itself"—though these observations are probably more about his lust for Maria Reynolds and other young women than about his politics.). Abigail personally supported the right of a free black boy to attend school against the objections of other parents, and won the day. She, like John, was a friend of Thomas Jefferson's, but political differences drove them apart, as she acknowledged when she said, on Jefferson's becoming Adams's vice president, that having a president and vice president of different "sentiments" could be a blessing to the country. A farm wife, she advocated new property rights for women to the Continental Congress in 1776 and was so active in her husband's presidency that outsiders called her "Mrs. President."

A Book You're Not Supposed to Read

John Adams by David McCullough (New York: Touchstone, 2001).

The Quasi-War with France

When Adams took the oath of office in 1797, war with either France or England remained foremost among the concerns of Americans, and the new president strongly endorsed Washington's policy of neutrality. The United States over which Adams presided was larger than the one George Washington had first been elected to lead, by three states—Vermont, Kentucky, and Tennessee. Slowly a third region was being added to the "North" and "South," namely the "West" with its own peculiarities and interests. "I have unshaken confidence" Adams said, "in the spirit of the American people…on which I have often hazarded my all." His inaugural address left nary a dry eye. Even the Republicans extolled Adams as a "man of incorruptible integrity."

Adams felt honor bound to take many of Washington's existing cabinet as his own for the sake of continuity and to honor the first president. This was a mistake that would plague him throughout his administration, as none were loyal to Adams and many schemed against him from the get-go. These lesser talents included Hamilton's recommendation for Treasury, Oliver Wolcott Jr., who, lacking Hamilton's genius, at least did nothing to unravel the brilliant structure already in place. There were also extreme Federalists, such as James McHenry in the War Department and Timothy Pickering at State, with Charles Lee of Virginia as the attorney general. Like Washington, Adams attempted to maintain a sectional balance. Of course, Jefferson was vice president. He met Adams in Philadelphia right before the inauguration and the two had a happy reunion, having not seen each other for three years. The good will between them lasted only a few days. Immediately after Adams was sworn in, he sought recommendations for emissaries to France. Jefferson, naturally, wanted James Madison—who was entirely unacceptable to the devout Federalists.

That led to a disagreement on Market Street, and Jefferson and the president never spoke about France again.

The threat of a war weighed extremely heavy on Adams's soul. He had not fought in the Revolution, but he had seen the results of the Boston Massacre. He operated out of a variation of the maxim Ronald Reagan would use two centuries later with respect to the Soviets, "Trust but verify." Regarding the rift with France, Adams said in a May 1787 speech, he had a "sincere desire" to see "it healed," and "to preserve peace and friendship with all nations," but at the same time he pointed out that no one would take the U.S. seriously if the young nation did not build up her military power. He therefore recommended increased measures of defense, citing the emblem of the United States: an eagle with the olive branch in one claw and arrows in the other. Predictably, the Jeffersonians called the president's speech a "war-whoop."

In fact, the United States government was not the one courting war. The French had stepped up their incursions at sea—it was no longer only the British who were attacking and capturing American merchant ships. Adams was informed that some three hundred such incidents involving the French had occurred in 1787 alone. Fortunately, things settled down, and Adams sought a new commitment from France to keep things quiet. Adams sent three diplomats—Charles Cotesworth Pinckney, John Marshall, and Elbridge Gerry—to France to meet with the French foreign minister Charles Talleyrand (a remarkable political survivalist). Talleyrand, however, after a brief initial meeting, instead dealt with the three through French agents referred to as "X, Y, and Z." Those agents, speaking for Talleyrand, insisted on bribes (*douceurs*, or sweeteners) and a loan before Talleyrand would even meet with the American trio officially again. An exasperated Pinckney issued the famous "No, no, not a sixpence!" All three American ministers decided on November 1, 1797, that they would not meet with anyone other than Talleyrand himself, although in fact they

★ ★ ★

What's In a Name?

Although they barely resembled modern political parties in other ways, the Founding-Era Federalists and the Republicans could be as partisan and bull-headed as our Republicans and Democrats. But the Federalists were the first party to master public relations—beginning with their name.

When a stronger central government was first proposed, those who supported it were known as "Nationalists." The Nationalists included George Washington, John Adams, Alexander Hamilton, John Jay, Robert Morris, Benjamin Franklin, and, at the time, James Madison. (By the time of Adams's election, Madison would switch parties to join the Republicans.) The opponents of strong central government were called … "Federalists," because they believed in a true federal system with division of power between the national and state governments, with the emphasis being on the latter. These Federalists included people such as Thomas Jefferson, George Mason, Samuel Adams, James Monroe, and Patrick Henry. (As we have seen, they also counted among their number a talented, highly literate, and outspoken woman, Mercy Otis Warren.)

You read that correctly: those who opposed a stronger national government under the Constitution originally went by the term Federalist. But

even before the new Constitution establishing it was drafted and debated in the summer of 1787, the Nationalists pulled a marketing coup of monumental proportions. They stole the name "Federalist" from their opponents, whom, in an even more brilliant twist, they began labeling in newspapers and speeches as the "Anti-Federalists." Sam Adams was one of the first to be so labeled publicly. As everyone knows, you never want to be called "anti" anything. (Today, for example, both sides of the abortion debate are "pro"—"pro-life" and "pro-choice.") In a lapse of monumental proportions—perhaps because Jefferson was in France during the drafting of the Constitution, or because Patrick Henry refused to attend the Constitutional Convention, or because Sam Adams did not participate—the opponents of a strong national government never effectively countered this rhetorical coup by its supporters. By the time of the ratification debates over the Constitution, the "Anti-Federalists" moniker had taken hold.

After the inauguration of Washington, the "antis" still hadn't learned their lesson: the opposition party to the "Federalist" administration referred to itself as the "Anti-Administration" at a secret 1790 meeting in Philadelphia. Because Jefferson thought the Federalists were opposed to the kind of "republicanism" that was spreading in France, soon the name "Republican" was being used in correspondence between Jefferson and Madison. These "Republicans" would be called the National Republican Party in 1824—after the Federalists died out completely and there was a uniparty. Sometimes the original Republican Party was called "Democratic-Republican," but rarely. As we have already seen, the true "Democratic Party" only appeared when Martin Van Buren created it as a vehicle to stop the slavery debate in 1824. The modern "Republican Party" was founded thirty years later to oppose the expansion of slavery.

continued to have conversations one-on-one with Lucien Hauteval ("Z"). When the two Federalists, Marshall and Pinckney, began to take sides against the lone Republican, Gerry, Talleyrand attempted to peel off the Jeffersonian. Indeed, Gerry communicated secretly with Talleyrand and was ultimately bullied into staying in France (by the threat of war) when Marshall and Pinckney departed.

A frustrated Adams had already begun to explore other options in case the commissioners failed. He called for raising an army of twenty thousand, and for the construction of frigates. When he heard the full story of what had happened in France, he only shared part of it with Congress, revealing in March 1798 only that the mission failed, but not that the French had treated the American diplomats with contempt. Predictably, the Jeffersonians were convinced that Adams was withholding information favorable to the French! So they fell in with the Federalists who were demanding full disclosure. In April, thinking his envoys were safely out of France, Adams released all the documents, which demonstrated to the entire House the impropriety with which France had acted. Predictably, once the Republicans learned how bad the information was for their side, they tried to stop publication of the dispatches. The *Aurora*, a spiteful Republican publication, pummeled Adams as "unhinged" and vain. Abigail thought her husband's critics possessed nothing less than the "malice...of Satan."

Most of the nation, however, saw the French as petty and childish, as well as belligerent. Congress passed measures for arming merchant ships, building foundries, fortifying harbors, and raising a provisional army of ten thousand men. (It should be noted that this army, enormous for the United States, would barely have made up a single one of Napoleon's divisions.) Congress also created a new Department of the Navy and authorized the construction of six new frigates, three of which were to have forty-four guns. Ultimately, only two sported that number. Adams referred to the vessels as "floating batteries with wooden walls." France had come foolishly close to pushing the United States into an alliance with England. Under Adams, Congress created the U.S. Marine Corps, abrogated a 1788 treaty with France, and enacted a direct tax on land (which was unconstitutional).

In addition to France and England, Adams also had to deal with the Lone Ranger antics of George Logan, a Pennsylvania Quaker who traveled to Paris on his own funds to obtain the release of some American sailors, thereby inserting himself into international negotiations (a practice Jesse Jackson, among others, would engage in over two hundred years later). By endangering those he sought to free, Logan inspired Congress to pass the Logan Act in 1799, prohibiting private citizens from negotiating with foreign powers in the name of the United States.

The Alien and Sedition Acts

Ironically, the addition of several more Federalists to Congress in the 1798 mid-term elections did not make Adams's job easier. The Federalists promptly passed the Alien and Sedition Acts, including a Naturalization Act that increased the time needed to qualify for citizenship from five years to fourteen. The Alien Act itself gave the president the authority to deport any foreigners considered dangerous. Of course, the Jeffersonians reacted with horror, claiming that Adams would ship out thousands of foreigners.

In fact, Adams never invoked the law. The Sedition Act outlawed any "false, scandalous, and malicious" writing against the government, Congress, or the president and any attempt to "excite against them...the hatred of the good people of the United States, or to stir up sedition." This law, in clear violation of the First Amendment, was nevertheless upheld by several Federalist judges, who convicted many people, including newspaper editors. And at first, the Acts were quite popular. Many newspapers came to Adams's defense. One must remember that the First Amendment notwithstanding, Americans' sense of personal honor at the time meant that they believed libel and slander should be taken very seriously. Defamatory comments often led to duels, and duels to death. Not for another fifty years would courts hold that a case for libel of a public figure had to meet a higher standard than that of a private individual.

Adams neither vetoed nor protested the Alien and Sedition Acts; he stood behind them. Later, to his discredit, he attempted to deny responsibility for them. They were certainly provocative. James Madison and Thomas Jefferson authored the Virginia and Kentucky Resolutions in 1788 and 1799, seeking to assert state sovereignty against the federal encroachment on citizens' rights. Relying on the "compact" theory of government, they argued that states had the right to "Interposition" between the federal government and the states—that is, the authority to protect their citizens from "unconstitutional and coercive federal laws." The Alien and Sedition Acts, they pointed out, exercised "a power not delegated by the Constitution." Jefferson, in the Kentucky Resolution, went further than Madison and claimed that "the several states...have the unquestionable right to judge of [the Constitution's] infraction...a nullification, by those [states], of all unauthorized acts...is the rightful remedy." No other states supported the Virginia and Kentucky Resolutions, and seven specifically rejected them. The newly formed Vermont expressly repudiated them, saying, "It belongs not to state legislatures to decide on the constitutionality of laws made by the general

A Book You're Not Supposed to Read

The Patriot's History Reader by Larry Schweikart, Dave Dougherty, and Michael Allen (New York: Sentinel, 2011).

government...." Adams and Congress were saved from a constitutional battle by the states themselves, though ironically later the New England states would use Jefferson's own reasoning to ignore the Embargo Act of 1807 under Adams's successor...Thomas Jefferson.

In February of 1799, Adams announced, with almost no consultation with anyone, that he had sent William Vans Murray to be a minister plenipotentiary to France, joined by Wolcott and Chief Justice Oliver Ellsworth. This time the French played no games with the ministers. Adams, demonized by the Jeffersonians as a Federalist "warmonger," had become the great peacemaker, navigating America safely through the "Quasi-War" with France, as it came to be known.

So Adams entered the final two years of his term preparing to make peace with the French government. In the meantime, however, he had to flee Philadelphia due to a vicious influenza epidemic. The U.S. government was temporarily relocated to Trenton, New Jersey (the final relocation of the government to the new federal city on the Potomac would occur in June 1800). Bad news arrived that December; George Washington had died.

Adams's Place in Presidential History

When John Adams arrived in the new federal District of Columbia, he found no city there at all—just shabby buildings and tormenting heat. He and his secretaries stayed at a local hotel, and he inspected the new "White House." After going home to Quincy, Adams returned again to find laborers hard at work on the presidential residence, and he penned the first ever letter from the White House on November 2, 1800. All of this had taken place during an "election," but Adams had done little campaigning (there was really no such thing then), and he calmly awaited the final results from the Electoral College, where he had learned there was a seventy-three-vote deadlock between Jefferson and the Federalist Aaron Burr. Adams came in third, at sixty-five. In reality, Burr and Jefferson had beaten not the president, but rather the Hamiltonian faction that wanted war with France. By holding firm to his—and Washington's—commitment to peace, John Adams became the first American president thrown out of office.

★ ★ ★

But Tell Us What You Really Think about the President

Journalist James Callender was outraged at the president's peace-making. Adams, he complained, was a "strange compound of ignorance and ferocity, of deceit and weakness," a "hideous hermaphroditical character which has neither the force and firmness of a man, nor the gentleness and sensibility of a woman."

CHAPTER 3

Thomas Jefferson, 1801–1809

"The Constitution on which our Union rests, shall be administered by me [as president] according to the safe and honest meaning contemplated by the plain understanding of the people of the United States at the time of its adoption—a meaning to be found in the explanations of those who advocated, not those who opposed it...."
—*Thomas Jefferson*

President Jefferson's Constitutional Grade: B–

More than any other president, Thomas Jefferson is associated with our modern concept of "small government." Perhaps that is because of a quotation attributed to him—but that he did not actually say, as far as we know: "That government is best which governs least." In reality, Jefferson's philosophy of government was a little more complicated than that. He first and foremost insisted on plain talk, chafing at any law that by its sophisticated language made easy application difficult or impossible. Long after his presidency, Jefferson wrote to William Johnson, "Laws are made for men of ordinary understanding and should, therefore, be construed by the ordinary rules of common sense. Their meaning is not to be sought for in metaphysical subtleties which may make anything mean everything or nothing at pleasure." (This sounds a lot like a quotation from our final presidential entry, William Howard Taft: "Don't write so you can be understood, write so that you can't be misunderstood.") In 1812 Jefferson had insisted, "Common sense [is] the foundation of all authorities, of the laws themselves, and of their construction."

Did you know?

★ Jefferson opened the White House door himself to greet guests, occasionally in his bedroom slippers

★ In 1802, Jefferson received a colossal wheel of cheese from the Baptists of Cheshire, Massachusetts, weighing over 1,200 pounds and spanning four feet in diameter, sent to commemorate Jefferson's victory over John Adams

★ The war against the Barbary pirates was America's first overseas war

★ ★ ★

A Small-Government Republican by Any Other Name Would Smell as Sweet

Americans in the nineteenth century didn't contrast big-government programs and politicians with small-government ones. Instead, they compared and contrasted two different ways of reading the Constitution. Jefferson was a "strict constructionist" who believed that the federal government should be limited to the powers explicitly delegated to it in the Constitution, and that all other powers were reserved to the states and the people.

Our third president was relying on the tradition of the Common Law, in which the "self-evident" natural moral law, which God created us all to know, is expressed in case law from decisions by judges; thus the law enforces what the people already know and believe. Common Law was an English tradition that had migrated from Great Britain to America. Every other European nation had some form of "Civil Law" instead, such as the Napoleonic Code (as in Louisiana today) or the Russian Civil Law (with roots in the Roman Empire's Justinian Code). Sharia Law in the Islamic world is another "code"-based legal system derived from the decrees of an authority (in that case, of Allah), in contrast to the Anglo-American Common Law tradition. Jefferson understood that the United States was unique, exceptional. He saw that the Common Law allowed a role for morality in our law, arguing, "When an instrument admits two constructions, the one just and the other unjust, the former is to be given them." There were instances, he insisted, when cases, "though within the *words* of the law, [are] notoriously not within its intention, and are therefore relievable by an equitable exercise of discretionary power."

Small-government Jefferson saw the presidency as not just the office of the "first man," but as the instrument of national will. As such, historian Cecelia Kenyon has argued, Jefferson agreed with his hated rival Alexander Hamilton and with his predecessor George Washington that the executive must occasionally act outside the law, or even against it, to serve the public good so long as he stands accountable before Congress, the courts, and the people for doing so. Jefferson also agreed with Hamilton that the central threat to a republic was tyranny of one sort or another. For Hamilton, it was tyranny of the masses voting themselves goodies from the public trough; for Jefferson, it was a monarch.

An Article You're Not Supposed to Read

In "Alexander Hamilton: Rousseau of the Right," *Political Science Quarterly* 75 (June 1958), 161–78, Cecelia Kenyon argues that Hamilton had absorbed Rousseauian principles. The strong executive he sought would reflect Rousseau's "General Will." Kenyon is extremely useful for revealing the concerns that both Hamilton and Jefferson had about a dictatorship.

The story of Jefferson's ascent to the Oval Office should be well known. After serving as Washington's secretary of State, then resigning in Washington's second term, Jefferson came within three votes of being elected president in 1796. Indeed, there was a question of the propriety of one of the delegation's votes, and when the votes were counted under rival candidate Vice President John Adams (as president of the Senate), Adams graciously stopped counting when he came to the disputed Georgia ballot to allow Jefferson and his associates to challenge it. They did not. It was a critical and defining moment in American history. As badly as Jefferson wanted the presidency, faith in the office and the process came first. He would not weaken the country over a few pieces of paper. Perhaps something inside him also said *it's not time*. Eight years of Washington's presidency had stabilized the young nation—but was it stable enough to allow a complete shift of governing philosophy almost as radical as the Revolution itself?

The Most Critical of All American Elections

Jefferson's time came in four short years, by which point Adams seemed more than eager to leave. In *A Patriot's History of the United States*, Mike Allen and I have described the election of 1800 as the most important

A Book You're Not Supposed to Read

A Patriot's History of the United States: From Columbus's Great Discovery to America's Age of Entitlement by Larry Schweikart and Michael Patrick Allen, 10th rev. ed. (New York: Sentinel, 2014).

election in American history, for it marked the first true test of the system. It's one thing for a president and his party to hand over control to someone of the same persuasion, another thing entirely to trust that the structure will survive one's political enemies. Yet Adams climbed in his carriage and left the capital for his beloved Braintree, Massachusetts, farm before Jefferson even took the oath of office. Not a cannon ball flew. America had truly become a land where the people ruled. (By an accident of the Electoral College, when there was a tie between the Republican Jefferson and the [despised] Federalist Aaron Burr, the House of Representatives settled the tie... with the prodding of Jefferson's nemesis Alexander Hamilton, who hated Burr more than he did the Virginian!)

Jefferson appreciated the magnitude of the change, and generously announced in his inaugural, "We are all Republicans, we are all Federalists." Of course, he said that to a mostly Republican audience, but the sentiments were sound.

The new president had the good fortune of inheriting, from John Adams, peace with both France and England. In his Inaugural Address he advocated freedom of "religion, press, and person," a veiled reference to Adams's Alien and Sedition Acts. Jefferson called for a devolution of power to the states and the strict construction of the Constitution—which he quickly abandoned. Along with Gallatin, Jefferson believed in sound money as defined by a gold standard, low debt, and low taxes. He urged Congress to repeal the Whiskey Tax and other internal taxes, and it did. Before Jefferson is given too much credit for lowering the nation's debt and cutting taxes, it should be pointed out that the revenue he used to replace the lost income came from tariffs and land sales—both the direct result of Federalist policies, namely Hamilton's tariff structures and the Jay Treaty securing the Western lands for settlement.

Green Acres

But that should take nothing away from Jefferson, whose own ideas had been behind the Land Ordinance of 1785 opening the Old Northwest for settlement. His proposal for ceding the territories of the "landed states" to the federal government in order to ensure that there be rough equality among the states was entirely visionary. Indeed, Jefferson, contemplating the land cession in the 1780s, argued that if there were no process whereby settlers could create entirely new states, Americans in the West would eventually think of themselves as colonists and rise up in their own revolution. He insisted that the citizens of the new states take an oath not only to the Constitution but to *Congress*, indicating they understood they were part of a whole. This would prove troublesome later for Jefferson, who often expressed a "compact" view of the Union, whereby states could come and go as they saw fit, as opposed to a holistic "body" view, whereby a state could not simply leave, any more than an arm can be chopped off without damaging or even killing the body.

Jefferson never shone more brightly than in his land policies. Here he resembled banker A. P. Giannini, the "retailer to the many, rather than a wholesaler to the few." Where Hamilton favored cash sales and selling large blocs of land to real estate speculators, Jefferson wanted ordinary farmers to get the land, and get it fast. In 1801 he had Congress set a minimum plot of 320 acres at a price of only $2 an acre, increased the number of land offices, and moved them closer to frontier areas. This caused sales to shoot up to half a million acres. More important, he waived cash payment in favor

★ ★ ★
Speak Softly...

It should be noted that Jefferson was not the powerful public speaker that one might assume, given the power of his written words. He spoke in a very soft voice, often causing people in the same room to have to lean in to hear him.

★ ★ ★

Jefferson's Agrarian Utopia

While Jefferson is sometimes viewed as championing "self-sufficiency," his ideal American farmer would have had to buy at least some manufactured objects that aren't typically produced on farms. As he once said of himself, "I cannot live without books." Jefferson's agrarian republic would have been populated by landholders who farmed in the morning, then read or engaged in politics or philosophy in the afternoon.

of a credit system whereby a farmer could put down twenty-five percent and pay the rest in four years. Under Jefferson, the government became a sort of precursor to Fannie Mae and Freddie Mac, extending $700,000 in credit to farmers.

Part of Jefferson's motivation in making land available to farmers was his desire to free America from its dependence on the bankers and their loans. Hamilton had seen them both as key to ensuring the survival of the Union. Jefferson condemned this reliance on "monied men," but failed to recognize that he had merely transferred leverage from one interest group to another. The farmers Jefferson favored over the bankers were not really apolitical. In the twenty-first century, long after the zenith of their political influence, farmers still wield a powerful club as a lobbying group. As late as 2015, candidates beginning their presidential runs in Iowa still had to tread lightly on the subject of ethanol subsidies, and sugar producers in Louisiana and Florida held tremendous influence in their states.

The Biggest of Big Government Projects

Jefferson and his Republican Congress proved faithful to his budget-cutting rhetoric, slashing the Federalists' annual $5 million budget in half. Gallatin's Treasury began paying off the national debt, so that by 1810 some $40 million of the $82 million debt had been retired.

Seeking to advance the interests of his natural constituency, the farmers, Jefferson tasked both Gallatin and Congress with finding ways to reduce the cost of getting goods to market. At the time roads were privately financed, but in 1802 Congress began to experiment with financing Western road construction with federal land revenues. Four years later, Congress funded the National Road to Ohio, and Jefferson did not veto the bill as unconstitutional. Of course, it could easily be defended as essential to the national defense—just as the construction of the interstates under Eisenhower's National Highway Act was. At this point Jefferson doesn't seem so small government. He pushed Congress, asking if there was anything else in the area of transportation Congress could do within the "pale" of its constitutional power to "advance the national good." He continued to become more aggressive in seeking to enhance roads and harbors, in 1806 acknowledging a federal role in transportation for the "improvement of the country."

In 1808, however, he took the most un-Jeffersonian step of all, urging Gallatin to outline a massive plan for government intervention in the transportation network to remove all obstacles to trade. Gallatin's proposal was for Congress to fund a ten-year, *$20 million* project in which the federal government itself would construct roads and canals, or provide direct loans for private enterprise to do so. Specifically, Gallatin detailed a $16 million expenditure for a canal that would connect the Atlantic Coast to the Great Lakes, and included some $3 million for local improvements. This proved too much for the president's own party, for it was five times the entire outlay for the rest of the government. Jefferson endorsed the plan; the only reservation he had—as a "strict constructionist" of the Constitution—was whether or not a constitutional amendment would be required. The president's friend and Republican ally James Madison did not dissent from the plan at the time, but as president he would veto the Bonus Bill, which contained what he believed to be unconstitutional funding for "internal improvements."

It is clear that Jefferson's small-government ideology was selective. When it came to the Department of War, his cuts knew no restraint, to the point

A Book You're Not Supposed to Read

American Sphinx: The Character of Thomas Jefferson by Joseph J. Ellis (New York: Vintage, 1998).

that the department barely existed. The Republican Congress eliminated all funds for deep-sea ships, maintaining only a small fleet of coastal gunboats—almost all of which would be quickly sunk in the War of 1812, while the few frigates the Federalists had built survived and fought gallantly. Republicans reduced the army to a paltry thirty-five hundred men, citing the fact that the Indian wars in the Northwest were over (thanks to Washington). Ironically, Jefferson established a new officer training academy for the U.S. Army—West Point—in part, though, to replace the Federalist officers with Republicans. Nevertheless, Jefferson was effective in his overall goal of cutting the budget by almost half, chopping jobs in every office, so that in the succeeding administration James Madison's State Department would conduct business with *fewer* employees than Washington's. His cabinet met once a week at first, but after 1807, with "grave matters of business piling up," Jefferson acquiesced to daily cabinet briefings.

Nevertheless, one major modern study of the administration of the Republicans has concluded that Thomas Jefferson's role as president was essentially the same role that Washington and the Federalists had adopted, although his methods "were more subtle and indirect," fitting Jefferson's personality. As contemporary observer John Quincy Adams reported, Jefferson's "whole system of administration [was] founded upon the principle of carrying through the legislative measures by his personal or official influence."

Deal of the Century

It is one of the ironies of American history that the strict constructionist (or, as we would say, small-government) Jefferson, in an act of questionable constitutionality, added more territory to the United States than anyone until Abraham Lincoln's secretary of State, William Seward, picked up Alaska for less than the modern price of an oil tanker. The Louisiana Purchase began with negotiations over New Orleans.

Any power that controlled New Orleans, Jefferson wrote, was the "natural and habitual enemy" of the United States, given that the port city was the egress from the Mississippi to the Caribbean and beyond. The French Emperor Napoleon had acquired the Louisiana Territory, including New Orleans, in the Treaty of San Ildefonso in 1800, although France never took actual possession and both France and Spain kept the treaty a secret for over a year. Now Jefferson was hoisted on his own Francophile petard: he couldn't allow a nation as strong as France to control American access to the Caribbean and its trade, but the U.S. Navy was still not powerful enough to fight the French. Jefferson glumly observed that the day French troops set foot in New Orleans, "we must marry ourselves to the British fleet and nation."

Jefferson's minister to France, Robert Livingston, received a letter from the president bemoaning the fact that while Spain, in "her feeble state" could have "retained [New Orleans] quietly for years," France's "temper [and] the energy and restlessness of her character," rendered coexistence impossible for the United States. Jefferson planned to beef up the Navy immediately and, if necessary, fire the first shots over French occupation of the city. These were astounding words from the Francophile who just three years earlier had sought to take the United States to war with England. Yet Jefferson did not send the letter only to Livingston: wanting to avoid any replay of the X, Y, Z affair and ensure that the emperor read it himself, the president sent a "back-channel" copy of the letter via his friend Pierre Samuel Du Pont de Nemours.

In the fall of 1802, the prospect of Americans' losing the "right of deposit" to keep their goods for export in New Orleans—which could amount to $1 million in cargo fees annually—sparked a national outrage against

France. Jefferson moved quickly, concluding, after researching the question and on Gallatin's advice, that he was within his constitutional rights to acquire territory from France, getting Congress to appropriate $2 million for "intercourse" between the U.S. and nameless foreign nations and in March 1803 sending James Monroe as a special envoy to negotiate with Napoleon Bonaparte, with authority to offer 50 million francs for New Orleans and the Floridas, or two-thirds of that sum for New Orleans alone.

Livingston was already at work, meeting with both Napoleon and Talleyrand. The latter got right to the point: "Have you any money?" he asked, in a grim reminder of the bribes that had been demanded in the X, Y, Z affair. But in this case the fortunes of war had already defined Napoleon's options. France had lost one fleet at the Battle of the Nile (1798), and Napoleon knew that when his current truce with Britain fell apart—as it surely would—the Royal Navy was far superior to his own. That meant he had no practical way of securing New Orleans from the British...so why not just sell it to the Americans? An April 1803 meeting between Livingston and Talleyrand began with the French minister asking if the United States was interested in the "whole" of Louisiana. Livingston repeated that his instructions only included New Orleans and the Floridas. Talleyrand reiterated that the only thing important to America *was* New Orleans. Again, how much for everything? Livingston, still without Monroe and with no authority to make any genuine offer, blurted out 20 million francs, which Talleyrand considered too low. Monroe finally arrived and the two met with Talleyrand, this time offering 60 million francs. France agreed. For $15 million, the United States added the entire Louisiana Territory—including what would become all or part of the states of Arkansas, Iowa, Kansas, Missouri, Nebraska, the Dakotas, Louisiana, Minnesota, Montana, New Mexico, Texas, and Wyoming—to the nation.

Now Jefferson had to sell the acquisition to the American people. Privately, in an 1803 letter to James Madison, he admitted that he thought the purchase was unconstitutional. John Quincy Adams and others claimed that because the vast amount of territory constituted a virtual "dissolution and recomposition" of America's territory, it required a constitutional amendment. Jefferson agreed in private, but feared that any delay would lead Napoleon to rescind the deal. So publicly, Jefferson claimed (ironically arguing from Madison's *Federalist* No. 10) that the larger the Republic, the "less it will be shaken by local passions." Sounding a lot like Hamilton, he also played the national security card, asking if it wouldn't be safer to have the opposite bank of the Mississippi under American control. In an action presaging Teddy Roosevelt's seizure of the Panama Canal zone ("I took Panama and left Congress to debate me"), Jefferson simply acted as though he had the authority and left the politicians and pundits to quibble over a *fait accompli.*

Jefferson's intent to obtain Louisiana is betrayed by the fact that even before the deal was done he had secretly secured funds for the exploration of the territory from Congress. Now he referred to the Constitution's provisions as "metaphysical subtleties"—and he would not let any such subtleties stand in the way of an "Empire of Liberty." As far back as 1783, the president had conceived of the names of new states to be formed from the West—Sylvania, Metropotamia, Saratoga, and Washington.

America's First War on Terror

Following depredations in the Mediterranean against American shipping, including widespread hostage-taking, which was a common revenue source for the Muslim pirates in Tripoli and other Barbary states, Jefferson was forced to take action. Both George Washington and John Adams, lacking a navy that would have empowered them to do anything else, had agreed to a policy of paying tribute, or bribes, to the Barbary pirates. There was an enormous amount of white slavery under the Muslims in the Mediterranean

A Book You're Not Supposed to Read

Jefferson's War: America's First War on Terror, 1801–1805 by Joseph Wheelan (New York: Carroll & Graf, 2003).

at the time, and it was supported by the governments in North Africa. Under a treaty negotiated in 1795 with Algiers, Tunis, and Tripoli the United States paid tribute in return for eighty-three American sailors held prisoner.

In 1801 the pasha of Tripoli, citing late payments, raised the amount of tribute due and chopped down the American flagpole at the U.S. consulate, declaring war on the United States. Jefferson, using the large ships provided by Federalist expenditures, and operating under a joint resolution of Congress (not an act of war) sounded much like George W. Bush two hundred years later ("Either you are with us, or you are with the terrorists") when he informed the Barbary states that the United States considered itself at war with *all* of them, not just Tripoli. And, like Bush, he initially sought help from allies, but found none, so he dispatched American ships. In 1804 Lieutenant Stephen Decatur landed with eighty men (mostly Marines) and set fire to the grounded USS *Philadelphia*, thus denying the Tripolitans the use of that captured American prize. A second, separate expedition under William Eaton, the ex-consul, and Marine First Lieutenant Presley O'Bannon mustered a force of mercenaries that crossed the desert to assault the city of Derna from the landward side in 1805, raising the U.S. flag on foreign soil for the first time and forcing the pasha to release his American hostages for a price of $60,000. Jefferson called it a "ransom," not "tribute."

While Jefferson's war on terror shocked both the Europeans and the Barbary pirates, showing America could execute military actions far from her shores, the expedition left the pasha in power and continued the practice of paying ransoms. A magnificent military victory was mucked up by the peace negotiations.

The Clock Strikes Midnight on the Midnight Judges

John Adams had sought to entrench a Federalist judiciary for generations with his appointment of the "Midnight Judges," but Jefferson was having none of it. Pursuant to the Judiciary Act of 1801, Adams had handed out as many circuit judgeships as he could, signing their commissions, as Jefferson said, up until midnight the night before Adams left office. The act, granting justices the power to hear "all cases in law or equity, arising under the Constitution and laws of the United States," opened the door for what would become known as "judicial review." That was exactly what Jefferson and the Republicans were afraid of—that Federalist judges could rule new laws passed by the Republicans unconstitutional.

The case that is always associated with the Midnight Judges in fact had to do with a different act of Congress, and involved William Marbury, who had been appointed Justice of the Peace in the District of Columbia, but whose commission was not delivered. After Jefferson's election, Marbury petitioned the new secretary of State, James Madison, to deliver his commission. Marbury filed his petition for a writ of mandamus (to force Madison to comply) directly to the United States Supreme Court, arguing that the Judiciary Act of 1789 granted the Supreme Court jurisdiction over these types of petitions. Chief Justice John Marshall, a Federalist, managed to establish the concept of judicial review, slap Jefferson, and yet not seat Marbury. The court ruled 4–0 that Marbury had a right to the commission, but that the Court couldn't require Madison to deliver it. The Constitution superseded any act of Congress, Marshall's court argued, and the Supreme Court could decide what acts of Congress were in fact constitutional.

Jefferson retaliated, having Congress impeach one federal judge and seeking the impeachment of Supreme Court Justice Samuel Chase, a Federalist. Chase was hardly popular. Even arch-Federalist Hamilton referred to him as "universally despised." But the Senate trial failed to come up with

Books You're Not Supposed to Read

Jefferson the President, First Term, 1801–1805 (Boston: Little, Brown and Company, 1970), and *Jefferson the President, Second Term, 1805–1809* (1974). Both volumes are by Dumas Malone, Jefferson's premier biographer.

sufficient votes to unseat Chase. In his conflict with the judiciary, Jefferson won some battles, but lost the war of precedent to Marshall.

No Free Lunch

Following his near-unanimous reelection (162 out of 176 electoral votes), and having bashed Adams repeatedly for his dealings in the "Quasi-War," Jefferson found managing two large potential adversaries, Britain and France, difficult. Napoleon had closed all European ports that he controlled to British trade and, by extension, to any foreign ships that came from a British port, including American ships. At the same time, the Royal Navy had imposed a blockade around all French-controlled ports. In short, American ships were bound to run afoul of either the British or French navies if they traded anywhere in Europe.

At this point, Jefferson's small government policies came back to bite him, for the United States had no navy capable of taking on either nation, let alone both of them. Jefferson got Congress to pass a bill authorizing 188 new gunboats carrying two to three cannon, to join the 75 already constructed. But these were next to useless when pitted against a British or French frigate and simply constituted a waste of money. They could not even enforce Jefferson's embargo against the warring powers. Overall, the Embargo Act was Christmas Day to smugglers: with American merchant ships confined to port and seamen out of work, an illegitimate trade sprung up. The embargo constituted an enormous burden not only on the New England merchants (the very group that had initiated the American Revolution), but also on farmers and planters in the South. Ship owners were put out of business, and exports plummeted from $110 million to

$20 million under the embargo. Bankruptcies soared in the five months after it was enacted.

For the first time as president, Jefferson was deluged with hate mail and newspaper editorials scorching him. Angry letters poured into the president's office. "Take off the Embargo," one wrote, "return to Carters Mountain and be ashamed of yourself and never show your head in Publick Company again." Another wrote, "I should think it would make you sink with despair," and yet another claimed "You are bartering away this Countrys rights honor and Liberty." The embargo cost America some $50 million worth of business and tarnished Jefferson's reputation. He had named Madison as his chosen successor, and Madison won the 1808 election, but the image of the Republicans as the "people's party" had suffered badly.

★ ★ ★
Two-Term Limit

Perhaps Jefferson's new unpopularity explains why early in his second term the president began to state in private mail—which he knew would become public—that two terms were enough for any president.

The Wolf by the Ear

Though he was given few opportunities to take action on slavery one way or the other, Jefferson instinctively knew it was bad personal practice and destructive to political harmony. Despite his unwillingness to free his own slaves, he knew slavery was immoral. "I tremble for my country," he wrote, "when I reflect that God is just; that his justice cannot sleep forever." Later, long after he was out of the presidency, he would utter the famous line regarding slavery, "we have the wolf by the ear, and we can neither hold him, nor safely let him go. Justice is in one scale, and self-preservation in the other."

Jefferson observed that separating states' rights and slavery was impossible, but he did not yet perceive the looming constitutional question—whether a person could be property. That was a decision that would be taken

Not Economically Feasible

Congress voted to end the slave trade in 1808, meaning that the slave population of the United States could only grow through native births, not imports of slaves. As many (including Abraham Lincoln) would point out, this had the effect of rendering meaningless any talk about "gradual, compensated emancipation." The impossibility of such a program lay in a simple fact of economics: the law of supply and demand. If someone is willing to pay for a product—or, in this case, a human being—the supply tends to grow. Or, to put it another way, if the number of slaves—through purchase and then emancipation—began to fall, the purchase price of slaves would rise, making emancipation prohibitively expensive.

out of the hands of the judiciary by the Civil War. For, as we will see, the slave states invoked states' rights almost exclusively to protect slavery, and nothing else. Ultimately, Jefferson was a living paradox on the question of slavery—a man whose rhetoric and written exhortations to liberty rejected slavery; yet a man who in most of his personal actions reaffirmed it and in his presidential actions ignored it.

Grading Jefferson on His Faithfulness to the Constitution

For all his strict constructionist rhetoric, like George Washington, Jefferson *acted* on the premise that if a power wasn't expressly denied the presidency, then he was free to use it. As Hamilton said of Jefferson, "it is not true that he is an enemy to the power of the Executive...." Rather, "while we were in administration together, he was generally for a large construction of Executive authority and not backward to act upon it in cases which coincided with his views." Such was the case in the Louisiana Purchase, in ordering a fleet to Barbary with only a joint resolution of Congress, and in his plan for a massive "infrastructure" program. At the same time, when assessing how well presidents adhere to the Constitution, one must examine the spirit of the document as well as the exact words, and the spirit was of limited power, especially of the federal government, and of leaving as much power in the hands of the people as possible. Through his land policies, Jefferson did this as well as anyone, making broad farm ownership possible and transferring land out of the control of the federal government to individuals.

His acquisition of Louisiana merely continued Washington's practice of negotiating treaties and only *then* seeking the "advice and consent" of the senate. For a Republic as large as the United States was, that was the only practical approach.

Jefferson, thanks to the fiscal policies of the Federalists (especially Hamilton) had inherited a "credit card" that paid itself down, almost automatically.

The embargo, while constitutionally passed, has been rightly characterized by historian Paul Johnson as an "absurdity," and one that severely damaged both Jefferson's administration and his legacy. It also exposed his weakness when it came to defending the country. Founding the U.S. Military Academy prepared generations of quality officers for the U.S. Army. Louisiana's addition strengthened the nation with resources and relieved threats on the borders, while New Orleans became a crucial port. But Jefferson's approach to the Navy was woeful, and he ended up—in his greatest military adventure, the Barbary Wars—relying on the frigates and other heavy ships that had been authorized by Federalists.

Finally, his unwillingness to even begin to confront the issue of slavery in a constitutional manner—by, for example, beginning to eat away at the government-supported infrastructure of supportive marshals, judges, postmasters, customs officials, and others—diminishes his presidential grade. From 1801 to 1809, one didn't have to be John Brown to begin to address slavery. A president, especially one with the reputation of Thomas Jefferson, could have done much to erode the institution and put it on the road to extinction.

CHAPTER 4

James Madison, 1809–1817

"Of all the enemies to public liberty war is, perhaps, the most to be dreaded, because it comprises and develops the germ of every other. War is the parent of armies; from these proceed debts and taxes; and armies, and debts, and taxes are the known instruments for bringing the many under the domination of the few. In war, too, the discretionary power of the Executive is extended...."

—*James Madison*

President Madison's Constitutional Grade: C+

If anyone should have known what the Constitution had to say about the office of the presidency, it was James Madison, who literally "wrote the book" by drafting large parts of America's founding document. Like his two immediate predecessors, Madison, despite holding the rank of colonel in the Orange County militia, had not fought in the American Revolution. Extremely plain in his dress—*Alexander Hamilton* author Ron Chernow has called him a crow next to Hamilton's peacock—and physically small and unassuming, not to mention stern and solemn-looking, Madison hardly had the presence of a Washington or Jefferson. Bookish and scholarly, learned in political philosophy and the law, Madison was a deep thinker, though not a polymath like the violin-playing, science-experiment-making architect Jefferson. Madison's family owned plantations at Port Conway, Virginia. James inherited numerous slaves from his father—none of whom he freed, because of his perilous financial straits (just like Jefferson). At least one recent biography suggests that Madison, though he is generally thought of as a deist, accepted general Christian principles and was particularly drawn

Did you know?

★ James Madison was the first U.S. president to request a declaration of war from Congress

★ He was the youngest delegate to attend the Continental Congress

★ In his 1790 congressional race Madison crushed his opponent James Monroe

★ Madison came under enemy fire while leading American troops in the battle of Bladensburg—the only president to do so while in office

63

★ ★ ★

Don't Judge a Book by Its Cover

A British minister who met Madison in 1809 called him a "plain and mean-looking little man, of great simplicity of manners, and an inveterate enemy of form and ceremony."

Treasury Secretary Albert Gallatin's sister-in-law described him as "a small man quite devoid of dignity in his appearance—he bows very low and never looks at the person to whom he is bowing.... His skin looks like parchment [but] a few moments in his company and you lose sight of these defects and will see nothing but what pleases you—his eyes are penetrating and expressive—his smile charming—his manners affable—his conversation lively and interesting."

to the Baptists in Virginia, who found themselves in disputes with the Anglican Church.

Father of the Constitution

Madison had made his reputation at the Constitutional Convention, where he spoke over two hundred times and impressed everyone. Somehow, he also found time to take minutes throughout the proceedings, providing our only complete firsthand account. Madison had concluded early on that the states had to be deprived of sovereignty, and a truly national government established. This nationalist blueprint for the United States formed the basis of his "Virginia Plan," which the Virginia delegation proposed at the convention. By the time the Constitution was drafted and approved by the convention in its final form, Madison's original proposals had been significantly modified, but even in his lifetime he was referred to as the "Father of the Constitution" ("a credit to which I have no claim," he wrote). To ensure its ratification, he authored numerous essays in *The Federalist Papers* defending it.

But Madison also strongly supported the addition of the Bill of Rights, which he hoped would help overcome opposition to the Constitution. In fact, Madison's political views changed radically between the proposal of the "Virginia Plan" and his own presidency. He had started out as one of the most enthusiastic "Federalists" (nationalists) but became a Republican and a strict constructionist of the Constitution and one of the fiercest opponents to federal encroachment on the states.

During Adams's presidency, as we have seen, Madison opposed the Alien and Sedition Acts by drafting the Virginia Resolutions, declaring the acts to be unconstitutional and claiming that states could "interpose" their own law over that of the Constitution "for arresting the progress of evil." That was an astounding position for the man who had argued just ten years earlier that federal law had to trump state laws. After serving as Jefferson's secretary of State and presiding (loosely) over the Louisiana Purchase, Madison was the heir apparent to the presidency for the Republicans. He was nominated to run in the 1808 election by the first political caucuses in American history.

Madison was not nominated without opposition from his old rival, James Monroe, who was a leading member of the "Tertium Quids" ("tertium quid" is Latin for a "third something," in this case, a third party), popularly known as the Quids. Jefferson's "We are all Republicans, we are all Federalists" had never been true, and now—or so it seemed to Quids like Anti-Federalists Monroe and John Randolph of Roanoke—not even all the Republicans were Republicans. The Quids saw Madison as a compromiser, too eager to go along with the Federalists to get along. Monroe was the radical. Madison defeated his Virginia rival (again) in the caucuses, then beat Charles Cotesworth Pinckney in the Electoral College, 122 electoral votes to 47. In Congress, however, the Federalists had made a modest comeback compared to their 1804 totals, and they would do even better in 1812. The country was divided. And Madison by and large neither led, followed, nor got out of the way. He became a captive to Jefferson's shortcomings and failed to address the growing anger and fear of the American people about the continual hostilities, insults, and incursions of the British Empire.

John Quincy Adams, who had attended many official functions, said of Madison's inauguration, "The crowd was excessive, the heat oppressive,

A Book You're Not Supposed to Read

James Madison, A Biography by Ralph Louis Ketcham (Charlottesville, VA: University of Virginia Press, 1990).

and the entertainment bad." Madison's Inaugural, like most presidential speeches of the day, was refreshingly short (only ten minutes) compared to modern bore-a-thons, and the oath was administered by Federalist Chief Justice John Marshall (a reminder of John Adams's "Midnight Judge" coup).

Almost immediately after taking office Madison ran into trouble. He nominated Jefferson's Treasury secretary, Albert Gallatin, as his own secretary of State, but Gallatin ran into strong opposition and Madison backed down, leaving Gallatin at Treasury. Other Madison appointments were less qualified than Gallatin. Washington literally had the best and the brightest in his cabinet, but partisan politics over two successive presidencies had now cut the pool in half, and Madison, lacking Washington's incredible aura, could not draw men of the highest talent to his administration. The mediocrity of Madison's appointments goes some distance to explain how such an anti-war president ended up in the nation's first declared war.

Assessments of President James Madison are perhaps the most polarized of those of any of the first four presidents. As Drew R. McCoy points out in *The American Presidency*, some see him as "an indecisive bungler, an almost colossally inept president whose naive, amateurish approach to diplomacy and whose lack of leadership over his own cabinet...helped draw the United States into a war for which it was woefully unprepared." But John Adams, a critic closer to Madison's time, said that Madison's administration "acquired more glory, and established more Union, than all three Predecessors...put together." Not bad coming from one of those "Predecessors"!

It must be remembered that *all* the Founding-era presidents, up to Monroe, strongly feared tyranny in all its forms, whether monarchy or the dictatorship of the masses ("the mob, the herd, the rabble" as John Adams referred to the public). But Madison seemed to swing wildly from one fear to another. The seemingly perpetual impending war with England (or France) only added to such concerns. Although the America James Madison inherited from Jefferson was far more prosperous than it was at the beginning of Jefferson's presidency, had much less debt, and was technically at peace, the United States seemed like a pimply-faced weakling in a schoolyard dominated by two large bullies.

Upon entering office, Madison found that the United States had a surplus of $9.5 million, or the equivalent of a full year's worth of congressional spending (in 2013 dollars, about $3.5 trillion!). The nation, thanks mostly to the efforts of a total of about thirty customs collectors, had chopped its debt and expanded its territory. Jefferson had not only purchased Louisiana but had sent Meriwether Lewis and William Clark to explore it, then dispatched Zebulon Pike to explore the southern portion of the territory. It is really difficult to say why—except perhaps for his own difficult relationship with Jefferson—Adams credited Madison with doing more to "establish the Union" than his predecessor.

A Book You're Not Supposed to Read

The American Presidency: The Authoritative Reference, edited by Alan Brinkley and Davis Dyer (Boston: Houghton Mifflin, 2004).

An Awkward Situation

Aware of the growing public enmity toward Jefferson's embargo, Madison nevertheless seemed content to just wait it out—in retrospect, a terrible decision, given that it took six more years for Britain, Prussia, and Russia to finally defeat Napoleon. Madison called for repealing the embargo and replacing it with the Non-Intercourse Act (1809)—a policy the president

★ ★ ★

You Had to Bring That Up

In 1811 the Republican majority in Congress allowed the charter of the Bank of the United States to expire, quoting Madison from 1791 on its unconstitutionality. But Madison's 1791 opposition to the bank was more nuanced than its Congressional opponents pretended. He had in fact proposed language to be added to the U.S. Constitution that would have allowed the U.S. government to charter corporations, including banks. (They were not adopted.) Madison's opposition to a national bank had rested almost entirely on partisan and sectional—rather than constitutional—concerns, namely, that the bank would not make sufficient loans in the South, and would be controlled by Northern interests. Only a handful of bank opponents had actually raised constitutional concerns in 1791, and Madison was not among them. And by 1811 Madison had argued that, since its founding, the Bank of the U.S. had been effective and in fact necessary. The Republicans refused to budge, allowing the charter to expire, and depriving Madison of the very institution he would need for war loans. But, hey: the Madison of 1791 could claim victory!

characterized as "an awkwardness in getting out of an awkward situation." Whereas the Embargo Act prohibited all overseas trade (lest American ships get hijacked by the British or French), the Non-Intercourse Act prohibited only trade with England or France, but with this stipulation: American trade would be reopened to whichever party first recognized America's rights as a neutral power. Whether an "awkwardness" or an intentional ruse, the "repeal" of a British blockade followed by its quick re-imposition left American ships on the high seas as potential hostages to the British navy. Worse, the temporary respite in the American embargo put considerable resources back in British hands and weakened America's bargaining position. Upon the embargo's repeal, some six hundred ships sailed for England, only to learn that Britain had imposed new Orders in Council establishing a new blockade of European ports.

The Non-Intercourse Act quickly gave way to a replacement of its own, Macon's Bill #2 (1810), which reopened trade with *both* Britain and France—but again only if the trade partner recognized America's right to trade. Naturally France jumped in. And naturally British ships began intercepting American vessels bound for France. America's international trade was just a pawn in a war between much greater powers.

Not a Shining Leader

Madison's weaknesses and tin ear to the American public were exposed further by the rise of a new political movement, a quasi-party from within the Republicans called the "War Hawks" who favored war with Britain. They included Henry Clay of Kentucky, Langdon Cheves and John C. Calhoun of South Carolina, Felix Grundy of Tennessee, and Richard Mentor Johnson of Kentucky. All the Westerners were particularly sensitive to depredations by the Indians on the frontier and believed (correctly, in most cases) that the British were instigating those attacks.

In 1811 the British-aided Shawnee were led by Tecumseh, who threatened to break the Treaty of Fort Wayne and form an outright alliance with the British. Governor (and future president) William Henry Harrison sent a petition to Madison warning him that it would take combat to secure the safety of American citizens. Harrison got a reply that gave him broad discretion in meeting any threat. He then met with Tecumseh and was assured all was well. But as soon as Harrison left on business, Tecumseh recruited other tribes to his alliance, including the "Red Sticks" faction of the Creeks. When Harrison returned, the acting governor had called out the militia, and Harrison sent Madison a letter announcing that he intended to march up the Wabash to confront the chief, but still thought peace was possible. In August 1811 Madison approved combat actions while opining that war was unlikely. Harrison did acquire some regular troops from Madison's government, and at the Battle of Tippecanoe on November 7, Harrison crushed the Indian alliance. But Madison had played no significant role in one of the most important American military victories up to that point—nor had he really even been aware of the threat.

Madison's ineptitude *vis a vis* Congress was on display when the War Hawks elected Clay Speaker of the House, allowing him to name the Foreign Relations and Naval committees. It concerned the War Hawks that Britain's ally against Napoleon was Spain, which still had control of

Florida and whose territory bumped up against the western boundaries of the Louisiana Purchase.

"We Fired Our Guns and the British Kept A-Comin'"

Ultimately, continued warlike actions by the British forced Madison's hand and, with the full support of the War Hawks, in June 1812 he became the first U.S. president to seek a declaration of war from the Congress. Ironically, Madison lost the support of the Federalists—who largely represented the coastal areas that suffered most from British impressment and other infractions of trade. Nevertheless, the Federalists were viscerally pro-British. It was just as predictable that the South and West, heavily populated by the virulently anti-British Scots-Irish, would be the strongest supporters of war. The final vote for war was 79 to 49 in the House and 19 to 13 in the Senate, a division that did not bode well for a united and successful war effort.

Nor did twelve years of ignoring the military under Jefferson and Madison seem wise in retrospect. The two Republican presidents shared a very unrealistic assessment of U.S. military might. Jefferson told William Duane in 1812 that "the acquisition of Canada this year as far as the neighborhood of Quebec, will be a mere matter of marching...." In fact, Jefferson predicted the United States would follow up with an "attack on Halifax [which would result in] the final expulsion of England from the American continent...." This was advice from one of the few Founders who had run from enemy fire.

The retention of James Wilkinson as the U.S. military commander of the Louisiana Territory by both Jefferson and Madison was another mistake. Madison placed Wilkinson in charge of Terre aux Boeufs along the Louisiana coast, where the general presided over a medical disaster. Outbreaks of malaria, dysentery, and scurvy killed dozens, but Wilkinson insisted on staying on the mosquito-infested coast. Congressional inquiries proved inconclusive, and the matter was dropped in Madison's lap. He retained

Wilkinson, arguably for political reasons, further tarnishing his legacy. Madison only sacked Wilkinson, finally, after he suffered two military defeats at the hands of the British.

The War of 1812 is best remembered for some notable military sayings— "We have met the enemy and they are ours," "Those are Regulars, by God!"—and for a battle that occurred after a peace treaty was signed (the Battle of New Orleans). It is often forgotten that Britain was up to its elbows in the war on the Continent, supporting Spain and Portugal with some thirty-six thousand troops at the same time as it was dealing with the Americans. For Britain, the war with America was a sideshow—Napoleon was the main event.

Still, the British always took war seriously. And the United States had only about seven thousand regulars with, to quote the British assessment of American naval capabilities, "a few fir-built frigates, manned by a handful of bastards and outlaws." Madison's rebellious House had already denied him additional taxes, and his Treasury secretary had to lower the defense budget for the United States to stay solvent. Congress did authorize Madison to borrow $5 million, but having killed the Bank of the United States—and with the U.S. virtually at war with the major potential lending powers— Madison had nowhere to borrow the money from.

America's strategy for winning against a more professional, better equipped opponent was to attack with divided forces. In July 1812, General William Hull entered Canada by way of Detroit, only to surrender to Anglo-Canadian forces without firing a shot. (He was subsequently court-martialed for cowardice, but Madison pardoned him.) Another land invasion of Canada in December 1813 failed, and a third incursion, in July 1814 along the Niagara Peninsula, resulted in a stalemate. (So much for Jefferson's predictions.) The upshot of the three failed invasions was that the United States learned once and for all that Canadians were not Americans, and did not have the same view of the British monarchy that the United States did.

★ ★ ★

Not Ready for Prime Time

In several incidents, New York militia refused to cross into Canada, claiming their responsibilities ended at the border and justifying misgivings that George Washington had expressed about a militia-based army.

But at sea and on the Great Lakes, things went differently, with a number of American victories. Indeed, the Americans won more than three-fourths of the naval engagements in the War of 1812. As Captain Oliver Hazard Perry, who defeated a British force at Put-in-Bay, Michigan, with ships he built from scratch, declared, "We have met the enemy and they are ours." Seeing most of Jefferson's gunboats sunk or holed up in their harbors, unable to move, Madison authorized all American merchant ships to become privateers, leading to the capture of over eighteen hundred British vessels. Yet most of America's naval victories, while impressive, did little to change the balance of power.

After the British and their allies defeated Napoleon's forces in the Battle of Leipzig in October 1813, Britain could focus more attention on the upstart Americans, launching an impressive three-pronged offensive—in the Chesapeake Bay area toward the nation's capital; along Lake Champlain; and in New Orleans. Before the British could move, however, an American counterattack by General William Henry Harrison pushed a retreating British-Indian force (with the Indians again led by Tecumseh) into Ontario and soundly defeated them at the Battle of the Thames. Tecumseh was killed and the power of the Indians in the Old Northwest was shattered.

And the first prong of the planned British three-prong invasion faltered. American regulars under General Winfield Scott advanced to the town of Chippewa and met British forces of roughly equal numbers. Scott had better cannon, and the British commander mistakenly thought he was facing militia. When it became apparent that the long grey lines were professionals, he exclaimed, "Those are regulars, by God!" The Americans nearly captured the British force, but engaging again at the Battle of Lundy's Lane a few weeks later, they only fought to a draw. But the British casualties were high; British commanders were horrified to see the losses inflicted on them by American professional soldiers. Although the British held the Niagara area, they could not advance.

The second British prong met with more success, nearly capturing President Madison. In August 1914, a large body of American militia (numbering between five and nine thousand men and including only about a thousand regulars) dug in at Bladensburg, Maryland, to prevent the British from taking Washington. Madison was on the field as preparations were made. Poor dispositions of men and guns allowed the British, despite heavy casualties, to take the American positions and resulted in a retreat that instantly became a complete rout (known as the "Bladensburg Races"). Madison and his staff were almost captured. When the British took Washington, D.C.—in one of the biggest humiliations in American history—they burned many of its buildings in retribution for a raid on Port Dover, Ontario, to which American troops had put the torch. The British then moved toward Baltimore but were blocked by Fort McHenry, which they assaulted for twenty-five hours without success, again losing substantial numbers of men. As Francis Scott Key's song went, "the flag was still there." With their cannonade, the British had unwittingly given us the national anthem.

Unaware that the British government was receiving reports of much higher-than-expected battlefield losses with little to show for them, Madison

★ ★ ★
Oh, Them Again

Apparently defeating the Tripolitan pirates once was not enough. Sensing that the United States was tied up with England, the Barbary states again returned to taking American hostages during the War of 1812. The U.S. Congress authorized naval deployments against the Algerian pirates three months after Jackson's victory in New Orleans. A squadron under Commodore Stephen Decatur set sail beginning in May 1815, and American frigates entered pirate waters, capturing two Algerian ships and bringing them in tow to the Dey of Algiers, who signed a new treaty that July. This second victory, like the first, was made possible only by the very "blue-water navy" that Jefferson and Madison had resisted.

A Book You're Not Supposed to Read

The War of 1812: A Forgotten Conflict, Bicentennial Edition by Donald R. Hickey (Champaign, IL: University of Illinois Press, 2012).

faced dark times. And a third major British army was on its way to New Orleans. In the South, however, General Andrew Jackson had finished clearing out the Indians in Georgia and Alabama, defeating the Red Sticks—Creeks who had aligned with Tecumseh and the British—at the Battle of Horseshoe Bend. He then swung back to New Orleans to defend the city against the British attack. Jackson's remarkable force of frontier militia, free blacks, pirates, and regulars was pitted against almost three thousand redcoats. Jackson's dispositions and cannon were both superior to those of the British, who advanced in open field and were decimated, losing men at a ten-to-one ratio compared to the Americans.

The Battle of New Orleans was fought between January 8 and 18, 1815. But already on Christmas Day 1814, the diplomats (including future president John Quincy Adams, Henry Clay, and Albert Gallatin) that Madison had sent to Ghent in Belgium had signed a treaty with England to restore the "status quo ante bellum," which was to say that England agreed to honor neutral rights of American ships and evacuate the last of the Western forts. Though not part of the treaty, the end of Indian power on the southern and northwestern frontiers was as significant as anything Madison could have hoped to achieve in the war. When news of the Battle of New Orleans came, the British counted their lucky stars that the Americans had not had such a powerful bargaining chip in Ghent.

Jackson and Harrison, not Madison, emerged as the heroes of the war. But the war gave him secure borders and, ironically, an unchallenged political future. The Federalist Party had committed suicide during the war when a group of delegates from Massachusetts, Connecticut, Vermont, and Rhode Island convened at Hartford, Connecticut, to issue a call for a separate peace between New England and Great Britain. (New Englanders had toyed with a plot to leave the Union in 1804 if Jefferson was reelected, then done nothing.) Former Federalists such as John Quincy Adams had already merged into the Republican Party, which for the time being seemed united. In fact, Madison entered his second term with as much opposition from the "nationalist" wing of the Republicans as he did from the dying Federalists.

"The Public Good May Require Them"

As we have already seen, in 1791 very few constitutional objections were offered by anyone (not even Jefferson) to the First Bank of the United States, and Madison had included a power to grant "charters of incorporation" where "public good may require them" including for a bank, in the additional powers he proposed giving Congress at the 1787 Constitutional Convention. But President Madison, like many in Congress, had made a long political journey since then. By the time the bank was up for recharter, it was seen as under the control of "foreign interests," especially the British. Treasury Secretary Gallatin insisted that the bank was useful in circulating sound money and in making needed loans, but by 1811 Madison had come to see it as a vestige of the Hamilton program, and the Republicans had allowed

Air Horse One

During the War of 1812, Madison attempted (without much success) to be an on-the-ground commander in chief. Without rapid transportation, however, he literally spent the majority of his time simply riding from location to location. For example, as the British approached Washington, D.C., Madison mounted his horse and rode to where the American army supposedly was located, in Rockville, Maryland, fifteen miles northwest of Washington. Upon arriving, he found the army, and General William Winder, had already left for Baltimore. Having already been in the saddle for eighteen hours, Madison rode another ten miles to Brookville, where he went into a home to rest, but had to receive visitors and write letters. The following morning Madison was back in the saddle, headed back to Washington, where he arrived on August 17 to find it "in ashes not an inch, but its cracked and blackened walls remain." He had ridden for virtually six days straight.

the charter to expire. During the war, however, it dawned on Congress that the main function of a national bank was to help government with emergency financing, and a re-charter bill passed. Madison vetoed that bill, but in 1816, when another bill to charter a new Bank of the United States was passed, Madison signed it.

The nationalist wing of the Republicans, led by John C. Calhoun and Henry Clay, hoped to use the new bank as a means of encouraging economic growth. But Madison quashed efforts by the two to set aside $1.5 million of the bank's establishment funds, as well as annual dividends totaling $650,000, into a special fund for "internal improvements" of the United States. Madison vetoed this "Bonus Bill of 1817," in one of his final acts as president. He was highly conflicted, believing that no country existed "which presents a field where nature invites more the art of man to complete her own work for his accommodation and benefit"—states alone could not build the canals and roads that would "bring and bind more closely together the various parts of our extended confederacy"—but arguing in his final address to Congress that the legislation would be unconstitutional without an amendment to the Constitution authorizing it. In addition to improvements such as roads and canals, Madison suggested that the nation build "a national seminary of learning" in the District of Columbia. Despite his caveat that an amendment would be needed for such "internal improvements," Madison's program elicited howls of concern from the old Jeffersonians. John Randolph said that Madison "out-Hamiltons Alexander Hamilton," Ralph Ketcham, the author of Madison's most recent major biography, has excused Madison's big-government proposals by arguing that "profound changes" had occurred under Jefferson and Madison, and that fifteen years of Republican leadership had "harnessed the Hamiltonian engine." Thus, in essence, Madison could support the Bank of the United States because it was "his."

Madison's veto message quoted the constitutional clause, "to provide for the common defense," which the president said he did not think applied to roads. He also noted, correctly, that the "general welfare" clause did not extend the powers of the federal government beyond those the Constitution enumerated.

Madison's Constitutional Grade

Many hoped the Bank of the United States would wield powers similar to those of modern "central banks," namely that it could restrain private banks—which each issued their own money at that time—impose a sort of market discipline, and guarantee long-term prosperity. Madison would be long gone before that theory could be put to the test. Nevertheless, by the end of his second term, with the Federalists gone and no significant dissent over policy in Washington, the "Era of Good Feelings" was now under way. On the surface the national harmony seemed to be an unadulterated blessing: Madison had left a united country, larger by two states (Louisiana and Indiana), free for the time being from Indian attacks on the frontier, at peace with both England and France, and ready to grow.

At many times Madison had used the power of the executive cautiously, but all too often the "young Madison" of Washington's time was in conflict with the "old Madison" of his own presidency, resulting in inconsistency of policy and approach. To his great credit, during the war Madison acted with tremendous restraint in dealing with the traitors who had called for

★ ★ ★
That's Our Bank Now

Madison's about-face on the Bank of the United States is reminiscent of an incident in 1993 when the liberal actor Ron Silver, on the day of Bill Clinton's inauguration, watched a flight of fighter planes fly over the Lincoln Memorial during an inaugural ceremony. Though at first Silver was agitated by the warlike display, he recollected that since Clinton was being sworn in, "those are *our* planes now." So it was with Madison: in Republican hands, all the institutions that once posed a danger were now safe. Under Madison, Nathaniel Macon, an old-line Republican senator, found himself "quite lost...I feel almost like I was in a foreign land."

A Book You're Not Supposed to Read

The Era of Good Feelings by George Dangerfield (Detroit: Ivan R. Dee, 1989).

the separate peace at the Hartford Convention. But to his discredit, his lack of judgment about the character of those he appointed failed him repeatedly. If Washington's administration was—to borrow the phrase from Jefferson describing the Constitutional Convention—"an assembly of demigods," Madison's administration was an assembly of underachievers, including many of the first true nameless bureaucrats to appear in the nation's government. His best appointees were his ministers to Ghent. Madison's success in war was due almost entirely to the efforts of Harrison, Scott, and Jackson (and a number of heroic sea captains), and his overall absence of strategy could have been catastrophic.

By conducting the war without resorting to abridgements of civil liberties, Madison laid the foundation for a quick healing after 1814. But Drew R. McCoy's judgment that his "executive restraint did more than confirm his principled commitment to, and abiding faith in, the Constitution [to] become a symbol for all Americans of their republican identity" is perhaps an overstatement. Madison was simply lucky that the Hartford Convention did not produce more disastrous or deadly results. He should probably have invoked Washington's model during the Whiskey Rebellion and arrested the ringleaders, charged them with treason, and then pardoned them after the war. Indeed, wartime is the *one* time when presidents are charged with placing national security above individual rights. The United States was extremely fortunate that Madison's shortcomings in a time of war did not yield much more painful outcomes. For all his insight in 1787, between 1812 and 1815 he fell short of the ingenuity and inventiveness needed to use federal powers in ways that would benefit the nation without greatly expanding the scope of government.

Madison's "Era of Good Feelings" owed as much to the fact that the Federalists were simply out of step with America in the second decade of the 1800s as it did to any achievement of Madison as president. Without the discipline of a strong counter-faction to challenge the administration with new and different ideas and policies, the political scene was temporarily tranquil. But that was a wasted opportunity. There was gaping division lurking beneath the smooth surface of American politics, and Madison could have taken steps to avert the impending crisis, right a terrible injustice, and ultimately save hundreds of thousands of American lives, if he had only been proactive. Like Jefferson, Madison had ignored the festering wound of slavery. The "Era of Good Feelings" under his successor would only put a Band-Aid™ on it. Avoiding the inevitable confrontation with slavery as the most divisive force in American society, Madison squandered a golden moment. Like his Virginia predecessors Jefferson and Washington, he was a Southerner who might have changed the course of American history at a time when a Northerner stood no such chance. Perhaps Washington was still too near the Founding to have made the attempt, but Jefferson and Madison, both with strong national support, had no such excuse.

CHAPTER 5

James Monroe, 1817–1825

"Never did a government commence under auspices so favorable, nor ever was success so complete."
—James Monroe

President Monroe's Constitutional Grade: A–

As the third Virginian to serve as the nation's president—and the last to be elected to that office—James Monroe, a Republican and friend of Thomas Jefferson, had more than a few difficulties with his predecessor James Madison. Despite having been friends with both Jefferson and Madison for years, Monroe was slighted by the two in a meeting just before the election of 1808. No one knows for certain the cause of their broken relationship, but when the three met in Washington, they failed to even bring up their disputes, let alone resolve them. Eventually President Jefferson repaired the damage, but Monroe never fully trusted Madison again. Monroe toyed with the notion of running for president in 1808, but had no money, and at any rate knew that Jefferson's first choice was Madison, "the Father of the Constitution."

Monroe was the last of the Founders to be president. He had fought in the Revolution and suffered a wound at the Battle of Trenton. He was the last to wear a ponytail ("queue") and the first president to visit all regions of the country. Like many of the Founders, he was a lawyer, and also like

Did you know?

★ Monroe was the first U.S. president to tour every region of the United States

★ He was the last president to wear a ponytail

★ By the end of his second term as president, Monroe had been in the service of the United States for fifty years

True Blue Republican

"I have always been a Republican. I have fought and bled for the cause of Republicanism. I have supported it for thirty years with my most strenuous exertions. Is it to be supposed that I will, in the noon of my life, abandon those principles which have ever actuated me? ... Mr. Madison is a Republican and so am I. As long as he acts in consistence with the interests of his country, I will go along with him. When otherwise, you cannot wish me to countenance him."

—James Monroe in the *Richmond Enquirer*, August 1810

many, he was a planter who had inherited his father's slaves. He had been a minister to France, minister to England (where the problems between Jefferson and Madison started), and governor of Virginia.

More than personal slights had driven Monroe to denounce the Jefferson administration for veering too far from Republican values. He became associated with the Tertium Quids, and there was talk of an alliance between the Quids and the Federalists to run him in 1808 that came to naught. In 1811, only four months after his election as Virginia governor for the second time, Monroe was appointed secretary of State by Madison, who hoped to unite the country as it faced war with England. When the war came with little opportunity for negotiation to stop it and Monroe had little to do as secretary of State, Madison moved him to the War Department; for about four months Monroe effectively held both positions.

Monroe performed brilliantly in setting up a defense of Washington after the British had burned the city and left. Monroe had warned John Armstrong, his predecessor at the War Department, that Armstrong should not lead troops himself but instead mount a defense of Washington, but Armstrong had ignored him. So Monroe found himself in complete command of the capital city's defense. It was also Monroe who sent express riders to summon as many militiamen as possible to aid Andrew Jackson at New Orleans. And it was Monroe, not Madison, who had the honor of announcing the news of Andrew Jackson's victory to the assembled federal government officials at the Patent Office Building in 1815. While Madison was still out of Washington—having fled—Monroe even briefly assumed the duties of chief executive. At one point Monroe essentially *was* the U.S. government. And at that point, he began to get too ambitious, drawing up plans for a hundred-thousand-man army. He was successful in convincing Congress to double the land bounties for new enlistees. It was fortunate for Monroe, though, that the Treaty of Ghent ended the war in 1815—as secretary of War he was formulating plans for yet another invasion of Canada! Reappointed secretary of State at that time, Monroe stayed the term until he won the presidency in 1816 and was inaugurated on March 4, 1817.

While it would have been quite impossible in 1808 for Monroe to win against Madison (and, by extension, against Jefferson's shadow), in 1816 the waters parted for him. The Federalists were dying out, and the War Hawk or "nationalist" wing of the Republican Party was split among William Crawford of Georgia, Henry Clay of Kentucky, and Daniel Tompkins of New York, none of whom had Monroe's political pedigree or link to the Founders.

His first real act as president was to tour the nation—something no one had done since Washington's brief visit to two areas of the country. Monroe's plan was to visit many of the nation's forts to see their condition for himself. In the summer, he went to the northern and eastern states, then went south and west. Harkening back to Washington's habits, Monroe paid for his own expenses and traveled without a procession (only a coach and a couple of aides—no military escorts). The president's modesty impressed everyone.

★ ★ ★
An Exemplary President

The *Baltimore Weekly Register* observed that "Mr. Monroe travels as privately as he can.... His dress and manners have more the appearance of those supposed to belong to a plain and substantial, but well informed, farmer...." Martin Van Buren, later a major force in politics, said, "Mr. Monroe's character was that of an honest man, with fair, but not very marked capacities, who, through life, performed every duty that devolved upon him with scrupulous fidelity." John Quincy Adams did observe "slowness, want of decision, and a spirit of procrastination in the President, which perhaps arises more from his situation than his personal character."

★ ★ ★

Making the White House a (Spectacular) Home

Elizabeth Monroe and her daughter Eliza, with $20,000 allocated for refurnishing, transformed the presidential mansion into a true national home for the elected leader of the Republic. They brought in some $9,000 in their own fine French furniture (for which the Monroes were reimbursed), ordered necessary pieces to fill out the rooms, and installed a beautiful piano and chandelier. Of course, the White House needed a wine cellar, stocked with twelve hundred bottles of Champagne and Burgundy. Elizabeth found carpets, chairs, drapes, and linens, which ultimately added $30,000 to the bill. Finally, in January 1818, the new White House was ready for the annual New Year's Day reception, but Elizabeth, who suffered from migraine headaches and rheumatism, had to be excused for a time and James Monroe entertained his guests alone. When she returned, she was a hit in her formal gown.

If Monroe thought he would have a quiet and uneventful tour, he was wrong: crowds turned out everywhere, and he was welcomed with a string of speeches from local officials, as well as parades and military salutes. He told Jefferson that he undertook the tour as a private citizen, but he quickly gave up on the idea and submitted to the wishes of the public. As he shook hands, Revolutionary War veterans would come up and say only the place of their combat service—"Brandywine, sir," "Monmouth, sir." The first half of his travels consumed almost Monroe's entire first year in office, and he arrived back in Washington in mid-September.

The $25,000 presidential salary was all that was allocated for his living expenses, and Monroe soon found it wasn't enough. He had to hire out-of-work relatives at a cut rate to handle some of his personal work in Washington. His wife, Elizabeth, truly made the White House into a national showcase.

"Plain." "Modest and unassuming." These were the typical assessments of President Monroe's appearance—and Madison had already been known for dressing down. But still waters ran deep with Monroe. He had chided James Madison for failing to toe the appropriate constitutional lines, but as president Monroe saw things differently. Presented with a series of pirate raids off islands near Florida and Galveston in the Gulf of Mexico, Monroe sent expeditions to end the attacks. General Jackson was ordered to Florida with a cryptic instruction to "adopt the necessary measures to terminate a conflict" and told that he should not withdraw until "our course is carried through triumphantly." That meant that Jackson would have to fight Spanish troops—very possibly starting a war, something he naturally wished to avoid. Still, during the War of 1812, Jackson had assaulted Spanish fortifications in Pensacola, Florida, without permission from Congress, and he knew Monroe's sentiment that the United States needed both Florida and Cuba to be secure. When he sensed that he was about to stumble into a war, Monroe changed his mind and sent a message to Secretary of War John Calhoun to tell Jackson not to attack any post occupied by the Spanish. Calhoun failed to transmit the message, so in accordance with his earlier, vaguer orders, Jackson rampaged through Florida, taking Spanish forts and hanging a pair of Creek chiefs. When he took Pensacola on May 24—giving the United States control of the Florida Panhandle—he hanged a British ship owner as an enemy agent and shot a second British trader on the same charge. At that point Jackson asked for reinforcement by regulars and promised to take all of Florida—and Cuba!

An elated Monroe quickly embarked on the second half of his national tour, this time visiting only military bases so as to avoid crowds and celebrations. But he soon learned that Jackson was being charged in Congress with disobeying his orders (which Calhoun had not sent) and so the president was forced to cut short his visits and return to Washington. There he walked a tightrope, publicly criticizing Jackson's conduct and encouraging Congress to censure the general, all the while knowing that Jackson's successes had the full approval of the American public, and no members of Congress were going to risk their wrath. The president also ordered Jackson to hand over Pensacola to any representative of the Spanish government who asked for it and quietly had John Quincy Adams, his minister to Spain, negotiate for the acquisition of Florida with a carrot and stick. The carrot was that if Spain handed Florida over to the Americans, the United States would renounce all claims by individual American citizens against Spain. These were not insignificant, totaling some $5 million. The stick was that the United States was content to leave Florida in Spanish hands... *if* Spain could guarantee an end to Indian attacks across the border—with the unstated threat that there would be an American response if Spain could not. Spain accepted the money, and not only gave up Florida in the Adams-Onis Treaty of 1819, but also agreed to extend the definition of the Louisiana Territory to the Pacific. In theory, Monroe had doubled the size of the Louisiana Purchase, this time for only a third of what Jefferson had paid! When the popular Jackson rode back to Washington to face his accusers in Congress, the censure motions failed.

It was a remarkable dance. By means of Jackson's guts (and ruthlessness) and his own extra-constitutional bluster, Monroe had backed down a teetering European empire. News of the treaty came right after the final payment on the national debt, extinguished through land sales. And only months later came word that the Cumberland Road had been opened, linking America's eastern seaboard with the Old Northwest and the new states of Indiana and Kentucky. A water route, the Erie Canal, was undertaken to connect the Hudson River with the Great Lakes.

Panic and Depression

But storm clouds were on the horizon. Monroe had inherited the re-chartered Bank of the United States, along with an economy in which there was considerable speculation in public lands. By 1819, the country had fallen into a depression, then called a "Panic." Historians and economists are still divided over the cause of the Panic of 1819, with many seeking to blame the bank itself for failing to regulate "runaway" state bank lending. In fact at the time there were too few state banks either located in the West or with the ability to make substantial loans to instigate massive financial swings. In reality, the Panic came because public lands were cheap, farmers massively overextended, and the whole bubble vulnerable to price fluctuations, which struck when English importers suddenly shifted to cheaper Indian cotton. All in all, the Panic was the result of a relatively small American economy tossed on the oceans of the post-Napoleonic readjustments in markets. What is undisputed, though, is that this

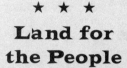

★ ★ ★
Land for the People

Monroe continued the Jeffersonian tradition of moving as much land as possible into individual hands. "The public lands," he said, "are a public stock, which ought to be disposed of to the best advantage of the nation," not hoarded in government preserves. Some say this generous public land policy helped cause the Panic of 1819. As the *Poison* song goes, "Every rose has its thorn...."

was America's first true national depression, with thousands of textile workers put on the street and businesses in every section of the country failing. Philadelphia alone lost over two thousand textile mills, and even the level-headed John Quincy Adams proclaimed the Panic a "crisis." The bank, under William Jones, may have mismanaged the downturn (as central banks often do), but hardly brought it on.

For the first time in American history, elected officials began to call for government action to restore balance to the economy. Congress slapped on immediate immigration restrictions to control the labor market. And there was enormous pressure to reduce the debt obligations of the farmers. Senator Richard Johnson of Kentucky introduced a resolution to allow debtors who had purchased land from the government to cede back a fourth of it in return for clear title to the rest, in a sort of reverse fire sale.

★ ★ ★
Mortgage Crisis Redux

Monroe's Treasury Secretary William Crawford argued that an "artificial and fictitious prosperity" had placed the debtors in their positions, not their "own imprudence." It was a line straight out of the Housing Bust of 2008, when people who defaulted on their mortgages claimed that they had been the pawns of "greedy bankers."

To his great credit, President Monroe, like Treasury Secretary Alexander Hamilton before him, insisted that the government stick to its knitting and rejected calls for intervention to bail out the debtors. He found support, of all places, from a former Federalist, John Quincy Adams, who noted that "merchants alone" were supremely acquainted with the economy and would be the ones to fix it. There were, however, things the president could do. Anticipating the essentials of the supply-side economics of the Reagan era, Monroe said, "Anxious to relieve my fellow-citizens in 1817 from every burden which could be dispensed with, and the State of the Treasury permitting it, I recommended the repeal of the internal taxes, knowing that such relief was then peculiarly necessary...."

A year later, when Congress sought what we would call a "stimulus" and "infrastructure" bill for $6,000 of repairs on the Cumberland Road, Monroe vetoed it, saying Congress "does not possess the power under the Constitution to pass such a law." While he believed "internal improvements" to be beyond the scope of the federal government's enumerated powers, he added that he thought perhaps the military might have some claim to road construction under the aegis of national defense, so Congress rushed through a General Survey Bill that appropriated $30,000 to have the Army Engineering Corps lay out a system of plans for roads and canals. Monroe, citing the Constitution's injunction that the federal government was charged with providing for "the common defense," signed the bill.

Monroe was not adverse to imposing taxes when they were needed: "To impose taxes when the public exigencies require them is an obligation of the most sacred character, especially with a free people." But in a variation on the "government governs best that governs least" sentiment ascribed to Jefferson, Monroe added that "To dispense with taxes when it may be done with perfect safety is equally the duty of their representatives."

Monroe did not realize that he was the beneficiary of some solid foundation-laying for business prosperity by the Federalist Supreme Court under Chief Justice John Marshall, who with the *Dartmouth College* case of 1819 firmly established the sanctity of contracts, then in *McCulloch v. Maryland* not only ruled the Bank of the United States constitutional under the "necessary and proper" clause of the Constitution but also established the important precedent that the states could not tax the federal government, saying, "The power to tax is the power to destroy." Just imagine what ultra-liberal cities could have done to the American military in the late twentieth century, by taxing the military bases within their limits! These Supreme Court rulings, in combination with numerous state-level decisions generally called "the Mill Acts," formed the basis of an American bias toward development over preservation of the land in its pristine condition (reversed almost entirely in the twentieth century, when the federal government set aside millions of acres for parks and natural habitats). By 1840, other Supreme Court rulings (*Bank of Augusta v. Earle, Charles River Bridge v. Warren Bridge*) would reinforce this institutional preference for developing the land, enforcing contracts, and ensuring competition, as legal historian James Willard Hurst demonstrates.

A Book You're Not Supposed to Read

The Jeffersonians: A Study in Administrative History, 1801–1829 by Leonard D. White (New York: MacMillan, 1951).

★ ★ ★

Feelin' Good?

"The Era of Good Feelings" was a phrase coined during Monroe's first term, though it applies to the end of Madison's presidency as well. This period was characterized by essentially one-party rule; in 1820 Monroe ran with no viable opposition—the first president to do so since Washington.

A Book You're Not Supposed to Read

Law and the Conditions of Freedom in the Nineteenth-Century United States by James Willard Hurst (Madison, WI: University of Wisconsin Press, 1964).

"A Question So Menacing to the Tranquility...of Our Union"

All the new territory Jefferson and Monroe had added to the Union came with a price. In 1819, Missouri applied for statehood, setting off Jefferson's "fire bell in the night." Initially unable to come to a resolution of the crisis over slavery, Congress set aside the Missouri statehood bill until the next session. Monroe recognized the slavery issue as supremely significant: "I have never known a question so menacing to the tranquility and even the continuance of our Union. All other subjects have given way to it, & appear to be almost forgotten." Like many, Monroe hoped the issue would go away. When the new American Colonization Society, formed in 1816 by both slave-holders and anti-slavery church groups, sought to return anyone taken from a slave trader to Africa, a solution seemed to present itself. In 1819 Congress appropriated $100,000 for an agency to oversee the returns, and the society negotiated with African chiefs for land that would become the nation of Liberia.

Monroe returned to the interrupted southern leg of his national tour in 1820, traveling through Georgia, Alabama, and Tennessee, where he visited Andrew Jackson's home. He thus became the first president to visit every section of the nation and to make a deliberate attempt to understand and make himself known to all Americans; he was also the first to travel by the new contraption known as the steamboat.

Upon his return, Monroe found the issue of slavery had been revived in the delayed Missouri statehood bill. Jefferson's "fire bell" was in fact a bomb. The sections of the United States were nearly perfectly poised in an even

★ ★ ★

A Singular Honor

The capital of Liberia was named Monrovia in honor of the American president. It is the only foreign capital in the world named after a U.S. president.

balance between slave and free states in the Senate and House. A compromise bill to admit Missouri as a slave state and Maine as a free state proved to be the first of several compromises that would only postpone disunion and war. By putting off a real resolution to the issue of slavery in 1820—at a time when an end to the "peculiar institution" still might have been brought about peacefully—the "Missouri Compromise" ensured a war at

★ ★ ★
A Lifetime of Public Service

When Monroe left office in 1821, he had served in more elected public offices than any other president; in one way or another he had been in the service of the United States for fifty years.

some point in the future to accomplish the same end. Under the compromise, an imaginary line was drawn, starting west of Missouri, at the 36 degree, 30 minute parallel, above which any future territory seeking statehood had to enter the Union as a free state, but any state below the line could choose to be a slave state. The deck was clearly stacked against the South; in the not too distant future the Missouri Compromise would ensure sufficient free soil votes in both the House and Senate that direct action against slavery could be taken. This so terrified the "Northern man of Southern principles," New York congressman and future president Martin Van Buren, that, as we have seen, he devised a new political party—the Democrats—to prevent *any* discussion of slavery in government. But ultimately all Van Buren accomplished was to ensure that over time the federal government would become so powerful that when an anti-slave president was finally elected, a war was guaranteed.

William Crawford of Georgia made an important contribution to Van Buren's scheme by introducing the Tenure of Office Act, which set the length of time for federal officers engaged in the collection and payment of bills at four years, although they could be reappointed. Monroe apparently knew little about the bill when he signed it into law, and he never acted on it, automatically reappointing all of his existing federal employees. But the

★ ★ ★

A Hands-Off Presidency

Monroe thought Congress should "make up its own mind on domestic matters without influence from the Chief Executive," a principle he violated only on occasion. John Quincy Adams was thinking along similar lines: "the exercise of actual control by the President over the opinions and wishes of a majority of the legislature will never be very palatable in what form soever it may be administered."

Act entrenched the spoils system that Van Buren would employ as a key weapon in forging his new party.

Monroe had almost nothing to do with passage of the Missouri Compromise except for working to ensure that Missouri came in as a slave state. His hands-off approach would not permit meddling on an issue such as statehood, and his desire for unity and his hostility to factions kept his role in the Missouri Compromise minimal.

By November of 1820, all looked bright on the surface. Monroe was reelected nearly unanimously (one legend has it that an elector voted for John Quincy Adams so as to preserve Washington's legacy as the only unanimous choice for president ever).

More trouble than just the Missouri issue greeted the reelected Monroe. His Treasury Secretary (and political rival) William Crawford had either accidentally misreported a $7 million surplus to Monroe or deliberately falsified the numbers; there was in fact a $5 million deficit. An embarrassed Monroe had to request that Congress slash three-fourths of the spending on military fortifications, and he also had to reduce the number of officers in the Army. Monroe found a way to avoid humiliating Andrew Jackson with a reduction in rank after so many victories by naming him governor of the Floridas. It came out later that Crawford had miscalculated.

Thinking he had put partisanship behind him with the elimination of the Federalist Party, Monroe soon learned why businesses are better when they have competitors. The Republicans lost all party discipline, with pockets of individuals increasingly going off on their own trajectories. With no opposition, the Republicans had no need of a party leader, and Monroe found his influence already waning by the first year of his second term. Moreover, the president did not want to involve himself in the internecine fighting among his subordinates, notably Crawford and John C. Calhoun. House Speaker Henry Clay reportedly told John Quincy Adams that the president "had not the slightest influence in Congress." His hands-off presidential style and distaste for partisan politics combined with the inflamed political ambitions of a number of younger men to make Monroe a lame duck.

★ ★ ★

You Telegraphed That One

One of James Monroe's presidential portraits was painted by an artist named Samuel Morse—who would later become famous for inventing the telegraph.

The Monroe Doctrine

Without Congress's approval, Monroe ordered an American vessel to sail around Cape Horn in 1821 and claim Graham Land, an island populated by seals, in Antarctica, claiming that it constituted an important naval base to protect American fisheries in the Pacific. With a stern warning, he brushed back Russia's attempt to set up fur posts 150 miles north of the American-Canadian border and to close off that part of the sea to foreign fishermen. Monroe's decisive steps opened the area to American fishing again. Then, in 1822, he convinced Congress to recognize former Spanish colonies Colombia and Mexico as independent states in the Western Hemisphere.

With Spanish colonies now splitting off, the Holy Alliance in Europe saw a threat to their power. They wanted to restore Spanish imperial possessions (as well as recapture some of the lost French ones). Britain, seeing an opportunity to weaken its potential European foes, tried to get the United States to join in an effort to keep the other Europeans out of the Western hemisphere. Monroe asserted that the Americas were by nature free and

A Book You're Not Supposed to Read

The Last Founding Father: James Monroe and a Nation's Call to Greatness by Harlow Giles Unger (Philadelphia: Da Capo Press, 2009).

independent, and should not be considered as subjects of any further European colonization. Some have credited John Quincy Adams with the wording of the "Monroe Doctrine," but biographer Harlow Unger makes the case that Monroe himself wrote it. The statement was formally delivered in his seventh "Annual Message" to Congress in December 1823:

> With the existing colonies or dependencies of any European power we have not interfered and shall not interfere.... But with the Governments who have declared their independence and maintained it...we could not view any interposition...by any European power in any other light than as the manifestation of an unfriendly disposition toward the United States.

Britain backed up the Monroe Doctrine with her Navy, but the precedent for American resistance to Old World intervention in the New World was set. Monroe, who had seemed consigned to irrelevance, had suddenly shocked the world by elevating the United States to spiritual leader of independence movements in the New World.

One at a time, Monroe began to lose the support of his allies, including his cabinet and his best general, Andrew Jackson, who got in more hot water by arresting the Spanish governor of Florida. Monroe stood by him, but rather than write the general personally had John Quincy Adams maintain correspondence with "Old Hickory" so that Monroe, as the president, could stay above the fray. Jackson felt betrayed, and Monroe had to write him a letter of apology. In the presidential election of 1824, Monroe disappointed perhaps his ablest supporter. Although John Quincy Adams had done yeoman's work as his secretary of State, and while Monroe thought him to be the best qualified for the job, he refused on personal principle to endorse Adams.

The race was thrown into a free-for-all among Adams, Henry Clay, Crawford, and Jackson. Crawford suffered a stroke in 1823, which took him out of contention. Van Buren, working behind the scenes to secure Jackson the election, did not yet have his new political structure up and running. Jackson had a plurality of the popular vote, but there was no clear winner in the Electoral College, so Clay instructed his supporters to back Adams—who upon winning named Clay secretary of State and heir apparent. The Jacksonians cried "Corrupt Bargain" (though no proof of a quid pro quo has ever been produced), leaving Adams a divided country from the outset.

Monroe, meanwhile, received a visitor from France: the Marquis de Lafayette, who was hailed a "guest of the nation" in 1824. Now the last Founder to be president was joined in a symbolic reunion with one of the American Revolution's great heroes. Lafayette slept in the White House before visiting the tomb of George Washington and meeting with the eighty-one-year-old Jefferson.

One last moment of drama occurred at John Quincy Adams's inauguration when Andrew Jackson arrived, armed (as was his custom) with two pistols. Monroe and his guest Lafayette feared the worst as Jackson looked frightening for a moment, then broke out in a broad grin and hustled forward to congratulate President-Elect John Quincy Adams. Although it wouldn't last, it was a scene reminiscent of Quincy's father pausing in the election of 1896 to allow Jefferson to challenge the Georgia vote. And it was a fitting tribute to the united, prosperous, and much larger United States of America that James Monroe handed over to the former president's son.

James Monroe, Constitutionalist

Few if any presidents have been as adept at staying within the letter of the Constitution while expanding its spirit broadly. When given specific choices on whether to go on record as expanding the power of government, such as the Cumberland Road Bill, Monroe always acted as a "strict construction-ist." But when not required to obtain Congress's consent, as with Jackson's escapades in Florida, Monroe often worked on the principle that it is easier to seek forgiveness than ask permission. Once in power James Monroe, like Thomas Jefferson, took a broader view of the president's responsibilities than he had once thought the Constitution allowed—to the nation's benefit.

Monroe's respect for the Constitution is all the more astounding given his brief possession of almost unlimited power in the last year of the War of 1812, when he served simultaneously as secretary of State, secretary of War, and, for all intents and purposes, president of the United States. As president he willingly deferred to Congress and the courts, except when it came to opportunities to expand American greatness. And, like all the other presidents before 1829, he never undertook to buy leadership or obtain legislation through patronage. Only his unwillingness to tackle the truly titanic issue of the day, slavery, detracts from a perfect "A" grade. Like his predecessors John Adams and Thomas Jefferson, James Monroe died on the fourth of July.

CHAPTER 6

John Quincy Adams, 1821-1825

"…without balance of powers there can be no good government among mankind.…"
—*John Quincy Adams*

President Adams's Constitutional Grade: B

Intimidating, almost wild-eyed, John Quincy Adams was the first president from one of four political families that have placed more than one member in the White House (the others being the Harrisons, the Roosevelts, and the Bushes). As a boy he had accompanied his father to France and seen the treaty process that ended America's War of Independence. Just over a decade later President Washington appointed him minister to the Netherlands. Then he served in the diplomatic corps in Russia and England, leading the delegation that negotiated the Treaty of Ghent to end the War of 1812. His crowning diplomatic achievement, however, was the Adams-Onis Treaty securing Florida for America. In between, he served as U.S. senator from Massachusetts. Adams's vast diplomatic experience allowed him to renew or achieve an array of treaties with Denmark, Mexico, Prussia, Austria, and the Hanseatic League as president.

Like his father, Quincy (as he was usually called) owned no slaves. (The Adamses were the only two of the first eight presidents never to have

Did you know?

★ John Quincy Adams took the oath of office on a book of constitutional law, not the Bible

★ He was the only president to serve in the House of Representatives after he lost his reelection bid

★ He had more impact on the slavery issue as a congressman than as president

★ Adams was key to creating the Smithsonian Institution

owned slaves.) Like his father, he did not serve in the army. Like Monroe, he had served in the U.S. Senate before being elected president. Although he did not write the Monroe Doctrine, his counsel certainly shaped it. Not the political manipulator that Jefferson or Hamilton was, Adams nevertheless knew how to play the political game, as demonstrated in his own election to the presidency, when he buttressed the candidacy of Henry Clay so as to diminish the electoral chances of Andrew Jackson. But the perception that he and Clay had made a "Corrupt Bargain" left him at enmity with two-thirds of the American public and proved an insurmountable obstacle to the success of his presidency. In the revolution in party politics that Martin Van Buren was concocting, Adams would soon be sidelined as part of the old guard whose leaders were still chosen from the elites by caucuses, not by the people.

Adams ironically lost the support of the patronage-heavy Post Office employees through his public commitment to retain all employees, even under the new "spoils system." Since the postal employees knew he would keep them regardless—but didn't know what his replacement might do—they sided with his opponent. (Already the Post Office was becoming one of the most important patronage arms in government, with thousands of jobs to be given away.)

More than any other president before him save Jefferson, Adams championed federal support of arts and science. He was also for the construction of a national university, something which George Washington had supported. Nevertheless, Adams did not use extra-constitutional means to advance such projects.

"The American System"

Adams did ride a new "nationalist" wave of thinking on policy that was led by Henry Clay and others who supported "the American System" of "internal improvements," a Bank of the United States, and import tariffs to protect American industry. Note that these were very different from the tariffs Hamilton had sought to ensure the United States could put an army in the field. The new "protective" tariffs were purely economic, intended to raise the price of foreign goods so that American manufacturers could charge more. The internal improvements were still paid for almost exclusively by private companies or with new state-backed private bond issues (in an example of what we might call mixed enterprise). The federal government had no role in building roads or canals.

The tariff issue came back to bite Adams. In one of the all-time worst political blunders in U.S. history, John C. Calhoun of South Carolina rallied other anti-tariff Southerners to support a very high tariff on raw materials that the New England states were importing for use in manufacturing, assuming that the pro-tariff New England representatives would vote against the poison pill legislation. By spreading the pain, the Southerners thought they would kill the tariff altogether. But a large portion of the New Englanders supported Calhoun's bill on general principles—tariffs were good, and so this one, while a little high, should be supported—and Adams signed it. Calhoun had to go to the floor of the Senate and make a speech opposing the very bill he had introduced. It was akin to the scene in 2005 and 2006 when Democrat politicians of both houses denounced the very Operation Iraqi Freedom they had voted for.

Soon the law became known as the "Tariff of Abominations" and most believed that anti-tariff Andrew Jackson, elected in 1828, would kill it, or at the very least scale it back. He didn't. By that time, Calhoun was the vice president and in open conflict with Jackson. In 1833 Adams, having been driven from the presidency, worked behind the scenes to craft a new compromise tariff bill, which removed the most onerous provisions.

The Handwriting on the Wall

Adams knew from the outset that the claims of a "Corrupt Bargain" would make his reelection difficult, if not impossible. Jackson had resigned from his senate seat in 1825 to begin campaigning—an unusual practice at the time. Using Martin Van Buren's new Democratic Party structure, Jackson won the election in a triumph for popular democracy that, as we shall see, historians such as Charles Beard and Arthur Schlesinger Jr. have exaggerated. But even if Adams hadn't been savaged by Van Buren's new partisan newspaper system, he simply did not have the party infrastructure that the "Little Magician" had created to elect Jackson. And, as we have already seen, Adams did not believe in patronage at a time when the "spoils system" was becoming the major tool political parties used in getting out the vote. Beaten by more than two to one in the Electoral College, Adams followed his father's example and did not attend his successor's inauguration. On his part, Jackson was typically classless, refusing to pay a traditional courtesy call to the outgoing chief executive.

Breaking tradition, Adams ran for the U.S. House of Representatives in 1830 and won, becoming the only American president to hold a seat in the House after his presidential term expired. He served until 1848.

The "Slave Power"

Other than his father, John Quincy Adams would have to be reckoned the most anti-slave president in the nation's young history—except that like most of his predecessors he did not use the office in any way to change, alter, or abolish the institution. Like Jefferson and Van Buren, Adams was afraid that slavery would dissolve the Union. But he fell victim to the illusion that prosperity could tie the nation together and even possibly eliminate the "peculiar institution." Thus his support for "the American System." As in Monroe's presidency, a case could have been made for federal support of roads and harbors on the grounds of national defense, but Adams did not take that approach. Quite the contrary, Adams adopted a much broader defense of such projects, claiming that "liberty is power" and that "the spirit of improvement is abroad upon the earth." Perhaps fortunately for the president, his faith in that "power" and "spirit" to justify federal involvement in road building was never put to the test of a Supreme Court case. He correctly stood aside during the tariff battle, reasoning that it was not a president's duty to oppose a bill having such widespread support (even if much of that support was based on a political trick) and that there was nothing unconstitutional about the tariff itself.

The tariff itself raised the very issue of slavery that John Quincy Adams tried to avoid in his

★ ★ ★
An Exemplary Ex-President

Adams's crowning achievements—both of which involved the slavery issue—actually came after he left the presidency. The first was his 1841 defense of the *Amistad* slaves before the United States Supreme Court, which decided in favor of the Africans who had taken over a slave ship; they were released and returned to their homeland. The second was the 1844 victory in his eight-year battle to lift the "Gag Rule" against even discussing slavery in Congress.

presidency. As the subsequent Nullification Crisis during Jackson's presidency would reveal, "states' rights" really only applied to one "right," the right to own slaves. William Freehling's book *Prelude to Civil War* shows that the debates over the tariff were often not really about the tariff itself but about the fear of federal action against slavery. If the North was powerful enough to impose tariffs in the teeth of the South's opposition, then one day the North might be able to abolish slavery. Thus, ironically, the single defining piece of legislation in John Quincy Adams's presidency—a tariff bill that deliberately sidestepped the entire slavery issue—would serve as a substitute for the slavery debate. It became a proxy of sorts. The fierce fight over the tariff made it clear that slavery could not be ignored, compromised away, or tolerated. At some point it would have to be killed. Adams saw a "slave power" conspiracy driven by "the machinations of a small yet purposeful proslavery cabal" corrupting the fabric of the Union, especially the federal government. This led

A Book You're Not Supposed to Read

Prelude to Civil War: The Nullification Controversy in South Carolina, 1816–1836 by William H. Freehling (New York: Oxford, 1992).

Adams, like many conspiracy theorists, to conclude that his setbacks were all traceable to this imaginary force. He told a friend in 1837, "[T]he principle of internal improvement was swelling the tide of public prosperity, till the Sable Genius of the South saw the signs of his own inevitable downfall in the unparalleled progress of the general welfare of the North.... I fell, and with me fell...the system of internal improvement by national means...."

No "slave power" conspiracy existed. It didn't need to. Slavery's power was out in the open, and it would soon be championed by a variety of Southern writers as superior to that of "free labor"—including the early sociologist George Fitzhugh. Just as imaginary as the "slave power" conspiracy is the fantastic vision of a modernized, industrial nineteenth-century South that, not needing slavery, would just release its human chattel. Historians who lament the failure of Adams's "internal improvements" as a sort of antebellum "New Deal" that would have magically raised the South to economic prosperity and caused it to reject slavery fail to grasp the social, political, and power relationships inherent in the slave system. Slavery was so tightly woven into Southern economics and culture that it no longer bound just slave-owners to the slave system, but courts, sheriffs, editors, ministers, and ultimately everyday people. As subsequent presidents would find, there was no unwinding the vine. It had to be ripped out. But this reality was not obvious at the time; it was only visible to some.

Grading John Quincy Adams

John Quincy Adams's great political disadvantage was that he served at a time when social foundations were shifting momentously—and he failed to realize it. With them went the old political structures: the caucus system was dying, and a new popular democracy was taking hold. Already, in Monroe's administration, many states had lowered property requirements for voting or eliminated them altogether, thereby greatly expanding the electorate. Within a few years, "King Caucus" would be dead entirely, replaced by presidential nominating conventions. Adams soon drifted into the new Whig Party, which was already as obsolete as the "Era of Good Feelings." John Quincy Adams operated well within the limits of the Constitution, but like his predecessors he kicked the can of slavery down the road yet again.

CHAPTER 7

Andrew Jackson, 1829–1837

"I weep for the liberty of my country when I see at this early day of its successful experiment that corruption has been imputed to many members of the House of Representatives, and the rights of the people have been bartered for promises of office."

—Andrew Jackson

President Jackson's Constitutional Grade: C–

There is no question that Andrew Jackson was the most important president between the tenures of George Washington and Abraham Lincoln. He changed the office dramatically from that of the first six chief executives, imposing a new activist presidential model. Martin Van Buren's novel political party structure transformed the nature of elections in 1828—although the first truly "Jacksonian" election did not occur until the election of William Henry Harrison in 1840. It was Jackson, however, who quarterbacked the team that Van Buren put together. Even though he would carp about patronage and spoils used by others, it was the administration of Andrew Jackson that truly invented the modern day "spoils system." Ironically, though "Jacksonian democracy" is associated with such innovations as the national nominating convention (and the associated demise of "King Caucus"), Jackson's own nomination was not the result of a convention. It was his opponent in 1832, Henry Clay—the man Jackson referred to as "the Judas of the West"—who was nominated that way. But states had eliminated the property requirements for voting, so essentially every male

Did you know?

★ Andrew Jackson, known for his hatred of the Bank of the United States, had his own plan for a national bank

★ The percent of the U.S. population voting in presidential elections nearly tripled between 1824 and 1828

★ Jackson was the first president to be the target of an assassination attempt

★ He repeatedly called for a constitutional amendment to eliminate the Electoral College

An Article You're Not Supposed to Read

James Stanton Chase, "Jacksonian Democracy and the Rise of the Nominating Convention," *Mid-America* 45 (1963): 229–49. Chase describes the early shift from "King Caucus" as a form of nominating political candidates to the nominating convention, a fixture in modern times.

"free white and over twenty-one" could vote for the presidential electors, bringing the percentage of the population that voted in 1828 to 9.5 percent, from just 3.4 percent in 1824.

Jackson was the first general elected to the presidency since Washington, and the first real soldier other than Monroe and Washington. He was the first true "Western" president (though today, as a result of the Civil War, most Americans would probably put Tennessee in the "South") and the first born of two Irish parents. As a young man he had served briefly in the House as an at-large member after Tennessee received statehood, then served a year as a U.S. senator before resigning. When he came to the Senate in 1823—for another abbreviated term—his time out of office would mark the second longest gap in that chamber's history. And, like all the presidents up to that point not named Adams, he was a slave-owner.

Although Jackson had legislative experience in both Houses of Congress, his name was most associated in the public mind with the Battle of New Orleans and the Indian wars. Having lost the disputed election of 1824, Jackson cared little for his predecessor. As we have seen, he did not visit Adams before taking office (and Adams, of course, returned the favor by not sticking around for the inauguration). He had been actively campaigning for the presidency since resigning his Senate seat in 1825, running the first full-time political campaign. Campaign buttons had been introduced in 1824, but now hickory poles were erected in towns across the country (in honor of Jackson's nickname, "Old Hickory") and hickory canes and sticks sold at rallies. One of the first ever campaign songs, "The Hunters of Kentucky," was written by Jacksonite Samuel Woodworth. Jackson's opponents referred to him as a "jackass," and in defiance he adopted a jackass as a symbol on some of his campaign posters. Decades later, when cartoonist Thomas Nast learned about this, he popularized the donkey as a symbol for the Democratic Party.

"Stealing from the Many to the Few"

As Martin Van Buren oiled the machinery of his new party, he also put the finishing touches on a new nationalized "newspaper" system of propaganda organs. None of these made money in the free market of subscriptions, and virtually all of them were partially or fully subsidized by the Democratic Party. Duff Green's *United States Telegraph* was the premier organ, but they all operated on the same basis. Their only goal was to advance party positions and candidates: as Duff Green wrote, "*party is everything.*" His paper's motto was "Power is always stealing from the many to the few."

Congress aided in the rise of these so-called "newspapers" by lowering the rates to send papers through the mail compared to other printed materials such as books. One expert on early papers has calculated that if papers had been shipped at the same postage cost as books, newspaper costs would have been seven hundred times higher! As a result, between 1800 and 1840, the number of newspapers shipped through the mail rose from two million to forty million. Papers received massive direct support from the political parties in power through printing and lithographing fees generated by business sent them by the Democrat Party. Francis Preston Blair's paper the *Congressional Globe* received the State Department's business to publish

★ ★ ★
What's in a Nick-Name?

Andrew Jackson, "Old Hickory," was the first president to be known by a nickname. Soon, "Old Tippecanoe" (William Henry Harrison), "Old Rough and Ready" (Zachary Taylor), and, of course, "Honest Abe" (Lincoln) would follow. The use of a nickname indicated that Jackson was viewed as a representative man, a man "of the people" (as opposed to the elites). He didn't hesitate to play upon that reputation.

A Party (News) Man

"[I]t is vain to talk of a free press when the *favor of power* is essential to the support of editors, and the money of the people, by passing through the hands of the Executive, is made to operate as a bribe against liberty."

—Duff Green

session laws. Asked what his view on particular issues was, Blair, in a rare moment of honesty said his paper's position was "determined by Jackson's stand on them."

With these subsidies in place, by 1840 newspaper circulations were growing at a rate five times that of the general population. By 1850, the U.S. Census Bureau estimated that eighty percent of American papers were entirely partisan—other estimates put the number closer to one hundred percent. Jacksonian editors viewed their readers as empty vessels that needed to be guided to appropriate views, then mobilized to vote. They abandoned all pretense of being "fair and balanced," to use a modern phrase. One Jacksonian editor stated, "We most of all abhor and detest…a neutral paper. It pretends to be all things to all men." Between 1847 and 1860, the ratio of so-called "opinion" pieces to "news" pieces nearly doubled. Papers such as the *Arkansas Democrat* and the *Richmond Whig* boasted their party loyalties on their mastheads. At least they were honest about whom they supported!

Van Buren spent much of 1827 riding around the country with Jackson posters, lining up political supporters, especially in the South. In the wake of the "Corrupt Bargain," Jackson refused to have anything to do with Adams: "From that moment on," he wrote, "I withdrew all intercourse with him." The election of 1828 got as nasty as any election had been. Opponents passed out "coffin handbills" noting the number of people killed under the general's command, including the British citizens Robert Ambrister and Joseph Arbuthnot. Jackson's political enemies accused Old Hickory's wife, Rachel, of bigamy (a charge that technically was true, although the case dated back to 1791–1794). "Ought a convicted adulteress and her paramour husband be placed in the highest offices of this free and Christian land?" asked the *Cincinnati Gazette*. When Rachel died just before the inauguration, Jackson blamed Adams's supporters for her death. But Jackson's own agents were far from unscrupulous: they had spread rumors that as minister to Russia Adams had handed a servant girl over to the Czar as a sex prize. Many

A Book You're Not Supposed to Read

Partisan Journalism: A History of Media Bias in the United States by Jim A. Kuypers (Lanham, MD: Rowman & Littlefield, 2014).

modern political traditions made their first appearance in the campaign, including party picnics and the widespread use of handbills. Jackson beat Adams in the Electoral College 178–83. Mobs broke into the White House on election night, and Adams, who escaped out the back, had liquored punch bowls set up outside to lure the partygoers out. On inauguration night, Jackson left revelers in the White House and dined alone at a local inn. In a scene straight out of a Barack Obama "Hope and Change" speech, crowds of people gathered in Washington until they numbered in the tens of thousands. Daniel Webster, a Jackson opponent, observed that "they really seem to think the country has been rescued from some general disaster" with Jackson's election. A Supreme Court justice saw only "the reign of *King Mob*."

Van Buren had chosen the leader for his new political system well, for in Andrew Jackson he had a man of popular appeal to commoners, and one who deeply believed in rotation in office. Jackson, who put his faith in "[T]he planter, the farmer, the mechanic, and the laborer . . . the great body of the people of the United States, they are the bone and sinew of the country—men who love liberty and desire nothing but equal rights and equal laws" was no believer in government by experts. As a man of the people, he believed that everyone had the ability to do almost any job, and therefore a regular turnover was desirable.

109

A Book You're Not Supposed to Read

Martin Van Buren and the Making of the Democratic Party by Robert V. Remini (New York: Columbia University Press, 1959).

Van Buren, who operated on a different principle—"to the victor go the spoils"—conveniently fit the two together. Since the president intended to put new people in anyway, why not make them people who had gotten the president elected? In fact, Van Buren dusted off *Federalist* No. 51, where Madison had asserted that "Ambition must be made to counteract ambition" to bolster his claim that "political parties are inseparable from free governments." He even argued that parties actually put a check on "the passions, the ambition, and the usurpations of individuals." Along with Thomas Ritchie, he had formed the Albany-Richmond Axis that put the two most powerful political states in the Union on the same side. Thus he was able to set Jackson up with a structure organized down to the grass roots, divided into wards, precincts, districts, counties, and states, each under the command of a party loyalist whose job was to get out the vote. The more successful the loyalist on election day, the bigger the "spoils" that would go to him as a reward.

Jackson's political opponents didn't have a chance. They were running a plow horse against a dragster. Political scientists like Michael Nelson want to give Jackson credit for seeing that "a Jeffersonian restoration would require a new form of politics," but in fact Jackson did very little to reimagine the political structure. To play his role in the drama Van Buren was staging, all Jackson had to do was be himself, and liberally lace his rhetoric with adulation for the "common man." Jackson could be exhilarating in his pro-Americanism, but he could also be petty and hateful in specific applications of his policies. So, for example, when he vetoed the funding bill for the Maysville Road—which was part of the National Road—he could play the "strict constructionist" and claim that that part of the National Road ran solely through Kentucky and therefore it was not

★ ★ ★

Don't Cross Andy

In 1806 Charles Dickinson accused Andrew Jackson of cheating on a bet over horses and, for good measure, insulted Rachel Jackson. Jackson challenged him to a duel (Dickinson had already fought several). Dickinson got off the first shot and hit Jackson in the chest—but the future president remained standing. "My God, have I missed him?" Dickinson asked. Jackson, holding his chest, misfired, then re-loaded his pistol and killed Dickinson.

Jackson was the first leader of the nation to be the target of an assassination attempt. In January 1835 Richard Lawrence, an out-of-work painter, came at Jackson as he left a funeral in the Capitol building. Lawrence shot at the president point blank, but this time it was his gun that misfired. An incensed sixty-seven-year-old Jackson clubbed Lawrence with his walking cane. Then Lawrence pulled out a second pistol and pressed the trigger—only to have that one misfire as well! The would-be assassin was fortunate that Jackson's aides dragged him away before Jackson got in still more licks. The odds of both guns misfiring in succession were thought to be 125,000 to 1. President Jackson was a very lucky man.

a matter of interstate commerce. More likely, the veto was really a chance for Jackson to gig his main political opponent, Henry Clay of Kentucky.

The new president was not like Jefferson at all. He was able to pay off the national debt—actually not a tough feat when the main form of government revenue, American land sales, were soaring. Indeed, by 1836 land sales had increased explosively, to the degree that Jackson felt he needed to slow them down, so he issued the Specie Circular, an executive order requiring that purchases of government land be made in gold or silver. Plus, in the early part of his administration, government revenues benefitted from the Tariff of Abominations, which Jackson did nothing to eliminate.

Due to a schism in his cabinet early in his administration over the Peggy Eaton affair, in which the secretary of War, John Eaton, had married the widow of a navy officer who had committed suicide (supposedly over Eaton's liaisons with Peggy), Jackson took most of his advice from the

★ ★ ★

Hometown Cookin' in the Kitchen Cabinet

Ever since George Washington established the "cabinet" in his first administration, presidents have followed his lead and assigned secretaries to handle the business of the various departments of their administrations.

Often these were close friends, but just as often the appointments were sops to political opponents who lost (so as to prevent them from excessive criticism) or to relatives or acquaintances of important people in the government. By the 1830s, the government had started to grow enough that selecting talented men who would pull together as a team grew more difficult. As we shall see, Abraham Lincoln corralled all his political competitors into the administration, resulting in great turmoil and resistance to his goals.

The idea of a group of advisors who met informally—outside the normal cabinet meetings—was hatched in Andrew Jackson's presidency. These men were editors, state officials who could swing votes, and other well-placed activists. While they did not take the place of the duly appointed secretaries, they nevertheless were highly influential. When, a hundred years later, Franklin D. Roosevelt took the office, he had a similar group called the "Brains Trust" (or "Brain Trust"), made up of Columbia professors, including Raymond Moley, Rex Tugwell, and Adolf Berle. Many of these men held official positions—Berle was assistant secretary of State—while Moley remained an informal advisor and speechwriter, but their impact on policy was often far greater than that of more prominent elected officials (such as Budget Director Lewis Douglas, for example). In a similar manner, John F. Kennedy would summon the "Best and the Brightest" both for his official cabinet and as unofficial advisors. While entirely un-democratic, the appearance of the Kitchen Cabinet was an admission that, as government grew, political favors often went to individuals who did not share either the confidence or the ideological direction of the chief executive.

"Kitchen Cabinet"—a group of supporters not officially holding any office. Francis Preston Blair, Amos Kendall, Duff Green, and Van Buren were among his foremost advisors.

Upon taking office, Jackson promptly booted a number of Adams appointees and replaced them with Democrats, citing "rotation in office" and laying the foundation for massive churning in the federal government with every new election. More importantly, he started a process in motion whereby the way to get elected was to promise more jobs than your opponent. Van Buren and Jackson had thereby consigned America to an ever-growing federal government. In many ways, then, Andrew Jackson, whatever he may have said about the virtues of limited government, ensured that government would quickly become anything but limited.

Jackson found himself dealing with three major issues: the Tariff of Abominations, Indians, and the early re-charter of the Bank of the United States. Much of Jackson's support in South Carolina came from tariff opponents who thought he would reduce rates as president. Yet Jackson left the rates in place. In response his vice president, John C. Calhoun of South Carolina, developed a variation on the Madison-Jefferson concept of "Interposition" that he called "Nullification." Calhoun,

Talking a Good Strict Constructionist Game

"It is well known that there have always been those amongst us who wish to enlarge the powers of the General Government, and experience would seem to indicate that there is a tendency on the part of this Government to overstep the boundaries marked out for it by the Constitution. Its legitimate authority is abundantly sufficient for all the purposes for which it was created, and its powers being expressly enumerated, there can be no justification for claiming anything beyond them."

—Andrew Jackson's Farewell Address

like Jefferson, based his doctrine on the so-called "compact" theory of the Union, whereby the United States was akin to a private men's club that members were free to leave anytime they wanted. Almost all the other Founders, including even Madison, had accepted the more traditional holistic understanding of the nation as a "body," from which you could not sever an arm or leg without fatally endangering the whole. Courts in the twentieth century would soundly reject the concept of nullification, but it was untested at the time. The first real Supreme Court ruling on nullification would come in 1859 with the *Ableman v. Booth* case involving the Fugitive Slave Act.

Calhoun insisted that South Carolina had the right to nullify the tariff within its borders. In 1832 he resigned from the vice presidency to run for the Senate, where he thought he could do more to advance his cause. Meanwhile, in that same year a tariff with lower rates was passed, and Jackson signed it. But that did not satisfy the Calhoun faction in South Carolina, which in November 1832 issued an Ordinance of Nullification declaring the tariff unenforceable in the state after February 1, 1833. Jackson would have none of it, and when South Carolina tried to implement its ordinance, Congress passed the Force Bill on March 1, 1833, authorizing the president to use force to collect the revenues. In stepped Henry Clay to accommodate Southern opponents of the tariff with federal legislation—which Calhoun, who saw the hopelessness of state nullification as a practical strategy, joined to support. The resulting Compromise Tariff of 1833 reduced any rates above twenty percent by ten percent every two years until 1842.

Jackson had staked out his position quite early. At an April 13, 1830, Jefferson Day celebration with Calhoun present, Jackson toasted, "Our Federal Union: it must be preserved." (Calhoun toasted back, "The Union. Next to our liberty, the most dear.") A more naked threat was issued by the president a few days later, when a South Carolina visitor asked if Jackson had any message to send to the people of South Carolina. "Yes," he replied. "Please give my compliments to my friends in your state and say to them, that if a single drop of blood shall be shed there in opposition to the laws of the United States, I will hang the first man I can lay my hand on engaged in such treasonable conduct, upon the first tree I can reach." Calhoun got the message.

While on the surface the debate was over the tariff, the real issue below the surface was always about slavery. Jackson understood that to some degree, as he wrote in May 1833 that "the tariff was only a pretext." But he saw "disunion and southern confederacy" as "the real object" and thought "the negro, or slavery question" was just another pretext. In fact, slavery was not a "pretext" for anything. Quite the contrary, as William Freehling and others have shown, the Confederacy was the pretext for perpetuating slavery. Jackson had the cart before the horse. The Nullification Crisis ultimately had an unexpected outcome, namely that after 1833 Southern states increasingly looked to the federal government as a source of protection for the right to hold slaves. The system that Van Buren had set up, only a few years earlier, to protect the institution of slavery with a weakened federal government and vibrant "states rights" was now undercut by the very first man that that system had succeeded in placing in power. Jackson, who was opposed by the "nationalists" such as Adams and Clay, had established the most nationalist doctrine imaginable for the Union.

★ ★ ★

Abraham Lincoln Could Not Have Said It Better

On December 10, 1832, Jackson issued a Proclamation to the People of South Carolina declaring "the power to annul a law of the United States, assumed by one State, incompatible with the existence of the Union, contradicted expressly by the letter of the Constitution, unauthorized by its spirit [is] inconsistent with every principle on which it was founded, and destructive for the great object for which it was formed."

Another set of problems came from a new round of Indian issues, the most notable of which involved the Five Civilized Tribes: the Choctaws, Chickasaws, Cherokees, Creeks, and Seminoles. The Cherokees had a written constitution and a written language, and many were Christians. But Georgians wanted their land, especially after gold was discovered there. Cherokee Chief John Ross had accepted George Washington's definition of a tribe as an independent nation within the United States, but the state of Georgia ignored the national treaties, declared an end to all tribal jurisdictions, and surveyed the Cherokees' land in preparation for selling it off by lottery. Jackson, who in his first inaugural had proposed a land exchange

A Book You're Not Supposed to Read

The Life of Andrew Jackson by Robert V. Remini (New York: Harper Perennial, 2010).

to move the Indians west onto federal territory, sided with Georgia. The appropriation of the Indian land was convenient for Jackson, lucrative for Georgia, and utterly destructive to the Cherokee. The Army moved in, forcing the Cherokee and the Seminoles on the "Trail of Tears" to Oklahoma. The Indian Removal Act (1830) revoked the Indian sovereignty established by Washington, shattered federal treaties, and authorized the forcible relocation of the Choctaws and Chickasaws as well. The Creeks proved more problematic, as they resisted in the U.S. court system, winning the *Worcester v. Georgia* case (1832), which ruled that Georgia had acted unconstitutionally. Jackson is supposed to have reacted to the Supreme Court decision by saying of the chief justice, "John Marshall has made his decision, now let him enforce it." In other words, Jackson was violating one constitutional principle—blatantly defying the separation of powers—so that he could ignore another, the sovereignty of federal treaties, which guaranteed the Indians' own sovereignty. Ironically, during the Creek War of 1813–1814, Jackson had adopted an Indian infant.

Jackson's deeply entrenched hatred of Indians dated from his military expeditions in Florida and Alabama, and even as far back as the American Revolution when the Cherokee allied with the British. Those attitudes, more than just "racism," go some distance to explain the Indian Removal. But his actions also clearly showed that he had no respect for other branches of the government if they disagreed with him. The Maysville Road veto—accompanied by a tendentious constitutional argument on Jackson's part, but almost certainly designed to punish his political rival Henry Clay—came next, followed by the initiative that defined the Jackson presidency, the "War" on the Bank of the United States. The Bank War, like all his other policies, involved Jackson's personal animosities in no small degree. His hostility to banks and paper money, which he viewed as unsound, dated from his difficulties in paying his own debts during the Panic of 1819.

"I Will Kill It"

The Bank of the United States, after being re-chartered in 1816 and surviving the Panic of 1819, had recovered and thrived, especially after Philadelphia banker Nicholas Biddle took the helm. Biddle had served in the Pennsylvania senate before taking over management of the bank from South Carolinian Langdon Cheves in 1822. It appears that Biddle was overplaying his hand at the instigation of Jackson opponents such as Henry Clay when he sought the bank's re-charter four years early, in 1832—on the theory that Jackson would not veto the popular bank in an election year. As the historians used to say, "Biddle blundered badly," and Jackson not only vetoed the re-charter bill but made that veto a central piece of his reelection campaign. "I will kill it!" he told one of his confidants. After reelection, Jackson went even further, removing all the government deposits from the bank and storing them in a string of "Pet Banks," so named because they were all owned by FOJs (Friends of Jackson). It was as blatant a political move as had been seen in the nation's presidency to that date, carried out without any consideration for the nation's economic health.

But the subsequent Panic of 1837, which for over a hundred years was laid at the feet of Old Hickory by the traditional narrative about the Bank War, in fact had little to do with the disruptions he caused. Peter Temin, an economist from MIT, wrote a path-breaking book in 1969 called *The Jacksonian Economy*, in which, using computers for the first time to process large-scale international money flows, he demonstrated convincingly that the Panic was caused by a cascade of events following the drying up of the flow of Mexican silver into the United States. The survival of the blame-Jackson storyline into late–twentieth century history books was due in part

A Book You're Not Supposed to Read

The Jacksonian Economy by Peter Temin (New York: W. W. Norton and Company, 1969), stands in sharp contrast to the traditional interpretations of Jackson—especially involving the Bank War and the economy—offered by Arthur Schlesinger Jr. and Bray Hammond.

to the work of Bray Hammond, a Federal Reserve banker who wrote *Banks and Politics in America: From the Revolution to the Civil War* (1957); supporters of the gold standard bought Hammond's explanation because it fit with their ideology.

Temin's research may have absolved Jackson from causing a national financial panic, but it doesn't let him off the hook for abuse of power, terrible management of the economy, and partisan bullying. He destroyed a perfectly good institution that was supported almost unanimously by private state bankers as a source of stability for the money system. Inflation was always a danger in an age of open competition in money. What we have learned since the publication of *The Jacksonian Economy* is that Jackson actually had an ulterior motive for destroying the bank—he intended from the outset to replace it with a new central bank of his own! Much as Jefferson had Gallatin lay out a massive federal spending plan for roads and canals, Jackson instructed Levi Woodbury, his Treasury secretary, to prepare a plan for a new central national bank that would be run by men of *Jackson's* choosing. Moreover, he intended to eliminate all paper money, even that issued by private banks (making the appearance of his face on the $20 bill all the more ironic).

Over the next thirty years, the nation functioned well without a national bank. Indeed, except for the Panic of 1857, which was brought on entirely by the decision in the *Dred Scott* case that threw open all the western territories to uncertainty about slavery—and likely violence—the nation prospered. Private state-chartered banks, free to issue their own paper money, proved quite stable, especially when (as in the South) they were allowed to establish branch systems. At best Jackson's Bank veto denied the U.S. government a source of loans in emergencies, and at worst it may have kept the economy of the subsequent thirty years from booming even more. There is little evidence, however, that killing the Bank severely hurt American business in general or banking in particular. But there is considerable evidence that Jackson picked the fight purely out of spite and fear of Biddle's potential patronage power, and also that Jackson refused to even consider compromises that met all his stated demands and concerns. The Bank War was, pure and simple, an opportunity for Jackson to stick it to the bankers and "the moneyed power" in New York and Philadelphia.

In keeping with Jeffersonian ideals, when the nation ran a surplus, Jackson presided over the distribution of the funds. But the Distribution Act of 1836 did not simply give the money back to the citizens who had been taxed to collect it in the first place. Championed by Henry Clay, this distribution was designed to be a loan of sorts to the private state banks, to replace some of the money taken out of circulation by the demise of the national Bank. Beginning in January 1837, some $5 million in surplus Treasury funds in the form of notes would be handed out in quarterly installments, with no real expectation that the loans would be repaid. The state banks were supposed to redeem the notes in gold or silver specie within a year, but they never acquired enough specie to repay the loans. Jackson, of course, signed off on the bill. The affair burnished Jackson's reputation as a "states' rights" supporter.

Jackson exited the scene just in time. His successor and political mentor, Martin Van Buren, would inherit the Panic of 1837, which became the worst

An Article You're Not Supposed to Read

Larry Schweikart, "Jacksonian Ideology, Currency Control, and 'Central Banking': A Reappraisal," *Historian* 51 (November 1988): 78–102. Using previously undiscovered plans by Treasury Secretary Levi Woodbury for the establishment of a new central bank once the Bank of the United States was gone, this article reveals Jackson's broader agenda of eliminating all paper money and forcing the United States onto a gold standard.

of the nineteenth century. Again, contrary to a hundred years' worth of historical writing, the Distribution had no part in starting the Panic.

Grading Old Hickory on a Constitutional Scale

Jackson should receive high marks for laying down the marker that the Union could not be dissolved through nullification, interposition, or secession. Despite his avowed states' rights principles, his actions in the Nullification Crisis were entirely in line with the spirit and the letter of the Constitution.

Yet his excellent performance there was more than offset by his damage to the Constitution elsewhere. In Indian relations, he eroded constitutional authority in two separate ways. First, he challenged Washington's long-standing definition of the Indian tribes as independent nations, yet under the sovereignty of the United States. That definition was derived from many treaties that the U.S. government had made with the Indian tribes—and the Constitution says that treaties, along with laws passed by Congress, are "the supreme law of the land.... any Thing in the Constitution or Laws of any State to the Contrary." Jackson ignored those treaties and sided with the states that wanted the Indians removed. Second, he damaged the separation of powers by defying a ruling of the United States Supreme Court. While the state of Georgia—and "states' rights" in general—may have seemed to be the winners, Jackson was merely installing his own dictates over those of legislatures and courts.

His war on the constitutionally chartered and popularly supported Bank of the United States was neither necessary nor in the nation's best interest. His veto of the bank's re-charter marked only one of many, with Jackson issuing more vetoes than all previous six presidents put together. In doing so, he dramatically shifted the nation away from the Founders' Whig principles, whereby the legislature should take the lead in making policy.

★ ★ ★

The Liberals' Bromance with Old Hickory

One of the more baffling historical "bromances" is between liberal historians and "King Andrew" Jackson, which has only come to an end in recent decades. Arthur Schlesinger Jr., the liberal's liberal, wrote glowingly of the "Jacksonian Era" and referred to the Jacksonians as the "Keepers of the Jeffersonian Conscience." Madison, Monroe, and John Quincy Adams were sellouts to the Hamiltonian agenda, and, Schlesinger lamented, "gloom settled deep on the Jeffersonians in the twenties." But then came Jackson. Marxist historian Charles Beard, who exaggerated the triumph of democracy in the election of Jackson even more grossly, gushed that as people swarmed to vote for Old Hickory "democracy foamed perilously near the crest." One can almost hear *The Marseillaise* rising in the background, see the red flags on the barricades, and catch a glimpse of Chairman Mao handing out little books backstage.

For a brief time, the hero worship only got worse: historians articulating class-based analyses of U.S. history saw in Jackson not just a man who opposed the elite Bank of the United States, but a foe of capitalism itself. So far—while not accurate—so good. At least the narrative hung together. But how did the bromance survive the Indian Removal? Schlesinger treated it as a footnote to Jackson's key role as the champion of the common man. Charles Grier Sellers, in a landmark article "Andrew Jackson vs. the Historians," *Mississippi Valley Historical Review* 44 (March 1958): 615–34, brushed off the criticisms of classic American historians such as James Parton, concluding that, "Looking back over a century of scholarship, students of Jacksonian Democracy may well rejoice that their subject has been so central to defining the American experience...."

More recent liberal historians, however, have focused heavily on the Indian Removal, seeing it as a character flaw in Jackson and a central feature of the oppressive regime of the white man in his quest to destroy natives. Whatever reasons Jackson offered for his actions are dismissed as little more than rationalizations, fabrications to cover his racism and White Americans' lust for land. In reaction, some conservatives have rallied around what they see as Jackson's defense of states' rights (in regard to the Indians) while ignoring his tendencies toward centralization—demonstrated by his role in upholding the tariff. Back on the other side of the political spectrum, the tariff is a point in Jackson's favor. And after all, it shouldn't surprise anyone that liberals celebrate Jackson's enforcement of a high tax and his expansion of federal and presidential power. To them, that's what defines greatness.

In many ways, Andrew Jackson ushered in the "first era of big government," when everything ran through Washington and particularly the White House. Like his predecessors, Jackson did nothing to stop the festering disease of slavery. Worse, he tacitly approved of the mechanisms by which his own Democratic Party perpetuated it (for example, the "Gag Rule" against even debating slavery in Congress). Expanding executive power dramatically while eagerly participating in the growth of government through Van Buren's "spoils system," Jackson was anything but the "small 'd' democrat" that liberal scholars such as Arthur Schlesinger Jr. have made him out to be. His nickname among his enemies, "King Andrew," indicated concerns about his abuses of power. Until very recently, when the Politically Correct Police have begun to bash him for his Indian policies and attitude toward slavery, Jackson has been a hero to historians of the Left. That alone should concern lovers of the Constitution.

CHAPTER 8

Martin Van Buren, 1837–1841

"As to the presidency, the two happiest days of my life were those of my entrance upon the office and my surrender of it."
—*Martin Van Buren*

President Van Buren's Constitutional Grade: C+

Despite the fact that the "Little Magician" had created the structure of a new party that twice elected Andrew Jackson as president, he himself got into the presidency only thanks to a split among the anti-Jackson candidates—former general William Henry Harrison, Daniel Webster of Massachusetts, Willie Mangum of South Carolina, and Hugh Lawson White. Although Van Buren outpolled all of them in the Electoral College 170–113, if a single candidate had emerged it would have been much more difficult for him to win.

The first of five presidents to come from New York (the others: Millard Fillmore, Grover Cleveland, and the two Roosevelts), Van Buren was known as the "Red Fox of Kinderhook" for the village near Albany where he lived. As a young man he inherited a slave from his father. Before he could take possession, however, the slave ran away. Like the Adamses before him, Van Buren never served in the military. All his adult life was spent in politics, much of it pursuing the presidency. In New York, he opposed DeWitt Clinton's plan for the Erie Canal, but when the political faction Van Buren

Did you know?

★ Martin Van Buren, born in 1782, was the first president never to have been a British subject

★ As a teenager, Van Buren inherited a slave, who ran away; thus he was the first Northern president to have been a slave-owner

★ Van Buren was the first Democrat to be nominated by a convention

An Article You're Not Supposed to Read

Lynn Marshall, "The Strange Stillbirth of the Whig Party," *American Historical Review* 72, no. 2 (January 1967): 445–69. Marshall shows that the Whigs were merely "me-too" Democrats, except they were more elite. So they could not appeal to the "common man"—and offered no real difference from the Democrats on the main issue of the day, slavery.

associated with, the "Bucktails" (named for wearing a deer's tail on their hats) won a majority on the Erie Canal Commission, Van Buren suddenly supported the canal. His Bucktail machine (also called the "Albany Regency") was the first real political machine in New York state, based on the "spoils system," and it primed the Little Magician for expanding his concept to the national level, which he did in 1825.

By that time the Whigs, a new party competitive with the Democrats, had appeared, born in 1832 as essentially an anti-Jackson party. The Whigs' platform consisted of three main planks: support for "Internal Improvements" (road-building, harbor clearance, and canal construction), a high protective tariff, and a national bank. Though neither of them ran for president in 1836, the leader of the Whigs was Henry Clay, and John C. Calhoun briefly allied with the Whig Party. Obviously the assortment of the anti-slave Webster, the radically pro-slave Calhoun, and the opportunist Clay were not the makings of a solid opposition to Van Buren, or any Democrat. As historian Lynn Marshall demonstrated in a groundbreaking article, the Whig Party was "stillborn," in that, in an age of increased democracy and popular participation in politics, they were still substantially a party of elites. In some ways, the Whigs were throwbacks to the now-defunct Federalists, but with a key difference: by 1836 the elephant in the room was slavery, and the Whigs wanted nothing to do with the subject, one way or another. This failure to take a stand on the issue of the day marked them for an early grave, since the Democrats, their opponents, had clearly positioned themselves as the protectors and defenders of slavery. From the outset, the Whigs were little more than a "me-too" party with little new to offer.

By the time Van Buren was elected, the Whigs were in disarray. But that didn't necessarily bode well for President Van Buren. The economic dislocations caused by the shriveling of Mexican silver inflows were already setting in. Thurlow Weed, a Whig enemy of Van Buren's from New York, predicted "Depend on it, his Election is to be 'the Beginning of the End.'" Weed meant the end for the Democrats in general, but his prediction was only to apply to Van Buren. He had pushed all the right buttons, worked tirelessly behind the scenes for the office, "rowing to his object with muffled oars," as John Randolph observed. He bided his time through eight years of Old Hickory's regime. And as soon as he stepped on the stage, it collapsed underneath him.

★ ★ ★
Know Thyself

It is doubtful that Martin Van Buren had himself in mind when he wrote, "There is a power in public opinion in this country—and I thank God for it: for it is the most honest and best of all powers—which will not tolerate an incompetent or unworthy man to hold in his weak or wicked hands the lives and fortunes of his fellow-citizens." Public opinion would turn against Van Buren after only one term in office.

America's economy, while rapidly becoming more industrialized, still was overwhelmingly agricultural, so its success or failure was closely tied to land values. In good times, if he had a bad crop a farmer could sell land, but when land prices fell he had no recourse, and the ripple effect spread quickly to the banks, then the rest of society.

Having watched his predecessor destroy the Bank of the United States, Van Buren tried to resurrect a form of a national central bank with the Independent Treasury System, which housed federal deposits in government sub-treasuries located in various cities. Government payments were to be made in specie or treasury notes, but the money did not collect interest and could not be used for making loans. Obviously Van Buren's Treasury System entailed withdrawing federal monies from the "Pet

Banks," which proved politically unpopular. After all, the political tug of war over the national bank had never really been about banks; it was about who got to control the money. So Van Buren was therefore unable to get Congress to approve the system, especially in the depression that lingered throughout his term. Once prices fell, the only way out of the depression was for land to recover its value—which began to occur in 1841, just in time for Van Buren's successor, William Henry Harrison.

Besides the economy, the other major issue Van Buren dealt with was the independence of Texas, a section of Mexico settled largely by Americans. In 1836, Texas acquired its independence from Mexico, but many there wished to join the Union. Southerners saw an opportunity to bring in a new slave state—and not just any slave state, but a massive one. Of course, controversy over slavery was *exactly* what Van Buren had attempted to avoid with the creation of the Democrat Party in the first place, and here, in one of the first challenges of his administration, was the elephant in the room once again. Van Buren kicked the slavery can down the road, refusing to discuss annexing Texas. He did, however, through a special envoy, engage the Mexican government on the prickly issue of claims owed to Mexico by Texans, something that would have to be addressed if and when Texas came into the Union. In 1838, an agreement on the claims was signed by Mexico and the United States.

Armed conflict nearly erupted in New York when Canadians in Lower Canada and Quebec rebelled against their government. Americans, sympathetic to the cause and still hoping to add at least parts of Canada to the Union, began raising companies of patriots to join the rebels. While encamped on the Niagara River, the Americans were met by a British raiding party who had crossed the border into New York to burn the ship *Caroline*. All this came at a time when Van Buren didn't need a war with Mexico, and certainly not one with Canada. He dispatched the respected general Winfield Scott to the area to meet with the Americans, call out the militia (but keep it under control), and successfully defuse the situation. That situation was no sooner resolved than a second conflict, the "Aroostook War," nearly erupted. Disputed land claims along the Maine border led the Canadians to arrest a Maine land agent. Maine's governor, John Fairfield, mobilized a thousand troops and asked the state legislature for the authority to raise another ten thousand militiamen. Van Buren acted quickly, contacting the British minister

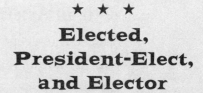

★ ★ ★

Elected, President-Elect, and Elector

Van Buren served as a presidential elector for both Franklin Pierce and James Buchanan, making him the only person up to that time to have held the presidency and then voted in the Electoral College for any of his successors.

Henry Fox, and a hasty arrangement provided for the withdrawal of all parties from the disputed region. He and Scott (known as "Old Fuss and Feathers") had managed to squelch the crisis.

Inheriting another of Jackson's policies, Van Buren was officially tasked with subjugation and resettlement of the Seminoles and the Cherokee that culminated in the "Trail of Tears." The removal cost a whopping $50 million.

As the Panic of 1837 lingered into 1839, Van Buren finally convinced Congress to pass the Independent Treasury Bill, which he deemed a "Second Declaration of Independence" from England (on account of the high interest rates British banks were charging). But the new Treasury System did not change the reality of the recession, which held on until land values recovered. In fact, central banking functions did little one way or another to affect the American economy. Rather, it was a largely Southern institution, the branch banking system, that began to smooth the financial upheavals by spreading regional risk across larger areas. Branch banking shared one of the characteristics that made the Bank of the United States so successful—it was a truly interstate bank.

Martin Van Buren, Constitutionalist with an Asterisk

Saddled with a depression, and having taken no major stand on the slavery issue (by design), Van Buren was turned out of office in the election of 1840. His foreign policy had been successful in that he had avoided two different opportunities for wars—one on each boundary. His economic non-policy was of no import. Nothing Van Buren could have done would have made things better or worse, except perhaps to deprive the U.S. government of some interest from private banks had his Independent Treasury Bill passed. Van Buren's small-government inclinations were laudable, but his role, in the time before his presidency, in laying the groundwork for the exponential growth of government—while it was not obvious at the time—was set to wreak havoc. He had hitched America's chariot to a team of wild horses, and by the time he climbed in, he was merely along for the ride. His constitutional grade is greatly lowered because by the time he took office, he could see the destruction his political party system was wreaking, and because he did not even attempt to deal with slavery. But why should he? He had created the Democratic Party precisely to protect it.

CHAPTER 9

William Henry Harrison, March 1841–April 1841

"There is nothing more corrupting, nothing more destructive of the noblest and finest feelings of our nature, than the exercise of unlimited power."

—*William Henry Harrison*

President Harrison's Constitutional Grade: N/A

No one knows what kind of president William Henry Harrison would have been. "Old Tippecanoe," as he was nicknamed after his victory against Shawnee chief Tecumseh at the 1811 Battle of Tippecanoe, took the oath of office on March 4, 1841, and thirty days later was dead. The former general, congressman, and senator had first run for president as a Whig in 1836, when he received the Whig nomination for president as the "Northern Whig" candidate, but the Whigs also ran a "Southern Whig" (Hugh Lawson White of Tennessee), as well as different candidates in South Carolina (Willie Mangum) and Massachusetts (Daniel Webster) making that election the only time a major American political party has run more than one candidate. In 1840, though, Harrison not only united the Whigs but employed a powerful ground game—as we would call it—that employed numerous powerful political symbols. For example, when Democrats ridiculed Harrison as "Granny Harrison," who would rather "sit in his log cabin drinking hard cider," Harrison's operatives adopted the log cabin and hard cider as political symbols and slogans, using them on banners and posters

Did you know?

★ William Henry Harrison was the first presidential candidate to travel from state to state making public campaign appearances

★ He served the shortest time in office of all the U.S. presidents

★ Harrison gave the longest inauguration speech in history—two hours and 8,445 words

★ He was the first Whig president

An Article You're Not Supposed to Read

Richard P. McCormick, "New Perspectives on Jacksonian Politics," *American Historical Review* 65 (January 1960): 288–301. McCormick's article challenged the popular notion that Andrew Jackson's election entailed a "roaring flood of the new democracy," as Charles Beard put it, or that, according to Arthur Schlesinger Jr., Jackson's election was a "mighty democratic uprising." McCormick used voting analysis to show that the portion of adult male voters actually voting was higher in 1840 than at any other time in U.S. history. Indeed, shockingly, in virtually every state the percentage of adult males who voted was over 70 percent. Indeed, in New Hampshire, 86 percent of adult males voted in 1840, in Georgia 88.9 percent, in Tennessee 89.6 percent, and in Alabama an astonishing 89.8 percent of all eligible voters voted! That's quite a contrast with today, with only 57.5 percent of eligible voters casting a ballot in 2012.

and creating bottles of cider that were shaped like log cabins—all to the delight of the "common man" so dear to the Jacksonians. To put it another way, William Henry Harrison out-Jacksoned Jackson.

Running with John Tyler of Virginia, Harrison's nickname provided another slogan: "Tippecanoe and Tyler Too!" He was the first career military man and general since Washington to seek the office, and he won a landslide victory. Harrison was the first candidate to tour different states prior to an election as a form of campaigning, holding gatherings that were the forerunners of our political rallies.

As Mark Kruman explains in *The American Presidency*, "The Whig's unprecedented log cabin campaign transformed the nature of presidential races.... Well organized, well financed, and active at the national level, Whigs carried out a remarkably thorough, enormously effective campaign." In fact, historian Richard McCormick has found that it was this campaign—and *not* either the Jackson or Van Buren elections—that truly marked the appearance of "Jacksonian Democracy" in the electoral process.

Tickin' Away

In the campaign Harrison developed the bad habit of making extremely long speeches, covering his military service, then the economy, and even presidential abuses of power. All in all, Harrison delivered more than twenty campaign speeches, a remarkable number for the day.

On Inauguration Day, the Whigs mounted a spectacular parade with rolling log cabins, bands, and marching militia companies. Then Harrison mucked it up with the most verbose and longest inauguration speech ever. It is not known if he contracted the cold that turned into pneumonia during that speech, but within a few weeks he was seriously ill, and he died on April 4. Harrison had not even had time to hand out jobs to most of the job-seekers, although he did have time to call for a special session of Congress to deal with the ongoing economic situation.

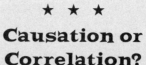

Causation or Correlation?

Both William Henry Harrison and Zachary Taylor died in office. Both were Whigs. Historians have not found a correlation between party affiliation and death in office. But they continue to look.

Not Grading Harrison

There is no basis for evaluating the presidency of Old Tippecanoe. The best lesson that can be taken from his presidency is that one should keep one's speeches short.

CHAPTER 10

John Tyler, April 1841–1844

"Popularity, I have always thought, may aptly be compared to a coquette—the more you woo her, the more apt she is to elude your embrace."

—*John Tyler*

President Tyler's Constitutional Grade: B+

As the first U.S. president to assume office on the death of a predecessor, John Tyler had to make an extremely important constitutional decision in his very first hours as president: whether to take the office. Since there was no precedent, what should Tyler do? How he answered that question has proved important to the functioning of the Republic ever since.

Tyler, born in Virginia during Washington's first term, lived on a plantation and was a slave-owner. For much of his life, he owned forty slaves. After practicing law and serving in Virginia's House of Delegates, Tyler won election to the U.S. Congress in 1816, then became a U.S. senator during the Jackson administration, during which time he came to oppose the "spoils system." He accurately identified it as an "electioneering weapon."

Understanding the constitutional significance of the situation arising from Harrison's death, Tyler made an immediate decision to take the oath of office as quickly as possible and move into the White House, precluding any shenanigans from either party. As a Whig who disliked many planks

Did you know?

★ Harrison and Tyler were born in the same Virginia county

★ Tyler named no vice president and served his term without one

★ Armed White House servants guarded Tyler's bedridden wife from a mob raging against his veto of a national bank bill

★ President Tyler was the first president to have his veto overridden by Congress

★ ★ ★
Love Is in the Air

John Tyler was the first president to lose a wife while in office. Letitia Tyler suffered from a stroke and died in the White House, having never left her bedroom except for one time—when her daughter was married. After her death a morose Tyler purchased a plantation and focused much of his attention on refurnishing it. Then he remarried, to Senator David Gardiner's daughter Julia. Between Letitia and Julia, Tyler had fifteen children, the most of any president (eight by Letitia and seven by Julia). Julia became the first first lady to donate a portrait of herself to the White House.

of his own party's platform, Tyler had to watch his back. But as an opponent of Jackson, he had no support among the Democrats either. Harrison had won the Whig Party's nomination in part because of the circulation of a letter by Winfield Scott—one of his opponents—suggesting that Scott favored abolition of slavery. That had swung the Virginia delegation behind Harrison, and Tyler, who had wept when Clay was defeated for the nomination, was selected because, as Thurlow Weed said, "we could get nobody else to accept."

In sharp contrast to Harrison's long-winded inauguration speech, Tyler's speech as vice president lasted only three minutes. Then he left Washington for his home in Williamsburg. He stayed there throughout Harrison's illness, not wanting to appear macabre. On April 5, 1841, Tyler was visited by Fletcher Webster, the son of Secretary of State Daniel Webster, who bore a letter informing him that he was the new president. While there was some question as to the meaning of the language in the Constitution saying that the "Powers and Duties" of the presidential office "shall devolve on the Vice President" in the case of the president's "Death, Resignation, or Inability to discharge [those] Powers and Duties," he insisted on being sworn in without any qualifiers as soon as he got to Washington.

As in the case of many vice presidents—placed on the ticket to get them out of the way or to balance the ticket and win certain states in the election—nothing much had been expected of John Tyler. Yet now the whole government rested on his shoulders. Given the circumstances of his ascent to office, it wasn't surprising that his opponents labeled him "His Accidency." Many in Congress (including John Quincy Adams) thought Tyler should merely be a caretaker president.

Harrison had told his cabinet that he would make decisions based on a majority vote of the cabinet. Tyler was having none of that: "I beg your pardon, gentlemen; I am very glad to have in my Cabinet such able statesmen as you have proved yourselves to be. And I shall be pleased to avail myself of your counsel and advice. But I can never consent to being dictated to as to what I shall or shall not do." If the cabinet members agreed on that, they could stay. If not, he showed them the door.

Tyler promptly signed a "preemption" bill allowing settlers to squat on public land with an eye toward ownership, and agreed to Congress's repeal of the Independent Treasury. But Tyler did not favor a new national bank bill (to Clay's chagrin) and vetoed it. He had approved an earlier version, but Clay had changed it. Then when Tyler suggested an alternative, called the "Exchequer," Clay and his allies torpedoed that. Then Clay instructed all the cabinet members to resign from their positions so that Tyler himself would be forced to step down and Clay could place Senate President pro tempore Samuel Southard in the White House. But Clay had overplayed his hand. Secretary of State Daniel Webster stayed, and so did Tyler. Shocked that they could not force Tyler out of office, the Whigs threw him out of the party and attacked him in Whig papers. Letters containing assassination threats arrived regularly. The congressional Whigs even denied Tyler the funds to repair the White House, which had fallen into a state of disrepair.

After the national bank veto, an angry mob stormed across the White House lawn, burning Tyler in effigy and threatening to assassinate him. He was not present at the time, and servants guarded the bedridden Letitia with guns until the mob left.

★ ★ ★

Play It Again, Sam

"Hail to the Chief" was first adopted and played at every presidential function in Tyler's presidency.

A Book You're Not Supposed to Read

John Tyler, Champion of the Old South by Oliver Perry Chitwood (New York: Appleton-Century, 1939).

In 1842, Webster finalized the Webster-Ashburton Treaty, which officially ended the "Aroostook War" and settled the dispute with Canada over the Maine border. The United States did not press for return of some twelve thousand fugitive slaves who had escaped to Canada, and got seven thousand square miles of wilderness area in exchange for five thousand square miles of disputed border territory. But, perhaps most importantly, the United States received sixty-five hundred square miles of land along the Minnesota border that contained the rich Mesabi iron ore range. To sell the treaty to the public, Webster released a map of the Maine-Canada border that he claimed had been drawn by Benjamin Franklin, showing the new border as drawn by the treaty was favorable to the United States. The Webster-Ashburton Treaty did not resolve other British-Canadian-American disputes in the Oregon Territory.

Meanwhile, the economic ravages of the Panic of 1837 continued. Both state and federal revenues had fallen. Tyler wanted to raise tariffs but still stay within the twenty percent ceiling imposed by the 1833 Compromise Tariff. To help the states with their debts, he proposed distributing some of the federal revenue from land sales, something which the Whigs supported in exchange for a higher tariff. The resulting Distributive Preemption Act of 1841 helped the states, but federal shortfalls in 1842 forced Tyler to seek even higher tariff rates, which would violate the promise made to the Southern states in the 1833 compromise. Not only did the Congress refuse to raise tariffs further, but they rescinded the distribution and again placed all revenues with the federal government. Whigs sought to separate the distribution from the tariff, and passed a higher tariff while rescinding the distribution. Tyler surprised everyone by vetoing both bills. When the Whigs combined the two, Tyler vetoed that as well. Finally, with the Tariff of 1842 ("the Black

★ ★ ★

Why the South Thought the Tariff Wasn't So Tarrific

Until the Civil War, there were no direct taxes (like the income tax) in America. The government was funded entirely by land sales and by import tariffs provided for in the Constitution and passed by Congress, with the rates adjusted as desired. (The Constitution prohibited any *export* tariffs.)

Most tariffs had the practical effect of benefiting New England, which had the most manufacturing, and punishing consumers in the South. There was almost no competition with Southern cotton or rice or tobacco on the international market—but there was plenty of competition with American iron foundries and textile mills. Thus, with a higher tariff on competing imported goods, Southerners paid more while Northern workers and factory owners made more. At the beginning of the Republic, as we have seen, Alexander Hamilton had justified the tariff in the name of national defense—so that America would never lack arms and weapons for lack of a manufacturing base. But in subsequent years the tariff became much more protective in nature, raising the prices of British and other European goods competing with American manufacturers. As a result, over time the tariff also became an issue of contention between different sections of the United States. Any high tariff benefited Northern industry while dramatically raising prices for Southern and Western consumers. Although later, from the nineteenth century up to today, Louisiana and Florida sugar growers would benefit immensely from American tariffs, before the Civil War the tariff was almost exclusively a sop to New England manufacturing. While Westerners paid the same higher prices on imported goods as everyone else, Southerners saw the tariffs as an attempt by the North to impoverish them in particular, and a threat to their slave-based economy, which they clung to more fiercely than ever, and, in turn, convinced them that they needed slavery more than ever. The economic impact of the tariff, especially on textiles and iron—the products Hamilton thought needed the most protection—remains a matter of debate among economic historians.

Tariff"), Congress set the tariff to pre-1833 levels (that is, higher, to almost forty percent) and sent in a second bill ending the distribution. Tyler signed the higher tariff but pocket vetoed the distribution bill, angering both sides:

★ ★ ★

Tippecanoe and Hawaii Too?

Tyler extended the Monroe Doctrine to Hawaii when he told Britain not to interfere there. This became known (to the extent it is known at all) as the "Tyler Doctrine."

Whigs disliked the uncoupling of the two issues, while Democrats hated the higher tariff. The Whigs were so incensed that they initiated impeachment proceedings against the Whig president they had already expelled from their party.

Needless to say, higher tariffs—especially on iron—caused a sharp drop in trade. By 1843, imports fell by almost fifty percent from their 1842 levels, while exports dropped by twenty percent. In the long run, the Black Tariff of 1842 hurt the Whigs so much that the Democrats were able to repeal it and scale rates back by about seven percent in the Walker Tariff of 1846.

Tyler's vetoes infuriated the Whigs not only because to them the bills were much-needed legislation, but because he was reviving the "King Andrew Jackson" mode of executive governance, as opposed to the legislative governance that was a staple of the older "Whig" philosophy on which the United States had been designed. A preliminary "Botts Bill" (named for Congressman John Botts of Virginia) for impeachment charges was rejected, thanks to the reluctance of Henry Clay to support it. A select committee headed by John Quincy Adams was formed thereafter and issued a report that fell just short of calling for impeachment. The report passed 98–90, but when the Whigs lost control of the House in 1842 they could not muster the votes needed to impeach Tyler. They did manage, however, to override a veto of a bill funding revenue cutters for the Treasury Department—the first ever override of a presidential veto.

Despite his difficulties with Congress, Tyler had a visionary plan for solidifying America's borders, disputes over which had not ended with the Webster-Ashburton Treaty. He requested an increase in the number of warships and introduced a plan to build a series of American forts from Council

Bluffs, Iowa, to the Pacific. Florida would be admitted as a state on Tyler's last day in office. When Rhode Island faced the "Dorr Rebellion" in 1842, with a group of insurrectionists trying to install a new state constitution, the governor of that state called for federal troops, but Tyler hesitated. He promised aid if actual fighting broke out but urged the governor to review the

A Book You're Not Supposed to Read

The Annexation of Texas by Justin H. Smith (New York: Baker and Taylor, 1911).

constitution and seek a peaceful solution. There was no violence, and Tyler never actually sent troops. Indeed the compromise led to a wider franchise in Rhode Island.

A much more important issue, the status of Texas, increasingly consumed Tyler's attention. Having obtained its independence in 1836, the Republic of Texas wanted to join the United States—a move blocked by two factors. First, Mexico had (contrary to its pledge by General Antonio Lopez de Santa Anna after the Battle of San Jacinto) refused to acknowledge Texan independence. Second, Texas had slavery, and adding such a large slave state to the Union could cause an imbalance between the free and slave states. Tyler leaked word that he was seeking to annex Texas, but his secretary of State, Daniel Webster of Massachusetts, opposed him. Webster was forced out and South Carolinian Hugh Legare was brought in. (Already the resignation of the other cabinet members, which had been intended to result in Tyler's resignation, had only opened the doors for him to appoint pro-annexationists.)

Tyler set out in 1843 across the nation on the first ever issue-oriented national tour, seeking to build popular support for the annexation of Texas. Just when Tyler seemed to have the wind in his sails, however, Legare died and Tyler canceled the remainder of the tour. He still had an ally in Abel Upshur, the secretary of the Navy, who extended assurances to Texas officials that the United States would provide military aid in return for a commitment by Texas to join the Union. This, of course, was unconstitutional—and made

★ ★ ★

Dodging a Bullet...or a Cannonball

Historian Edward Crapol has called the *Princeton* explosion the "most severe and debilitating tragedy ever to confront a President" up to that point in U.S. history. If John Tyler had not narrowly escaped death when the "Peacemaker" cannon exploded, the United States would have had *two* presidents die in office in a three-year period. It was a near miss.

worse by Upshur's rumor-mongering: he accused the British of sending agents to bring Texas into its empire. Upshur insisted he had a majority of senators in favor of annexation, and a final draft of the treaty was ready by February 1844. But on February 28, 1844, the day after the treaty was completed, Upshur, Tyler, and four hundred guests happened to embark on a ceremonial cruise down the Potomac on February 28 on the USS *Princeton*. The ship was state-of-the-art—the first American warship to have a steam-powered screw propeller—and it sported a large new cannon, the "Peacemaker," which was fired several times for the entertainment of the passengers—until it misfired and exploded.

Upshur was nearby and killed instantly. A number of military and government officials were killed. Tyler, who had hung back from the display and thus escaped injury, was badly shaken by the event.

Tyler nominated John C. Calhoun to replace Legare (who had so recently replaced Webster) at the State Department. It was a poor choice, for Calhoun, more than any other prominent American, was associated with slavery as its most vocal and prominent defender. Calhoun's nomination only exacerbated Whig concerns that the addition of Texas was all about adding another slave state to the Union. Clay and Van Buren held a private meeting that concluded with their public opposition to annexation. (For Clay, this proved yet another political blunder.) Tyler sent the annexation treaty to the Senate in April 1844.

The next month at a special Baltimore nominating convention that was neither Whig nor Democrat, Tyler had to run for office without a party supporting him—the same position Theodore Roosevelt would find himself in seventy years later. Earlier Tyler had tried to gravitate back to the Democratic Party, but it was still hostile toward him since the Virginia Senate days and it was backing Van Buren. By the time of the Democratic nominating convention, though, the "Little Magician," had cost himself desperately needed support by failing to back annexation for Texas. Tyler supporters, reviving the practices of Harrison, started holding "Tyler and Texas" rallies. They hoped to create a groundswell of support within the Democratic Party, but they were unable to

★ ★ ★

Only Tyler Can Go to China

With the Treaty of Wanghia, ratified in 1844, Tyler opened American trade with China. The treaty gave the United States favored nation trading status with China, access to five critical trading ports, and fixed tariffs, in return for the U.S. supporting the Chinese diplomatically.

influence delegates. Van Buren, however, also proved unable to secure the nomination for himself. After nine ballots the delegates turned to James K. Polk of Tennessee, a pro-annexationist Democrat (and Westerner—fitting Van Buren's model for preventing a war). Considering Polk's nomination an endorsement of his own policies, Tyler was unruffled by the Senate's rejection of the annexation treaty. Andrew Jackson wrote pro-annexation letters from his deathbed, and Polk won a narrow victory over Clay, the Whig Party's nominee, in the November general election. The following year the Senate approved a joint resolution (not a treaty) annexing Texas. Tyler had the pleasure of signing the annexation bill into law on March 1, 1845, just days before he left office. He had achieved a national goal, but lost a personal battle to be reelected.

Grading Tyler's Constitutional Scorecard

The most important thing Tyler did was to unequivocally, forcefully, and coolly assume the office of the presidency. In just twenty-four years, another assassination—under much more difficult and contested circumstances—would hurl another vice president into the presidency. Thanks to Tyler's deliberate action, even the unpopular Andrew Johnson was able to take over the reins of power without controversy. Without Tyler's example, one can imagine the incredible chaos that would have accompanied an event such as the John F. Kennedy assassination over a century later.

However, Tyler's use of an extra-constitutional joint resolution of Congress, rather than a treaty, to annex Texas damages his claim to be a strict constructionist. And his inability to get along with either party was a cautionary tale for the post–Van Buren era: no longer could a "lone ranger" president get anything done. The party structure was fully in place by now and demanded fealty to its processes, most notably the spoils system. Except for the despised Southerner Andrew Johnson, who assumed office on the assassination of the savior of the Union, no president since has been as isolated as John Tyler.

CHAPTER 11

James K. Polk, 1845–1849

"The great object of the Constitution was to restrain majorities from oppressing minorities or encroaching on their just rights."

—*James K. Polk*

President Polk's Constitutional Grade: B

Probably the second president born in North Carolina—Andrew Jackson likely was born there, though he claimed in an 1824 letter that he was born in South Carolina—James K. Polk had served as a colonel in the militia, been elected to the House of Representatives from Tennessee, and served as Speaker of the House. A prominent leader of the Jacksonian Democrats, he idolized Jackson and was known as "Young Hickory." He carried Jackson's water on the House floor during the Bank War, then served two years as Tennessee governor. Known for his role in the annexation of Texas and the Mexican War, President Polk expanded the Union more than anyone else except Thomas Jefferson.

In 1844, when James K. Polk began campaigning, he expected to win the vice presidential slot. After all, it was a sure thing that no one could beat the founder of the Democrat Party, Martin Van Buren. But as Van Buren had always sought to keep slavery from dominating the national political debate, he opposed the annexation of Texas, and lost the support of much of his own party, especially the slave South. At the convention, Van Buren could

Did you know?

★ James K. Polk was the only Speaker of the House ever to win the presidency

★ He attended the nominating convention hoping to be nominated vice president

★ Polk was the first candidate to promise to serve only one term

not muster enough votes to win, but then neither could anyone else. Future president James Buchanan of Pennsylvania, General Lewis Cass of Michigan, and John C. Calhoun of South Carolina all vied for the nomination as well—but of course Calhoun had no real hope of winning because, as Van Buren already had established, only a "Northern man of Southern principles" or a westerner could be elected. That left Buchanan and Cass, both Northerners who would not interfere with slavery if elected president.

After eight ballots, however, none of the candidates won a majority, and Polk emerged as a likely candidate. Polk himself had initially told his managers to support Van Buren, and Van Buren reciprocated after it became clear that he could not win himself. When informed that he had won the nomination, Polk (in language quite common in the antebellum era) said that "the office of President of the United States should neither be sought nor declined. I have never sought it, nor should I feel at liberty to decline it." Then Polk added a promise that, if he won, he would only serve one term. He thought that pledge would unite the Democrats around him.

Having done battle with the Whigs for over a decade, Polk had honed his skills in countering his opponents' arguments and forging alliances necessary to pass legislation. His attacks on Whigs in newspaper editorials were widely reprinted around the country, and gave him a national reputation—something unusual for politicians at the time. Polk was a "hard-money" Democrat and wanted to reduce the tariff rates that the Whigs had raised and get Van Buren's Independent Treasury set up. But beneath the surface, the increasingly urgent and titanically divisive issue of slavery was stirring. The political conflict over the annexation of Texas as a slave state proved that Van Buren's scheme for enforcing party loyalty through the spoils system and keeping the slavery issue out of sight and out of mind would not defer the crisis forever. Polk's pro-annexation stand largely won him the nomination and the presidency. But up until Van Buren failed to get the Democratic nomination, it had seemed that his system was working to perfection. Until that point the ostensible leaders of *both* parties, Henry Clay and Van Buren himself, had adopted positions that prevented them from addressing the slavery issue.

Whigs thought that the boost the annexation of Texas had given to slavery could be minimized by admitting a free state or states from the territory in the Pacific Northwest, so they pressed American claims on the northern Oregon border at the 54 degree, 40 minute parallel, using the battle cry "Fifty-four forty or fight!" By this time America's westward expansion—a natural tendency since the nation's birth—was coming up against the slavery issue everywhere. Since the 1836 "Gag Rule" requiring the House to automatically table every petition or bill for the restriction of slavery, the two sides fought the war over slavery in battles over proxy issues—first tariffs and then westward expansion. Both sides thought further expansion westward favored their position—depending on whether "free soilers" and Whigs could add more free states to the Union, or if the determined pro-slave forces were somehow able to add slave states (despite the Missouri Compromise). The claim of Texas, which permitted slavery, to the Rio Grande River as the state's southernmost border—whereas Mexico insisted that the border was the Nueces River farther north—would lead to territorial expansion that would further roil the issue.

Polk told insiders that he had four objectives as president: to reduce tariffs, to reestablish the Independent Treasury, to settle the Oregon

★ ★ ★

The "Natural Limits of Slavery"

Beginning in the 1830s, a doctrine captured the minds, or at least, the emotions, of many leading politicians and writers. Abraham Lincoln believed it for a time, and so did James K. Polk as president. This notion, called the "Natural Limits of Slavery," held that slavery was limited "by nature" to the cotton lands in the South and could not survive farther west. Polk wrote in his diary that slavery could not exist in what would be called the "Mexican Cession" territories—but in fact Arizona and California became important cotton producers and slaves were increasingly being used in mining and industry. Lincoln came to realize that he was wrong. Polk did not.

A Book You're Not Supposed to Read

Ordeal of the Union: Fruits of Manifest Destiny, 1847–1852 by Allan Nevins (New York: Scribner's, 1947). This is the first volume of an eight-volume series covering the decade leading up to the Civil War and the war itself.

boundary dispute, and to acquire California. The last point was an astounding statement of "Manifest Destiny," especially since California was still a part of Mexico! The congressional Democrats gave Polk a victory with the tariff reduction, but the Walker Tariff, with lower rates on manufactured goods, alienated many Democrats in Pennsylvania in particular. Polk also vetoed an internal improvements bill that some Midwestern Democrats backed.

Americans wanted a border with Canada at the forty-ninth parallel to allow them access to Puget Sound, but Britain was pushing for the forty-second parallel. The president hoped to bluff the British into the more northerly border. As Polk said, "The only way to treat John Bull was to look him straight in the eye." In fact, he astutely recognized that Britain no longer needed the Pacific Northwest and its fur trade as it once had, and that in any case British political energy was absorbed in the repeal of the Corn Laws. So Polk requested funds from Congress to build a series of forts at the 53 degree, 40 minute parallel as the northernmost border of Oregon. As a result the British became convinced America would fight for the 54 degree border (known as "All Oregon"), and in 1846 agreed to the forty-ninth parallel, which allowed the British to retain Vancouver Island. Polk did such a good job of selling his bluff that many in his own party resisted, especially slaveholders such as Calhoun, who fought the addition of Oregon.

Yet Polk's ingenious solution to the Oregon question left many Democrats thinking the president was in the grasp of the "slave power" conspiracy—fears that would soon intensify when he would add California and the Southwest to the Union through the Mexican War. Polk was deeply interested in the San Francisco Bay area, acquisition of which would not only allow trade with China for America but would also deny it to England. To that end, Polk sent a special envoy, John Slidell of Louisiana, to Mexico with an offer of between $24 and $30 million for California and New Mexico—but not to make any offer for the loss of Texas. Mexican officials refused even to meet with Slidell, claiming his credentials were not in order. Mexican politicians were already boiling over the annexation of Texas, and Mexican military leaders were telling the government they could easily win a war with the United States.

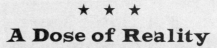

★ ★ ★
A Dose of Reality

Polk noted, "The passion for office among members of Congress is very great, if not absolutely disreputable, and greatly embarrasses the operations of the Government. They create offices by their own votes and then seek to fill them themselves." Apparently Mr. Polk came face-to-face with the reality of the spoils system his own party had engineered.

In early 1846 Polk sent troops under General Zachary Taylor to the disputed region between the Nueces and the Rio Grande. Three months later, Slidell returned, feeling dishonored. Polk claimed the slight was a just cause of war and began to sow the seeds for a war declaration from Congress. General Taylor had been actively demonstrating in the area of the Rio Grande, even crossing it and occupying Matamoros, while Mexican forces in turn crossed and killed American soldiers on the American side of the river. That was enough for Polk, who asked for a war declaration based on the fact that Mexico had "invaded our territory and shed American blood upon the American soil." Whigs, naturally, criticized him. John Quincy Adams voted against the war, and one Whig in particular, a congressman from Illinois named Abraham Lincoln, demanded to know the precise "spot" where American blood had been shed (introducing resolutions that came to be called the "spot resolutions").

Guilt-ridden Americans often see the subsequent Mexican War purely in terms of Yankee land-lust. Forgotten is the push within Mexico to regain Texas and the near-universal view at the time that the Americans would lose—and badly. Mexican leaders viewed U.S. citizen-soldiers as "totally

A Book You're Not Supposed to Read

America's Victories: Why the U.S. Wins Wars and Will Win the War on Terror by Larry Schweikart (Point Pleasant, NJ: Knox Press, 2015).

unfit to operate beyond their [own] borders," and overseas observers reinforced their confidence. An English weekly sneered, "America, as an aggressive power, is one of the weakest in the world...fit for nothing but to fight Indians." The Mexican newspaper *La Voz del Pueblo* begged for war: "Let us make it, then, and victory will perch on our banners." Polk's perspective was different. "The cup of forbearance has been exhausted," he noted.

War with Mexico was brief, although Polk, despite having craved it for so long, did not prepare for it well. Enlistments were short, and he was stingy with supplies. Moreover, Polk was as much concerned about keeping Whig generals from winning too much glory as he was about defeating the Mexicans. When Taylor had the enemy on the ropes, Polk did not reinforce him. Instead, hoping to win an even cheaper victory, Polk indulged a silly whim he had of negotiating with exiled dictator Antonio Lopez de Santa Anna with the promise of providing for his return in exchange for a treaty giving California to the United States. Santa Anna betrayed Polk and tried to make a fight of it, which proved no more successful than his efforts to crush Sam Houston years earlier. General Winfield Scott captured Mexico City in September 1847, while John C. Fremont had taken California. Mexico surrendered in 1848.

Once again, Polk—having been so masterful early in his administration—fumbled. He sent Nicholas Trist to negotiate the surrender, but then recalled him. A miffed Trist ignored the recall and stayed to finish the job, obtaining the Treaty of Guadalupe Hidalgo, which Polk ratified. It gave the U.S. 1.2 million square miles consisting of modern-day Arizona, Utah, Nevada, California, and parts of Colorado, New Mexico, and Wyoming. The Texas border was settled at the Rio Grande. Mexico was paid $15 million.

Added to the cost of the war itself Polk ended up paying a great deal to try and fight on the cheap. He also authorized a representative to attempt to buy Cuba from Spain for the outlandish sum of $100 million. Spain refused.

Polk was the first president since the early days of the Republic to add a new cabinet-level position; he signed a bill creating the Department of the Interior in March 1849. He claimed to lack the time to find constitutional grounds for a veto, but in erring on the side of big government, Polk diminished an otherwise impressive four-year term.

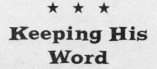

★ ★ ★
Keeping His Word

Politicians are routinely criticized and ridiculed for making promises they can't—or don't—keep. James K. Polk was different. He achieved all four of the goals he had campaigned on and kept his promise to step down after one term. In four years Polk reduced the tariff, restored the Independent Treasury, settled the Oregon boundary dispute, and acquired California.

Grading President Polk

Polk should be commended, first and foremost, for keeping his promises. That alone does not suffice, however, to earn a president a high constitutional grade. (Barack Obama fulfilled most of his promises, to the detriment of the Republic.) Lowering the tariff was laudable, but failing to distribute Western lands somewhat offset that action. Reinstituting the Independent Treasury was an acceptable policy, although it did little to inspire trust in the financial system. The acquisition of California and the Southwest was done for (mostly) the right reasons and through the correct constitutional procedure. Paying a defeated foe, whose capital American forces actually occupied, up to a trillion dollars in modern money was highly questionable. If Democrats had learned anything it should have been, "to the victor belong the spoils," not to the loser. Polk's worst two moves were creating the Department of the Interior—today a major source of domestic regulatory tyranny—and failing (as his predecessors had) to deal with slavery. Indeed, by not pressing for the passage of the Wilmot Proviso, which would have banned slavery in the newly acquired Mexican Cession territories, Polk missed a grand opportunity to take a definitive stand against the continuation and spread of slavery. Since Polk was a slave owner himself, however, that was never going to happen.

CHAPTER 12

Zachary Taylor, 1849–July 9, 1850

"It would be judicious to act with magnanimity toward a prostrate foe."
—Zachary Taylor

President Taylor's Constitutional Grade: C

The fourth general to be elected president, and the second (and last) true Whig, Zachary Taylor was also the second president to die in office. Taylor was another president born in Virginia, although his parents had migrated to Kentucky. Like most of his predecessors, he was a slave-owner. Like George Washington, he wanted to be a soldier from an early age, and during the War of 1812 he distinguished himself defending Fort Harrison against attacks by Tecumseh. He saw action at the Battle of Wild Cat Creek, ending the war a captain after several brevet (temporary) battlefield promotions.

The Second Seminole War burnished the reputation of "Old Rough and Ready," as he became known, and by 1841 Taylor was commander of the United States Army's Second Department, Western Division. In July 1845 he was directed by President James K. Polk to deploy his forces in the disputed area north of the Rio Grande River in Texas. When war started, Taylor led troops at the Battle of Palo Alto and the Battle of Resaca de la Palma, where, despite being greatly outnumbered, the American forces saw victory. Already there was talk of his running for president, though he claimed,

Did you know?

★ Zachary Taylor sailed into the presidency on a wave of glory from the Mexican War

★ The future President Taylor's daughter Sarah defied his disapproval and married another future president…Jefferson Davis

★ Taylor was the first to call a president's wife "First Lady"

"Such an idea never entered my head." It certainly entered Polk's head, who was concerned about the growing glory that was accruing to the Whig general. After defeating another large Mexican force at the Battle of Monterrey, Taylor accepted a truce rather than a full surrender, leading Polk to transfer half of Taylor's men to rival Whig general Winfield Scott at Veracruz. When General Antonio Lopez de Santa Anna, the Mexican dictator, saw Taylor weakened, he attacked with a massive advantage in troops at the Battle of Buena Vista in February, only to be defeated again. Upon Taylor's return home in December 1847 he received a hero's welcome, and his path to the White House was clear.

Taylor had remained largely quiet about his political beliefs. He did not approve of government funding of internal improvements, but he still considered himself a Whig. He had disagreed with Jackson's attack on the Bank of the United States, and he was aligned with the "Whig" (in the older sense) concept of legislative governance, as opposed to the new president-dominated style. He made many comments that led Whigs to think he was on their side. For example, despite the fact that he himself owned slaves, he let it be known that if elected he would not veto the Wilmot Proviso prohibiting slavery in the Mexican Cession territories. Still, this was considered a half-way measure by northern Whigs, who wanted a more forceful statement in favor of the Proviso.

Taylor received the Whig nomination for president, with the convention choosing Millard Fillmore of New York for vice president to offset the slave-holding Taylor and balance the ticket. Unlike the previous Whig general who had run for president, William Henry Harrison, Taylor did not actively campaign, but rather let Kentucky Senator John J. Crittenden, his campaign manager, handle the general election effort. Taylor defeated

Democrat Lewis Cass of Michigan—who was beginning to develop a new compromise on slavery called "popular sovereignty" (let the people of each state decide). Polk, in what would become a regrettable habit among American political elites, looked down his nose at the non-politician Taylor, seeing him as "without political information" and "wholly unqualified" to be president.

As president-elect, General Taylor did not resign his military commission, creating an awkward situation *vis a vis* his commanding general, Winfield Scott. "Old Fuss and Feathers," as Scott was known (to Taylor's "Old Rough and Ready"), took a "sabbatical" as general-in-chief of the Army and confined his activities to the Eastern Command, thereby leaving the soon-to-be commander in chief in command of the Western Command.

Once in office, Taylor was faced with the same thing that each new president was encountering: scores of job-seekers lining up, literally walking in off the streets, sometimes disturbing him at work. Taylor felt obliged to indulge them all with his attention, at least for a few minutes.

As president he was anything but a Whig's Whig. He did not name Henry Clay, the most prominent Whig in America, to any position, and most of his appointees were not party leaders at all. This made Clay a regular enemy, even though

Differing Opinions

Impressions of Zachary Taylor were all over the map:

"He has not one spark of genius in his soul. His mind works slowly—his purposes are honest. His education is extremely limited. The mass of his knowledge is indeed small enough."

—**Alfred Balch, Tennessee politician**

"Old Zack is a good old soul but don't know himself from a side of sole leather."

—**Horace Greeley, newspaperman**

"He is an honest, plain, unpretending old man, but about as fit to be President as any New England farmer."

—**B. B. French, later known as the "architect of the Capitol"**

"General Taylor is the greatest man, *in truth before God*, I ever knew! He is to a common observer only a kind benevolent man—a sensible man, and a brave man. But he grows greater every day and is the wisest man in *every thing*. You would be astonished if I should tell you what I know about his knowledge of both men and things." [emphasis in the original]

—**John Clayton, Taylor's secretary of State**

★ ★ ★

Birds of a Feather Don't Flock Together

According to John S. D. Eisenhower's *Zachary Taylor* (New York: Times Books, 2008), Taylor and Henry Clay should have been the strongest of allies. Yet they were nearly enemies. Part of the problem lay in Clay's forgetfulness, or claimed forgetfulness: when Clay, traveling by steam ship, made a stop in Baton Rouge, Taylor came aboard the boat to see off some guests. As Taylor worked his way to the saloon, he saw Clay sitting at a dinner table, faced the Kentuckian, and bowed. Clay ignored him until his dinner partner said, "Mr. Clay, that is General Taylor." Clay's demeanor changed and he hopped up, followed Taylor out and extended his hand. "General," said Clay, "you have grown out of my recollection." "You can never grow out of mine," replied Taylor.

as both a slaveholder and Whig he should have been *simpatico* with Taylor. Clay referred to Taylor as "exclusively a military man," "bred up and always living in the camp with his sword by his side and his Epaulettes on his shoulders."

Taylor predicted that his cabinet would be "harmonious, honorable, patriotic, talented, and hardworking." John Crittenden, as secretary of State had, perhaps, the most important place in the Taylor administration, but Taylor relied a great deal on an up-and-comer, William H. Seward (later, with the purchase of Alaska from the Russians, of "Seward's Icebox" fame). Like Monroe, Taylor undertook a tour, focusing on the northeastern states to familiarize himself with the region. Everywhere Taylor stopped, great crowds gathered and lavishly planned gala events were scheduled. The stress of so many of these events may have impaired Taylor's health.

Taylor immediately faced the thorny issue of slavery—always bubbling below the surface and ready to erupt. When he met with a group in Pennsylvania, he assured them "the people of the North need have no apprehension of the further expansion of Slavery." This was a powerful statement coming from a slaveholder.

The California Compromise

California and the other Western territories were causes for alarm, as California lay both above and below the 36 degree 30 minute line drawn by the

Missouri Compromise. Would it be free, or free to choose slavery? Taylor wanted to admit California as a state and install a civilian government immediately, bypassing the territorial process (much as the U.S. had with Texas). California already had enough of a population to be admitted directly as a state. That way, Taylor reckoned (in a deviation from typical Whiggism), he could avoid putting the slavery issue into Congress's hands. But then the people of California prohibited slavery in their state constitution, upsetting the balance between free and slave states and alarming slave-state senators. The prevailing institutional structure that had prevented the slavery issue from reaching the point of genuine public debate was under siege.

A number of smaller issues were resolved quickly. The dispute between New Mexico and Texas over the location of their mutual border briefly threatened to blow up, as Texans claimed areas of New Mexico that Texas had never actually controlled. Some of the more aggressive Texans wanted Santa Fe itself. Taylor was fortunate in that a body of American troops were on the spot to stop the mischief. Texas, having just joined the Union, briefly threatened secession. When a Texas delegation met with Taylor to deliver the secession warning, the president responded like the general he was: "If it becomes necessary I'll take command of the army myself and if you are taken in rebellion against the Union I will hang you with less reluctance than I hanged deserters and spies in Mexico." The dispute was resolved in favor of New Mexico, the threats ended, and New Mexico drew up a constitution, with its borders intact, in 1850.

Then there was Utah. To counteract the creation of a new "State of Deseret" by Mormons in the northern part of the Mexican Cession, Taylor

★ ★ ★

The Appearance of Impropriety

Alexander Hamilton had been the first prominent American political figure to find his reputation severely damaged by merely the perception of official wrongdoing. Jefferson was sure that Hamilton had committed some kind of fraud, but no examination ever found him guilty of anything when it came to the Treasury. A similar issue in Zachary Taylor's presidency damaged his secretary of War, George Crawford, and, by extension, Taylor himself. Before the American Revolution, George Galphin had filed a claim against the British government related to some losses involving land dealings with the Indians. Galphin was about to collect when hostilities broke out in the colonies and the British decided not to honor claims by anyone who was not a Tory. When the Revolution ended, Georgia agreed to assume Galphin's claim along with many others and pay the debt. Then, under Hamilton's recommended assumption of the states' debts, the United States became responsible, but the process for payment moved glacially. George Crawford was the lawyer hired to press the claim, and under President James K. Polk the original $43,000 was ordered to be paid, but not the accrued interest—which was considerable. Galphin's heirs were pressing on to collect the interest when Crawford became the secretary of War under Taylor. In April 1850 the claim for interest finally reached Treasury Secretary William Meredith, who approved the payment, which had now reached $191,000. Crawford was due half that sum for his legal work. And Crawford took the money! While the award was lawful, and Crawford entitled to it, the image of a sitting secretary of War coming into an enormous sum of money thanks to a ruling by the secretary of the Treasury smelled of corruption. This "stressor," as we would say today, was weighing on Taylor when the president prepared for the Fourth of July festivities and ate the foods that likely killed him.

had the Territory of Utah organized, but reassured Mormons that the federal government would not interfere with their religious freedom there.

There were international issues, most notably the constant nagging problem of American "filibusterers" moving into Cuba to try to foment a revolution there—with the support of Southerners who saw Cuba as another potential slave state. A large group of them were taken prisoner by the

Spanish at Contoy and were pending execution. Against the advice of his entire cabinet, Taylor issued an ultimatum to Spain in the filibusterers' defense, saying that they had only intended to commit crimes, but had not committed any yet. Eventually, Spanish courts released the prisoners.

Taylor also sent ships along with a British effort to find the lost team of Arctic explorers led by British Admiral John Franklin and negotiated the Clayton-Bulwer Treaty of 1850 with Britain, establishing that neither nation would claim control of an inter-oceanic canal proposed to be built through Nicaragua. Britain held both exits of a potential canal route (though nothing had been built yet), so Taylor deftly dealt with the Nicaraguans themselves, pledging U.S. support for Nicaragua's claim to its own coasts and putting the British in a bind. In the resulting Clayton-Bulwer Treaty both Britain and the U.S. renounced "exclusive control" over "said ship canal" and agreed not to erect forts there. Since America had no place to put a fort—but the British did—the treaty was a remarkable American diplomatic coup.

Meanwhile, something had to be done with the new territories. The "Great Compromiser," Henry Clay, stepped up once again, to offer a solution that would be known as the Compromise of 1850. With the aid of Daniel Webster, Clay proposed giving statehood to California, which would enter the Union as a free state; banning slavery in the District of Columbia (the first actual rollback of slave territory since the Constitution); the organization of New Mexico and other areas as federal territories; and a new Fugitive Slave Law. During the contentious debates, Senator Henry Foote of Mississippi and

★ ★ ★

The First First Lady

In his short time as president, Taylor had to attend several funerals, including that of James K. Polk and James Madison's wife, the eighty-one-year-old Dolley Madison. It was at her funeral that Taylor himself coined the term, "First Lady," causing no small discomfort to the other prominent ladies there, Mrs. John Quincy Adams and Mrs. Alexander Hamilton (who thought she *should* have been a First Lady!).

Missouri's Thomas Hart Benton got into such a heated argument that Benton rose to approach the Mississippian. Foote drew a pistol, and Benton threw open his coat and yelled "I have no pistols.... Let him fire. Stand out of the way. Let the assassin fire!" Others grabbed the men and pulled them away before anyone died. But the debate was better known for the great speeches of Clay, Webster, Calhoun, and William H. Seward, who insisted there is a "higher law than the Constitution"—a line that sent Taylor into a frenzy: "The speech must be disclaimed at once, authoritatively and decidedly," he exclaimed. "We can't stand for a moment on such principles."

Clay's great scheme for a single omnibus bill broke down, and the individual parts of his compromise were still being debated when Taylor died on July 9, 1850, at age sixty-five. The illness that killed him was diagnosed as cholera at the time, but in 1978 a theory was proposed claiming that pro-slavery Southerners poisoned Taylor. Subsequent studies of the remains showed no evidence of poison.

Taylor had not cared for his vice president, and Fillmore was never included in any of the president's endeavors. Instead, William H. Seward of New York was treated as Taylor's heir apparent—a fact that cast a shadow on Fillmore's presidency.

Taylor: Barely Avoiding the Incomplete

Whereas William Henry Harrison was not in office long enough for his adherence to the Constitution to be judged, Taylor was—just barely. Taylor's handling of the New Mexico situation was commendable. His part in advancing the Compromise of 1850 was less so. As with many of his predecessors, everything Taylor did must be weighed in light of his unwillingness to use his constitutional powers to stop slavery. Though a Whig, Taylor behaved like a typical Jacksonian Democrat. Government grew under his administration, and while the Compromise of 1850 was not yet complete, the wheels were already turning. The Fugitive Slave Act, while legal, was an infamous piece of legislation, doomed to fail and to accelerate the drift to violence, not suppress it.

CHAPTER 13

Millard Fillmore, July 1850–1853

"May God save the country, for it is evident the people will not."
—*Millard Fillmore*

President Fillmore's Constitutional Grade: B–

F**ew** presidents have been the butt of as many late-night comics' jokes as Millard Fillmore. Probably some of that has to do with a name—"Millard"—that is un-hip today. *Tonight Show* host Johnny Carson, who called Fillmore "one of the most forgettable presidents in U.S. history," kept his memory alive by placing a bust of Fillmore on his *Tonight Show* desk. On Fillmore's hundred and seventieth birthday, the comedian paid an elaborate tribute to the former president. But even the politicians of the day had their quips about Millard Fillmore: "God save us from Whig vice presidents," said one contemporary.

Part of Fillmore's reputation, or lack thereof, is perhaps due to the absence of both "big" legislation and wars during his administration. As the last Whig president, Fillmore headed a dying party. As the second New Yorker to fill the presidency, Fillmore was "anti-slavery" except when it came to excluding slavery from the Mexican Cession territories. There, he supported "compromise." Typical of "me-too" Whigs, Fillmore did not join the new Republican Party when it was formed, as the new party stood for actually stopping the

Did you know?

★ Fillmore appointee Benjamin Curtis was the only Whig United States Supreme Court justice in history

★ Presiding over the Senate as vice president, Fillmore watched as Senator Henry S. Foote of Mississippi pulled a pistol on Senator Thomas Hart Benton of Missouri (no shots were fired)

★ Under the Fugitive Slave Act, you could go to jail for giving a runaway slave food

expansion of slavery. Critics saw him as weak. Allan Nevins wrote of Fillmore that he was a "man of dignified bearing, suave manners, conciliatory temper, and limited powers of the mind." Future Secretary of State William H. Seward said of Fillmore, "Providence has at last led the man of hesitations and double opinions where decision and singleness are indispensable." But a phrase associated with Fillmore attests to greater respect in other quarters: "Fillmore says it's right; we'll go it." Henry Clay, who did not get along with Taylor, found Fillmore "able, enlightened, indefatigable, and…patriotic."

Fillmore was a well-prepared politician who had served in the New York State Assembly, where he associated with Thurlow Weed, head of the Anti-Mason Party. In 1832, Fillmore won a House seat in the 32nd district, then after a two-year hiatus was reelected as a Whig, serving until 1842. After a stint as New York's comptroller, where his focus was improving the New York banking system, Fillmore was nominated as vice president under Zachary Taylor, in part to keep the anti-slavery firebrand William Seward from the spot.

When Taylor died and Fillmore—thanks to the precedent set by John Tyler in 1844—took over immediately, the entire cabinet, which was friendly to Taylor's heir apparent Seward, resigned. Fillmore accepted all the resignations, save that of Treasury Secretary Thomas Corwin. After setbacks to his favored version of the Compromise of 1850, Fillmore signed the act. Senator Stephen Douglas of Illinois had taken over from Henry Clay in ramrodding the Compromise through the chamber. Douglas had a much different strategy than Clay, who had submitted an "omnibus bill" thinking that senators from each section of the country would find enough to like in it that the whole thing would pass. Instead, the Senate voted it down. Douglas peeled off each individual part of the Compromise and cobbled together a coalition big enough to pass each in a separate bill.

One difficulty Senate leaders and Fillmore encountered was that to pass the Compromise they needed to get many recalcitrant Whigs on board, and that in turn required solving the Texas–New Mexico border dispute inherited from Taylor. Fillmore satisfied the Whigs by rejecting Texas's claims on the New Mexico border. He advocated that Texas's debts be paid, but only if the state would abandon its claims to New Mexico. By deploying federal troops to New Mexico, Fillmore helped shift Whig support away from the Wilmot Proviso and ensure passage of the Compromise. With the New Mexico issue settled, and with the help of Daniel Webster, Fillmore managed to use threats and promises of jobs to line up the necessary votes from Northern Whigs.

The most contested part of the Compromise was the Fugitive Slave Act. It put the federal government on the side of slave-owners seeking return of runaway slaves in the North. The implications of the law were that ordinary anti-slave Northerners could be dragooned into assisting with the return of runaways or face criminal charges. For local officials, the incentives for returning a runaway slave were much higher than for finding that the slave was free. The Act penalized officials who did not arrest alleged runaways with a fine of up to $1,000. Officials were required to arrest alleged runaway slaves merely on the word of a claimant. Providing food or shelter to a runaway was punishable by jail time.

Fillmore thought he could walk the tightrope by enforcing the Fugitive Slave Act while appeasing the North by cracking down on Southern filibustering operations in Cuba, more strongly enforcing the Neutrality Act of 1818. In the long term, he was grossly wrong, but so were most of the politicians of the day. His single U.S. Supreme Court appointee, Benjamin Curtis, proved one of the two dissenters in the infamous *Dred Scott* case in 1857, so Fillmore's judgment on the appointment, at least, was sound.

In the short term, however, Fillmore exercised surprising influence over passage of the Compromise. Future Treasury Secretary Salmon Chase estimated that in his first message alone the president swayed six New England senators in favor—and while neither it nor any other sectional agreement

A Book You're Not Supposed to Read

The Coming of the Civil War, 2nd ed., by Avery Craven (Chicago: University of Chicago Press, 1957).

could have solved the issue of slavery permanently, Fillmore achieved a brief peace, as is testified by his annual messages to Congress.

Brief was the key word. In March 1852, Harriet Beecher Stowe wrote *Uncle Tom's Cabin*, which quickly became a bestseller of titanic proportions. Stowe, who had never even been on a plantation, nevertheless captured the horrors of slavery in fiction that almost unwound the Compromise by itself.

Fillmore also faced a "Citizen Genet"–type episode when Louis Kossuth, a Hungarian revolutionary who had arrived in New York, demanded, to the acclaim of large crowds, that America change its non-intervention policy toward Austria-Hungary. He even began trying to raise arms. Whigs were concerned that Kossuth would have an appeal among Whig-voting German immigrants, but Fillmore did the right thing and ignored him. American policy remained unchanged.

One of Fillmore's greatest accomplishments, if it can be called that, was to preside over the effective death of his party. He was the last Whig president. Northern Whigs opposed slavery, and the number of Southern Whigs shrank by the day, but the Whig Party was not a true anti-slavery party. By 1852, Democrats were strongly entrenched in the South and nationally were committed to the expansion of slavery—not just its protection where it existed. Whigs, on the other hand, didn't know what they were for. The best they could come up with was "union." Fillmore therefore worked to create a new party called the Union Party. But the Union Party, just like the Whigs, could not go all the way and become the *opposite* of the Democrats, which was exactly what was needed: a true anti-slavery party. When Fillmore was turned out in 1853, it was a profound commentary on the reality that no compromise would suppress the issue of slavery, and no party that wasn't dedicated to removing it could survive.

Millard Fillmore and the Constitution

Fillmore did everything by the book, defying no constitutional boundaries and creating no new vast powers. But with each passing administration, the unwillingness to tackle the single greatest threat to the Union must require significant downgrading.

CHAPTER 14

Franklin Pierce, 1853–1857

"The dangers of a concentration of all power in the general government of a confederacy so vast as ours are too obvious to be disregarded."

—*Franklin Pierce*

President Pierce's Constitutional Grade: C

The age of Founders had long passed, and after 1852 the age of political giants was at an end, too, with the deaths of Henry Clay (1852), Daniel Webster (1852), and John C. Calhoun (1850). Jackson had departed in 1845, James K. Polk in 1849, and Zachary Taylor the next year. Of all the prominent politicians who had directed American policy since 1800, only Martin Van Buren and John Quincy Adams were still alive.

Franklin Pierce, the youngest president to date to hold the office, represented a new generation of politicians. Although winning his party's nomination was a struggle—he wasn't even voted for in the first round—Pierce emerged to beat out James Buchanan of Pennsylvania and Lewis Cass of Michigan. In the general election, he soundly defeated the Whig candidate, "Old Fuss and Feathers," General Winfield Scott. Part of Pierce's attraction was that he was, in the words of Joel Silbey, "an unswerving acolyte of the Democratic ideological heritage...." A less generous description might be "party hack." His opponents characterized him as a coward and a drunk (a popular accusation at the time), noting that he was the "hero of many a

Did you know?

★ At forty-nine, Pierce was the youngest president before Ulysses Grant

★ He was the only president born in New Hampshire

★ Pierce was a friend and classmate of the writer Nathaniel Hawthorne at Bowdoin College

A Book You're Not Supposed to Read

Calculating the Value of the Union: Slavery, Property Rights, and the Economic Origins of the Civil War by James Huston (Chapel Hill: University of North Carolina Press, 2003). Huston shows that the oft-overlooked value of slaves themselves, as property—not just labor—made the South by far the richest section of the country in the 1850s. More wealth was tied up in slave property than in all the Northern railroads and textile mills put together. The conflict eventually came down to a simple proposition about property rights: Were people property, or not? If so, how could one type of property be excluded from any section of the country (that is, the North). Ultimately, just as Lincoln said, the United States would have to become either all free or all slave—it could not exist a "house divided."

well-fought bottle." (A colonel in the Ninth Infantry Regiment in the Mexican War, Pierce had suffered an unfortunate accident when his horse fell on him, leading others to think he fainted. It earned him a reputation as a coward, but in fact he had so badly injured his leg that he passed out from pain trying to command troops in the field, then got acute diarrhea—not a great legacy for a future president.)

After Pierce's election to the presidency, a New Hampshire friend said "Frank goes all right for Concord, but he'll be monstrous thin spread out over the United States." When Nathaniel Hawthorne, Pierce's famous writer classmate at Bowdoin College, undertook to write his biography, education reformer Horace Mann (who knew both men) said that if Hawthorne "makes out Pierce to be a great man or a brave man, it will be the greatest work of fiction he ever wrote." Hawthorne's *Life of Franklin Pierce*, which appeared in 1852 to help with his election campaign, told the story of a "beautiful boy, with blue eyes, light curling hair," who grew up to be a distinguished military man, concerned about preserving the Union by ensuring the South's right to slaves and placating the Northerners who were not abolitionists. While it was not exactly a work of fiction, if it were a television movie today, it would be called a "docudrama."

Pierce had a tragic event befall him just after his election. He had already lost two sons. Then, on January 6, 1853, before he had even taken the oath of office, the train in which he and his family traveled derailed, and while he and his wife survived, their eleven-year-old son was crushed. Both parents suffered from severe depression as a result. This affected Pierce's tenure in office, and his wife wondered if the accident wasn't some sort of divine punishment for his pursuit of the presidency. Pierce referred to the tragedy in his Inaugural Address, saying "You have summoned me in my weakness...." But even before that horrible accident, as we have seen, Pierce had a reputation as a drunk. Pierce was said to outdrink Daniel Webster—no small feat.

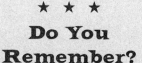

★ ★ ★
Do You Remember?

It is a good thing Franklin Pierce wasn't called before a House or Senate investigation, as he could not plead faulty memory: he was the first president to deliver his entire inaugural address from memory (although, in later years, it was highly likely that Ronald Reagan, used to memorizing long sections of script, could also have done so).

Much as twenty-first-century president Barack Obama wouldn't use the term "radical Islam," Pierce wouldn't even use the term slavery in his inaugural, referring to it only as the "important subject" the nation had to deal with. Like presidents before him (but it was getting worse), Pierce confronted hundreds of job applications for government "spoils." Van Buren's system had now reached full maturity and less than thirty years after its creation was already bogging down the presidency in a sea of job-seekers. Pierce didn't even speak with his vice president, William King of North Carolina—who only lasted six weeks in office before he died of tuberculosis shortly after returning from Cuba; Congress had passed a special law allowing King to be sworn in while in that country, where he had gone in an attempt to improve his health. As was the case with Tyler and Fillmore before him, Pierce named no vice president.

Before delving into the specifics of Franklin Pierce's one term, it is necessary to review just how critically divisive the slavery issue had become, and how the presidency had evolved into an institution crucial to preventing a

★ ★ ★
It's My Party

Like James Madison, Franklin Pierce saw the necessity of political parties. "A Republic without parties is a complete anomaly," he wrote. "The histories of all popular governments show how absurd is the idea of their attempting to exist without parties."

civil war. Recall that Martin Van Buren had created the Democratic Party specifically as a mechanism to avoid a war, and that the essence of his strategy for doing so was the assumption that people could be bought. By providing party—and later, government—jobs, party leaders could effectively coerce people to hold their tongues about slavery. Democratic legislators would refrain from debating slavery or even raising it as an issue. After Democrats passed the "Gag Rule," no one in the House of Representatives could debate the issue. No slave-related legislation would even be introduced to the floor, where it might start a debate or, even worse, be passed into law.

By 1853, the presidency—which Van Buren had meant to remain relatively weak—had (thanks mostly to Van Buren's first chosen candidate, Andrew Jackson) instead assumed enormous powers in comparison with those that had been wielded by President Washington. Under Whigs such as Harrison and Taylor, and then their vice presidents, who were necessarily weaker, few observed or appreciated the incredible power that had slowly been building up in the executive office. None of those presidents had used this power to attenuate the spread of slavery in any way.

A Book You're Not Supposed to Read

Franklin Pierce by Roy F. Nichols (Newtown, CT: American Political Biography Press, 1931).

So Pierce had inherited the Compromise of 1850 and, most significantly, the Fugitive Slave Act, which was already generating resistance in the North. Yet Pierce continued to play the game as usual, hoping to balance his cabinet with regional and party groups. Aware that he had faced many defections to the "Free Soil" party, Pierce tried to mollify everyone by giving some posts to members of each party, and even to factions within each party. But (as has proven the case in subsequent presidencies as well), rather than insulating him from criticism, that only divided his administration. He named Northern Democrat William Marcy of New York as secretary of State and Mississippi's Jefferson Davis as secretary of War, and showed no animosity to the disaffected Northern Free Soil group either.

> ★ ★ ★
> ## Blaming the Victim
> According to historian Joel Silbey, during Pierce's administration the Democrats "were united…behind a notion of eternal vigilance against persistent Whig efforts to expand and alter the nature of the American government." Too late—the Jacksonian Democrats had already done that!

That the nation drifted (one might say, sprinted) toward civil war was not an accident. It was inevitable. Sooner or later the issue of slavery would be raised in the national context in a way no one could avoid.

And that's precisely what happened when Illinois Senator Stephen Douglas introduced a bill that would organize territories west of the Mississippi to secure a route for a future transcontinental railroad. Since the admission of California as a free state had essentially nullified the "36 degree 30 minute" line prohibiting slavery, no constraints on the expansion of slavery existed any longer. Douglas hoped to organize two new territories—Kansas and Nebraska—on the basis of "popular sovereignty," whereby the people of each territory would decide if the state was to be a slave state or free state when they drafted its constitution. "The people decide" was Douglas's framework. Anyone could have foreseen what would follow: both slaveholders and free soilers began a race into Kansas to populate the territory with their own voters. And where they came up against each other, there would be violence.

Actually, "popular sovereignty" had already been in place in the Utah and New Mexico territorial bills as part of the Compromise of 1850, but a new element was galvanizing the debate over the Kansas-Nebraska bill: Southerners wanted the new law to explicitly repeal the Missouri Compromise. Suddenly Pierce began to see the handwriting on the wall, namely that the Compromise of 1850 had already destroyed the Missouri Compromise, and there was no putting the genie back in the bottle. Douglas, of course, wanted the president's help with his Kansas-Nebraska Bill, and Pierce, having trouble with Congress as it was, could use the support of a powerful senator such as Douglas. But it was no easy task to get the bill through Congress. The Democrats were not responding to the "carrot" of government and party jobs as they once had, as had been evidenced by their successful opposition to David Wilmot's Proviso that would have banned slavery in the Mexican Cession territories. Concerns about slave labor competing with free farmers joined with concerns about large-scale Irish immigration in the North pushing down wages to peel off large numbers of Northern Democrats concerned with economic realities. Neither Democrats nor Whigs seemed intent on stopping either driver of low wages, and a firestorm in local elections in 1854—with the Free Soil Party and the famous "Know Nothings" taking votes from both major parties—revealed just how badly Pierce and his predecessors had underestimated the coming conflagration over slavery. Each of those interim parties brought only one of those issues—slavery and immigration, respectively—to the table. It would take a completely new party to fuse the two.

The overriding reality that presidents from Jackson onward had to deal with was the fact that, increasingly, the South wanted not merely to protect slavery within its borders, but to expand it—because only through expansion could its preservation be ensured. The protection of slavery rested on the definition of property rights, and eventually such a definition had to be national in character. If slave states were overwhelmed by newly admitted free states, then the free states' representatives in Congress could curtail slavery, or even abolish it. If, on the other hand, the definition of people as property triumphed in the territories, it was inevitable that it spread back to the North—as it already seemed to be doing as a result of the Fugitive Slave Act in the Compromise of 1850. Thus the fight over slavery in the territories became *more important even* than the fight over slavery where it already existed. In fact the issue became so important that it threatened to swamp every other issue in almost every area of government. Understanding this fact is crucial to understanding Pierce's challenges as president.

The first place Pierce confronted the issue of the expansion (or not) of slavery was in foreign policy, in 1854 when Southern expansionists sought to acquire Cuba as a slave state. Pierce was clear: "The policy of my Administration will not be controlled by any timid forebodings of evil from expansion." If Cuba could be acquired peacefully, Pierce was open to annexing it as a slave state. In March 1854, a steamer, *The Black Warrior*, stopped in Havana to trade, but it did not have a cargo manifest, so Cuban officials seized it and its crew. Complaints to Spain did not resolve the situation. After a year, the episode was resolved peacefully, but Southerners saw it as a missed opportunity to take the island from Spain.

The U.S. minister to Spain, the pro-Southern Pierre Soulé, received an order from Secretary of State William Marcy to approach Spain about negotiating the purchase of Cuba. If the Spanish wouldn't entertain the option, Marcy wrote Soulé, "you will then direct your effort to the next desirable object, which is to detach that island from the Spanish dominion...." Marcy was necessarily oblique, but most historians agree he meant "Threaten to take the damned island!" Soulé and other ministers, James Buchanan and John Y. Mason, met in Ostend, Belgium, in October 1854 and sent a dispatch from Aix-la-Chappelle known as the "Ostend Manifesto" that said "Cuba is as necessary to the North American republic as any of its present members, and...it belongs naturally to that great family of states...." The U.S., the manifesto warned, would not allow Cuba to become "Africanized" through a slave revolt (as had happened in Haiti, for such a revolution would

A Book You're Not Supposed to Read

The Political Crisis of the 1850s by Michael F. Holt (New York: W. W. Norton, 1983).

"endanger or actually…consume the fair fabric of our Union." The United States would be "justified in wresting" Cuba from Spain if the Spanish failed to comply with American demands.

Publication of the "Ostend Manifesto"—which had no backing whatsoever from Pierce—caused a firestorm in the North. (The *New York Tribune* labeled it the "Manifesto of the Brigands.") Now the pro-Southern Pierce was forced to step back from expansionism, and the Southern expansionists turned to Kansas, where they wasted considerable energy that could have been more effectively expended on Cuba—in what historian David Potter described as trading the substance of Cuba for a "Kansan shadow."

At the urging of Secretary of War Jefferson Davis, Pierce sent James Gadsden to Mexico to acquire additional land in the southwest for a southern transcontinental railroad. (Davis originally proposed trying to acquire all of Sonora and Baja California, but this would have added too many slave states to the Union, and Congress scotched all talk of it.) After negotiating with President Antonio Lopez de Santa Anna—the man who had slaughtered the inhabitants of the Alamo in 1836—Gadsden bought a strip of land now in southern Arizona and New Mexico for $10 million (money Santa Anna desperately needed for his army). And whereas Pierce's predecessor John Tyler had opened up trade with China, under Pierce Commodore Matthew Perry entered Japanese waters and negotiated a small trade treaty.

But the slavery issue, and Kansas, continued to boil. Pierce hoped for the quiet passage of the bill, while he judged that none of the "acts prejudicial to good order" on the ground in Kansas justified "the interposition of the Federal Executive." Insisting to the Northerners that the Missouri Compromise had already been effectively repealed by the Compromise of 1850, the prooidcnt uoed lil influence to bring Democrats in behind Douglas's Kansas-Nebraska bill, which passed in May 1854.

Bleeding Kansas, Bleeding Congress

Tensions were already high in Kansas. Slave forces quickly organized a legislature at Lecompton, while late-coming Free Soilers set up a mirror government in Topeka. By May of 1856, a pro-slave mob attacked Lawrence, Kansas, training cannon on the hotel and sacking the governor's house and several anti-slave newspapers. Then, on May 22, Congressman Preston Brooks of South Carolina marched into the U.S. Senate and used his cane to mercilessly beat the U.S. senator from Massachusetts, Charles Sumner, who had just delivered a vicious speech on the "sack of Lawrence." The two episodes combined to reveal not just how important slavery had become as an issue, but how close the nation was to irreparable violence. They also revealed the inability of Pierce to stem the tide. Midterm elections led to a massive upheaval in which the Democrats lost almost all the states outside the South. Whigs were hardly better off, losing ground to the new Republican Party.

Although Pierce expected to be re-nominated, his support of the Kansas-Nebraska Act meant he had no chance of gaining Northern support. He briefly hoped to forge an alliance with Stephen Douglas, but James Buchanan of Pennsylvania emerged with the nomination. In his final months in office, Pierce attacked the new anti-slavery Republican Party.

Assessing Pierce

As president, Franklin Pierce did not abuse his power or manipulate the Constitution. Certainly he didn't have enough allies in Congress to do much of that, and neither did the events of his term lend themselves to the application of presidential power. Short of sending in the army, he had no way to quell the violence in Kansas. In fact, inserting large bodies of armed men into the state might not have defused the situation. On the other hand, he made no effort to exert power over the friends he had, to trade favors, or to bribe and cajole when necessary. He allowed his ministers to Belgium to get out of control, and nearly provoked a war with Spain. Most damaging of all to his grade, he didn't seek any real solution to the "peculiar institution" but was content to allow Congress to muddle along with meaningless compromises. There is a reason that Pierce is often forgotten among the presidents—and that his successor was equally forgettable.

CHAPTER 15

James Buchanan, 1857–1861

"What is right and what is practicable are two different things."
—*James Buchanan*

President Buchanan's Constitutional Grade: D

Of the nation's first seven presidents, five were reelected for a second term. Of the next eight, none was. Two died and six either failed to be reelected or decided at the outset only to serve one term. The presidency had become a symbol of how divided the nation was over slavery. James Buchanan was the last in this line of men often termed as failed presidents for their inability to prevent the nation from sliding into war.

Buchanan was the final Van Buren–created, party politician—the essential "Northern man of Southern principles." A Pennsylvanian and a congressman then senator under Jackson, Buchanan was a true believer in the Democratic platform. Like Van Buren, he opposed slavery—except when it came to actually doing something about it. A former secretary of State under Polk, Buchanan had lobbied for the acquisition of Cuba for the South for years. While in the Polk administration, he had negotiated the Buchanan-Packenham Treaty that settled the Oregon boundary. He lost the 1852 nomination to Pierce, who named him ambassador to Great Britain. Ironically, this insulated Buchanan from the sectional vitriol that had overwhelmed

Did you know?

★ Buchanan was the only president who never married

★ James Buchanan had very small feet, which he took great pride in showing off to the ladies he danced with

★ Buchanan was the last president born in the 1700s

★ ★ ★

No, No, Honey I'm Good

Buchanan's consumption of liquor was impressive. He would begin drinking each night after dinner, often consuming three bottles of liquor at a time. He used his Sunday ride to visit the Jacob Baer distillery in Washington to pick up his weekly ten-gallon cask of "Old J. B. Whiskey." The White House staff thought that stood for Old James Buchanan Whiskey.

the nation in the Pierce administration and opened the door for his nomination in 1856. Former President Millard Fillmore, running as the "Know Nothing" candidate, siphoned votes from the decaying Whigs and ensured the defeat of John C. Fremont, the standard-bearer of the newly formed Republican Party. But the signs were ominous: Fremont only missed winning the Electoral College by a few Northern states, and a matter of a few thousand votes in the next election could turn the Democrats out and usher in an entirely new party...one dedicated to stopping slavery in the territories.

Afflicted with an eye disorder—he had one nearsighted and one farsighted eye, and in any case they were not perfectly aligned—Buchanan had to constantly cock his head and close one eye when he conversed. He also winked a lot, causing one writer to describe him as a "winking, fidgeting little busybody." A worse drinker than Pierce, Buchanan could consume two to three bottles of cognac in a sitting. A generous man, he loaned money to friends and distributed to the poor. A slave-owner, he frequently bought slaves in Washington, then transported them to Pennsylvania where he freed them. His campaign manager unflatteringly described him as "a sort of masculine Miss Fribble."

In the campaign, he was told (by a Navy surgeon who would serve under Union hero David Farragut in the Civil War), "The people have taken the next presidency out of the hands of the politicians.... the people and not your political friends will place you there." While the people elected Buchanan, the people also wanted a solution to the slavery issue, and if he could not provide it, someone else would. Like most of his immediate predecessors, Buchanan sought to restore harmony and end sectional tensions.

To achieve that harmony, he attempted (like Pierce) to balance his cabinet posts sectionally and by party. One of the first presidents to appreciate the growing influence of the Supreme Court, Buchanan was close to two of the justices and was kept informed of pending cases—especially those related to slavery. He maintained that the Supreme Court was the final arbiter of the meaning of the Constitution—an attitude that made the case that soon engulfed his presidency all the more important.

Dred Scott was a slave in Missouri, the property of Army surgeon Dr. John Emerson, who took Scott to a U.S. army fort in Illinois, then to Wisconsin Territory—both of which were "free soil." While at Fort Snelling Scott got married, something he wouldn't have been able to do if he had been deemed a slave. When Emerson was transferred to Missouri, he left Scott behind to be hired out, essentially bringing slavery into a free state. When Emerson died, his widow inherited his slaves, and Scott attempted to purchase his family's freedom. The widow refused. Missouri and Maryland both had "freedom statutes" that allowed slaves to sue for wrongful bondage, and he was financially supported in his lawsuit by the children of a former master, Peter Blow. Already, Missouri courts had heard ten other cases, under

A Book You're Not Supposed to Read

Cannibals All! Or, Slaves Without Masters by George Fitzhugh (Richmond, VA: A. Morris, 1857). George Fitzhugh was a nineteenth-century communist who had read Karl Marx's work and fully subscribed to his ideas. He believed slaves in the South were better treated than factory workers in the North, and that all would be better off as slaves (hence "Cannibals All!"). His work was buried by liberal historians because Fitzhugh unabashedly called slavery the perfect form of communism. Not too many liberal scholars wanted to hear that! Fitzhugh even managed to reverse the meanings of "Free Labor" and "Slave Labor." The original meaning of "Free Labor" was that men had the right to bargain freely for their pay, but Fitzhugh argued that free workers' labor was being stolen from them by factory owners. So they, in fact, were the slaves. But "Slave Labor" was in fact free, because slaves had no responsibilities, no worries, no concerns. Everything in life was provided for them…exactly as the liberals want things to be, in their utopian vision of America.

freedom statutes, based on slaves taken into free territory, and in all cases freed the slaves. Scott first lost on a technicality, then won, but the victory was appealed. Subsequent appeals landed the case in the U.S. Supreme Court (where it was misspelled *Scott v. Sandford*, instead of "Sanford," the name of Scott's new owner, who had acquired the slave in a transfer).

President-elect Buchanan, informed by his friends on the Court, knew the case was coming and knew it would be big. He hoped it would decide the issue of slavery for a long time, removing it from the hands of Congress and the president. And just before Buchanan's inauguration, the Supreme Court handed down what is generally considered to be one of the two or three worst rulings in Supreme Court history (along with *Plessy v. Ferguson* and *Roe v. Wade*). Chief Justice Roger Taney, writing for the majority, denied Scott's right to sue, claiming that he never was or could be a citizen, and so the Court lacked jurisdiction over the case. Nevertheless, despite having asserted that the Court didn't have jurisdiction, Taney's decision addressed the Missouri Compromise, claiming that Congress had exceeded its power in curtailing slavery in the territories and that the Fifth Amendment protected slave owners who wished to take slaves into free states. Ultimately, he said, Congress couldn't keep slavery out of a territory—and neither could popular sovereignty. Only once a state had already been created as a slave state could it amend its constitution after the fact to prohibit slavery. This tortured ruling, of course, threw enormous weight on the side of the slave South. If the Civil War had not intervened, *Dred Scott* would have made it very difficult ever to attenuate the expansion of slavery.

While the political explosion that followed the decision was immense, an even more rapid reaction came from the financial markets, where Taney's ruling had opened up *all* of the Western territories to the violence that was besetting Kansas. Overnight, stocks of railroads running to the West crashed, and the contagion spread to the New York banks, precipitating the Panic of 1857. Since the Democrats were in power, the Panic hurt them badly, especially with laborers in Ponnsylvania and other Northern states. Enough Republicans were elected to Congress in 1858 that it became impossible to elect a Speaker of the House, as the two sides could not agree.

Meanwhile, in the Western territory of Utah, the Mormons had been harassing federal officials, threatening to create their own Mormon state. Buchanan sent twenty-five hundred troops and new federal officials to Utah, and even before the soldiers arrived the Mormons promised to behave. In foreign affairs, Buchanan's administration got a new treaty with China and expanded relations with Japan. His administration also suffered some scandals involving government printing contracts.

But the economic upheaval and the issues with the Mormons were eclipsed by the all-encompassing issue of slavery, which continued to cause conflict in Kansas. Buchanan had sent Robert Walker to Kansas as the territorial governor, and Walker had promised to hold a plebiscite on slavery there. The Lecompton Assembly that was preparing the new Kansas state constitution—which could not be amended for seven years—was pro-slavery. But free soilers outnumbered the slave forces in Kansas by the time Walker arrived, so the Lecompton constitution could not get ratified.

Walker urged Buchanan to denounce and reject this action, but that would have risked the wrath of the Southerners. The president tried every bribe he could think of—party posts, contracts for building in Kansas, even direct cash—to get the pro-slavery constitution adopted, but to no avail. It all was humiliating to the president and the Democrats, costing the party Northern seats in the House in the 1858 election.

Stephen Douglas, Buchanan's looming rival in the Senate, was reelected after a memorable campaign against a new Republican in Illinois, Abraham Lincoln. Douglas, the leading advocate of "popular sovereignty," had stood by and watched as Buchanan sought to override the will of the majority of Kansans. Worse, Douglas, in his Illinois senate debates, had been forced into a corner by Lincoln, who asked if he supported the *Dred Scott* decision or popular sovereignty—for it was impossible to support both. Douglas's answer was the "Freeport Doctrine": that the people should decide, so that no matter what the Court said, the people could elect officials who simply would not enforce the law. The hypocrisy of a sitting U.S. senator calling on the public to deliberately disregard federal laws while at the same time giving lip service to those laws marked Douglas for political death. The South abandoned him after the "Freeport Heresy."

Lincoln became a well-known figure and emerged from the Republican convention in 1860 as the nominee. Van Buren's scheme for using the federal bureaucracy to contain the passions over slavery would die with the election of Lincoln. In fact, Van Buren's elaborate scheme actually made the Civil War inevitable, once it became clear that the power of the federal government, which had grown so great under the ministrations of the Democrats, in the hands of a Republican could be turned against the South. When Lincoln was elected in 1860, the vast powers that had aggrandized the presidency over time through the spoils system meant that Southerners felt they had to secede from the Union.

Buchanan's cabinet was split over the possibility of secession, and he was now a powerless lame duck. He existed in a limbo "execrated now by four-fifths of the people of all parties," as a friend put it. The president was obviously unhappy, confined himself to his study, and was often too sick to come out. His Democratic heritage came out in his final message to Congress, when he denounced secession—but insisted he didn't have the authority to prevent it. Perhaps here he should have channeled Andrew Jackson! But this was *real* secession, not a group of disgruntled Mainers carping about the border, or a bunch of malcontent Federalists opposing the war with England. The South had already started writing a constitution for a confederation. But Buchanan, seeing a massive storm ahead, sought simply to get to shore before it hit and hand the boat over to Lincoln.

The fact that the South had taken over federal property in Southern states, including forts, posed a dilemma for Buchanan. At Fort Sumter, South Carolina, the secessionists wanted control of the post but refrained from firing at it, knowing the fort would eventually run out of supplies. When Buchanan sent a relief vessel, fire from shore batteries drove it off. That was an act of war, but Buchanan refused to act. He announced that he would not send new supplies to Fort Sumter unless Major Robert Anderson, the commander, requested them. Buchanan was surprised at how fast things had moved, and how far. Yet he did nothing to stop this illegal act of the Confederate States.

Buchanan's Sorry Record

From Kansas to the secession crisis, James Buchanan proved utterly incapable of leading. He abused his power by trying to force free soilers in Kansas to accept slavery, acquiesced in one of the worst Supreme Court cases in history, and literally did nothing to stop the Southern states from leaving the Union. While it is true that his predecessors had greased the skids by taking no steps to interdict slavery, ultimately it was Buchanan's time to put his little foot down. To his dishonor, he did not.

CHAPTER 16

Abraham Lincoln, 1861–April 15, 1865

"I know the American People are much attached to their Government;—I know they would suffer much for its sake;—I know they would endure evils long and patiently, before they would ever think of exchanging it for another. Yet, notwithstanding all this, if the laws be continually despised and disregarded, if their rights to be secure in their persons and property, are held by no better tenure than the caprice of a mob, the alienation of their affections from the Government is the natural consequence; and to that, sooner or later, it must come."

—*Abraham Lincoln*

President Lincoln's Constitutional Grade: A–

Amidst a recent spate of revisionist history from both the libertarian Right and the radical, often racist Left, a constitutional grade of A– for Abraham Lincoln may surprise some. Lincoln haters on the Right point to violations of free speech, the imposition of a draft, and the printing of Greenbacks as just a few of his egregious violations of the Constitution, while those on the Left insist that Lincoln did not use the powers at his disposal to create a permanent, genuine "social revolution" that reordered American institutions. In fact, Lincoln was the ultimate constitutionalist, who began with first things. The very first was that he had taken an oath to protect and defend the Constitution against all enemies, foreign *and* domestic; and in 1861, the secessionists constituted the greatest threat to the existence of the United States of America since George Washington was forced to retreat from New York in defeat in 1776. For more than a decade, Lincoln had been formulating his correct view that without the Union there

Did you know?

★ Lincoln remains the only U.S. president ever to have held a patent (for a floatation device that lifted boats off sand bars)

★ Lincoln's name was not even on the original list of candidates for the 1860 Republican nomination

★ His depression was often so bad that he joked to friends and family not to allow him near a knife

is nothing—without the United States itself, there was no Constitution. The life of the body politic came first. To kill the body of the Union was also to kill its soul: the Constitution.

Lincoln's personal story is well known and does not demand a detailed retelling here: after his family moved about, Lincoln, self-educated, became a Springfield, Illinois, lawyer (and a very good one) who worked mostly defending corporate clients. Over the years he made powerful defenses of private property rights and the rights of businesses to operate without undue regulations. His early political career appeared to be a failure. He served in the House of Representatives for only two years, when he issued the famous "Spot Resolutions" during the Mexican War, and before that he served in the Illinois House of Representatives. After his defeat in the 1858 Illinois Senate race at the hands of Stephen Douglas, Lincoln thought his political life was through.

Lincoln was a dark horse candidate for the Republican nomination—not even on the original list of candidates—and once nominated he found himself running for president of a brutally divided country. The 1860 race included four main candidates: himself for the Republicans, Stephen Douglas for the Northern Democrats, John Breckinridge for the Southern Democrats, and John Bell for the new Constitutional Union Party. Bell took Virginia, Tennessee, and Kentucky; Breckinridge, the rest of the South; Douglas, Missouri and a split delegation from New Jersey. Lincoln won every other Northern state plus Oregon and California for 180 electoral votes (compared to the 123 *total* for his opponents). But no electoral votes at all were cast for him in ten of the fifteen slave states, and he won only two of almost a thousand Southern counties. He had a strong popular vote edge over Douglas (1.8 million to 1.3 million, but the other two candidates split another 1.4 million). Hence the results could be read any number of ways. A "slave power" conspiracist, for example, might conclude that the country had voted for slavery by about two to one (combining Douglas, Bell, and

Breckinridge's votes) A paranoid Southerner might assume the opposite—that 2.6 million Americans (all but the Breckinridge voters) had voted against slavery.

A Book You're Not Supposed to Read

The Lincoln Nobody Knows by Richard N. Current (New York: Hill and Wang, 1963).

No matter how you cut it, the divisions meant more than a difference of opinion, as the secessionist movement was ready to leave the Union even before Lincoln took office in March. South Carolina seceded in December, then Florida, Mississippi, Alabama, Georgia, Louisiana, and Texas followed in February. North Carolina, Tennessee, and Virginia warned that, while they would remain in the Union for the time being, they would leave if any federal action was taken against those states that had already left. By February the Confederate States of America had been formed and a new, anti-constitutional (in essence, treasonous) government established in Montgomery, Alabama.

This was entirely uncharted territory. Washington had dealt with a minor Whiskey Rebellion, not secession, and the Hartford Convention that opposed Madison in the War of 1812 did nothing more than talk. Forming an entirely new "nation" out of part of the United States was unacceptable. To Lincoln, it was even worse, for he believed that neither the United States nor the Confederacy could survive alone, any more than an arm could survive without a body or a body stay alive with massive bleeding from an unattended severed limb.

In Lincoln's Inaugural Address, he asked Southerners more than twenty questions. He assured the country that he supported the nation's laws in all cases, including even the Fugitive Slave Act. He pointed out that those included the laws against insurrection, and he promised to protect and defend federal property inside the Confederacy, including the forts. But he wavered on the issue of allowing the Confederates to replace federal officers and agreed not to deliver "irritating" or "obnoxious" mails. Lincoln was

A Book You're Not Supposed to Read

Crisis of the House Divided: An Interpretation of the Issues in the Lincoln-Douglas Debates, 50th anniversary edition, by Harry V. Jaffa (Chicago: University of Chicago, 2009).

hoping for a peaceful resolution to the secession crisis. But in many ways, his conciliatory gestures only encouraged the Rebels. Ultimately secession was treason, and it is an interesting question how someone like Andrew Jackson would have dealt with this overt lawlessness, especially given the large number of people in rebellion.

William Tecumseh Sherman warned Lincoln on inauguration day that the South was building up its military force and that the country was "sleeping on a volcano." Lincoln still hoped for an amicable solution and refused to fire the first shot. When another resupply effort at Fort Sumter on April 12, 1861, drew Confederate fire and Major Robert Anderson surrendered the fort the following day, Lincoln called for the states to send seventy-five thousand state militia troops, and he put out an enlistment call for forty-two thousand regulars. He blockaded Southern ports as well. He also took the immediate step of labeling the conflict a "rebellion," thereby sending a signal to England and France that they would be meddling in internal American affairs if they aided the Confederacy.

Rebel troops were visible in the distance from the White House, causing Lincoln to suspend *habeas corpus* in Washington and along the railroad lines to Philadelphia. It was an expansion of presidential power, but then an exceptional, and exceptionally dangerous, situation had gripped the nation. Lincoln intended, he said, to deal with "the enemy in the rear"—an "efficient corps of spies, informers, suppliers, and aiders and abettors."

But when John Merryman of Maryland was arrested in May and a Union Army officer refused to present him to the local court, Chief Justice Roger Taney ruled the suspension of habeas corpus illegal. Lincoln ignored Taney and informed Congress that whether or not the suspension was "strictly legal," ho was acting on the grounds of "public necessity." Lincoln's broader argument was that in times of emergency, as the only nationally elected official, he had a constitutional duty to exercise authority normally wielded by Congress. Over the next four years, there would be six other suspensions of the writ of habeas corpus. Democrats howled, expectedly. Lincoln argued that the presidency alone had the wherewithal to act quickly and decisively to raise an army, prevent insurrection, protect

A Book You're Not Supposed to Read

With Malice Toward None: A Life of Abraham Lincoln by Stephen B. Oates (New York: Harper Perennial, 2011), remains one of the best one-volume biographies of Lincoln.

lines of supply from saboteurs, and so on—including a blockade of Southern ports. Congress ratified Lincoln's argument in August 1861. Then, in 1863, the Supreme Court declared his actions in the blockade legal.

The overarching philosophical approach of Lincoln's argument was based on the preamble to the Constitution ("We the people"), and the Declaration of Independence, with its frequent references to "the people." By looking to "the people" as a whole and tracing the establishment of the United States back to the Declaration, Lincoln definitively rejected the "compact theory" whereby the states were the enabling agents who had created the United States after the drafting of the Constitution. As the Union was a living body, secession was unthinkable. Lincoln took his oath of office seriously and interpreted it to mean that he had not only the authority but the responsibility to prevent the nation from fracturing. Moreover, Lincoln, more than Madison ever had, saw himself as a true commander in chief of the Army, and took his duties seriously. He studied a book on tactics and military terms by "Old Brains" Henry Halleck, and continually checked telegraph dispatches coming into the War Department.

Lincoln spent money before Congress allocated it, instructed his Treasury secretary, Salmon Chase, to develop a means to fund the war, and in

★ ★ ★
Lincoln's T-Mails

Tom Wheeler, in *Mr. Lincoln's T-Mails* (New York: HarperBusiness, 2006), argues that Lincoln embraced the new technology of the telegraph and used it in a military setting as few others did. The president adopted a folksy style when communicating by "T-Mails" and, more importantly, endeavored to bring his generals into the nineteenth century by convincing them to adopt it too. Ulysses Grant, especially, became comfortable using the telegraph while traveling with the army in the field, rather than trying to manage the battles from Washington. The greater mileage in telegraph lines in the North proved yet another military advantage contributing to victory.

August 1862 signed a Confiscation Act that authorized the confiscation of slaves from Rebels, followed by their emancipation. While minimal in its immediate effect, the Confiscation Act began to lay the groundwork for the Emancipation Proclamation. Yet Lincoln reversed a similar move by General John C. Fremont in Missouri, where Fremont had not only declared martial law but begun freeing slaves on his own authority. Lincoln knew that the Border States were crucial to victory ("I hope to have God on my side," he quipped, "but I must have Kentucky") and after Lincoln countermanded Fremont's orders, Missouri sent an additional forty thousand men to fight.

The blockade produced at least one ticklish international incident, in which Union ships intercepted the *Trent*, a British merchant vessel carrying two Confederate envoys to Great Britain. The men were seized, but soon released, with the delicate negotiations handled by Lincoln's Secretary of State William Seward. A conflict with England was averted.

More than many of his generals, Lincoln instinctively knew that the destruction of the Army of Northern Virginia and opening the Mississippi River by eliminating the fortress at Vicksburg were the central goals. A number of his military advisors were mired in obsolete strategic thinking in which capturing Richmond (it had replaced Montgomery as the Confederate capital) was the objective. After a disastrous initial battle at Bull Run, Lincoln installed a new general, George B. McClellan ("the Napoleon of the West") and instructed him to seek out the enemy. But McClellan was cautious to a fault, always believing he was out-numbered and under-supplied. Lincoln sent an indirect message to McClellan, saying to a mutual acquaintance, "If General McClellan isn't going to use his army, I'd like to borrow it for a time." In the Peninsula Campaign, McClellan finally moved in to capture Richmond, where Rebel General Robert E. Lee, aware of McClellan's paranoia about being outnumbered, had one of his officers (who was also an actor) stage elaborate marches of troops to impress McClellan's scouts. Ultimately, the campaign failed and McClellan was sacked as general-in-chief. General John Pope replaced him at the head of the Army of the Potomac, and promptly lost again, this time at Second Bull Run. Again Confederate troops threatened Washington.

Rotation in Officers

Following Pope's failure, Lincoln brought back McClellan, just in time for the first of two ill-fated Confederate offensives in the North, this one at Antietam in September 1862. Even possessing a copy of Lee's battle plans that had fallen on the ground and been picked up by a Union soldier, McClellan hesitated. Nevertheless, with superior forces, McClellan finally drove Lee back and gained a technical victory. This allowed Lincoln to issue his Emancipation Proclamation on January 1, 1863, addressing the critical definition of private property that the nation had struggled to avoid for eighty years. Even in the Proclamation, however, Lincoln was cautious,

★ ★ ★
Death and Madness in the White House

William Wallace Lincoln, known as Willie, was Lincoln's third son. In early 1862, he became ill—likely with typhoid fever—and died in February. Letitia Tyler had died while her husband John was president, but no chief executive up to that point had lost a child in the White House. Mary Todd Lincoln "collapsed in convulsions" of sobbing, while Lincoln sank into his customary depression. But after a time Lincoln knew that Mary's perpetual melancholy, occasionally drifting to mental illness, would infect the presidency itself. He brought her to a window, from which the local mental institution could be seen. "Try and control your grief," he instructed her, "or it will drive you mad, and we may have to send you there."

A Book You're Not Supposed to Read

Emancipating Slaves, Enslaving Free Men: A History of the American Civil War, 2nd ed., by Jeffrey R. Hummel (Chicago: Open Court Publishers, 2013). Hummel provides an excellent economic analysis of the impact of slavery, but goes overboard in his assessment of the constitutional overreach by Lincoln.

emancipating only those slaves in "states still in rebellion." Technically, that only applied to the South and the members of the Confederacy not yet controlled by the North, exempting Missouri, Kentucky, West Virginia, Maryland—all of which were still needed for the war effort. Lincoln knew that soon slavery in even those states would have to be dealt with eventually, but that Congress needed to be the agent to effect that change, not the president.

In his long journey toward the Emancipation Proclamation, Lincoln had moved from the "natural limits of slavery" position through "gradual compensated emancipation" to full emancipation.

The "natural limits" theory was that the South's cotton lands would eventually play out, and that as plantation owners kept moving south and west, they would run out of land suitable for slavery. Consequently, slavery would just die out on its own. Most soon abandoned that theory when they discovered that not only were Western lands, including mining areas, quite suitable for the use of slaves, but slavery was increasing in urban areas and for use in industry. Lincoln's next position, "gradual compensated emancipation," proved equally ill-grounded in economics. First, slavery was not just an economic system—it was a social system of power, which in the South meant as much to the non-slaveholder as to the plantation master. Even poor whites had someone to look down on. Second, as we have seen, even if slave owners had been willing to go along with graduated emancipation, the price for remaining slaves would by necessity increase as they became scarcer. Finally, a corollary of most "gradual compensated emancipation" schemes was a resettlement in Africa, which very few American free blacks wanted. Sooner or later, the United States would have to deal with the end of slavery and the position of blacks in the social and political system after that.

While Lincoln said, "If I could save the Union without freeing any slave I would do it, and if I could save it by freeing all the slaves I would do it; and if I could save it by freeing some and leaving others alone, I would also do that," he still recognized that a final reckoning with the *definition of people as property* lay ahead. What brought him to the inevitable decision to issue the Emancipation Proclamation, though, was no idealistic drive to arrive at that final definition. It was a separate revelation: that only by destroying the institution of slavery could the South ever be brought back into a peaceful Union. Once in place, the Proclamation had the added benefit of bringing in over 179,000 free men of color to the Union Army and 19,000 to the Navy. (It is worth noting, though, that over 100,000 *white Southerners* fought for the Union as well.) And since he confined the Proclamation to those parts of the country that he had military authority over as commander in chief, it was fully constitutional.

At his Gettysburg Address, Lincoln further expanded on the unbreakable connection between the Declaration and the Constitution, noting that the "new nation, Conceived in liberty" was "dedicated to the proposition that all men were created equal." The "new nation"—and its Constitution—were meaningless if the United States was not "dedicated" to this proposition. Lincoln referred to the Declaration as the "sheet anchor" of republican values.

Even after the key victory at Gettysburg, Lincoln's generals dawdled. General George Gordon Meade, had he followed up to attack Lee's retreating force after Gettysburg, could have ended the war (or most of it) in July 1863. But by permitting Lee to escape, Meade prolonged the war and lost his job. Lincoln appointed Ulysses S. Grant, who had become a star in the West with his capture of Vicksburg on the Fourth of July 1863, lieutenant general—the first to hold that rank since Washington. During 1864, despite heavy losses,

★ ★ ★

Running Out of Men?

A common leftist claim about the Emancipation Proclamation, made by Howard Zinn in his *People's History of the United States*, is that Lincoln was running out of men and needed black bodies to reinforce the army. Such a notion is hogwash, reflecting Zinn's ahistoricism and inability to place things in the context of the day. Yet the meme is picked up in textbooks such as Irwin Unger's *These United States*: "Another consideration was the potential value of black soldiers. If the North could tap this human reservoir, it could offset the immense losses on the battlefield and the declining zeal of white volunteers." Even the great David Donald, who wrote the Civil War section for the *Great Republic* textbook by Bernard Bailyn, focused his analysis of the Emancipation Proclamation on the supposed need for black soldiers.

There is only one problem. Virtually no military man in either the Union or Confederate Army thought blacks could fight. The earliest free black recruits were routinely placed as guards or in supply positions, never in combat. As is shown in the film *Glory*, black regiments had to struggle to see combat.

Never in any of Lincoln's writings about emancipation, and never in his discussions with the governors of the Border States, did the military necessity of black troops even come up. More importantly, Lincoln had already made up his mind about Emancipation in *the summer of 1862*, long before the horrific casualty counts of Antietam, Fredericksburg, and Gettysburg rolled in. As to the notion the North was losing a disproportionate number of men, Grady McWhiney found that in the first twelve major battles or campaigns of the war where the casualty toll exceeded five thousand, the South lost a *higher* percentage of men committed to the battle than the North in every instance save the battle of Fredericksburg. Of course, at Gettysburg, Lee lost an astounding thirty percent of his force killed or wounded. If either side in the war needed black soldiers, it was the Confederacy.

Grant announced his intention to "fight it out on this line if it takes all summer." Grant was the first Union commander to perceive that merely having superior numbers and equipment was insufficient: troops and supplies had to be used. "As we say out West, if a man can't skin he must hold a leg," he announced, indicating that all units were to go on offense, all the time. With Lincoln's approval, General Philip Sheridan rode roughshod through the Shenandoah Valley and destroyed it as a food source, while General William Tecumseh Sherman made good on his promise to "make Georgia howl" by marching from Atlanta to the sea, leaving a trail of destruction in his path.

A Book You're Not Supposed to Read

Attack and Die: Civil War Military Tactics and the Southern Heritage by Grady McWhiney and Perry D. Jamieson (Tuscaloosa, AL: University of Alabama, 1984).

Nevertheless, Lincoln's re-nomination, let alone his reelection, was considered touch and go. So-called "Radical Republicans," who wanted to severely punish both the South and the Democratic Party, had carped mercilessly about Lincoln's war policies. In 1864, Radical members of Congress introduced the Wade-Davis Bill. Already looking ahead to what would be called "Reconstruction," the Radicals wanted to require over half of a Southern state's voting population to swear loyalty to the Union before the state could submit a constitution to Congress for approval. Lincoln elicited howls of outrage and further cut into the support for his reelection campaign by vetoing the bill.

To buttress his electoral chances in 1864, Lincoln brought Tennessee Senator (and Democrat) Andrew Johnson onto the ticket. This was the second instance of members of separate parties running together since the change in the Electoral College rules putting the president and vice president on one ticket. Lincoln also took precautions such as giving the Army a furlough on Election Day. His general election opponent was none other than former general George B. McClellan, whose Democratic Party platform called the war a failure. Lincoln's reelection seemed precarious right up until news of Sherman's conquest of Atlanta, Sheridan's destruction of the Shenandoah, and Admiral David Farragut's capture of Mobile all arrived in short order, refuting the Democrats' claim.

Bloody combat still had several more months to run, but the final Union victory was no longer in doubt, and the Confederates surrendered in April 1865. Just a month earlier Lincoln delivered his famous Second Inaugural Address in which he publicly asked forgiveness for America having accepted slavery:

> Fondly do we hope—fervently do we pray—that this mighty scourge of war may speedily pass away. Yet, if God wills that it continue, until all the wealth piled by the bond-man's 250 years of unrequited toil shall be sunk, and until every drop of blood drawn with the lash, shall be paid by another drawn with the sword...so it must be said, "the judgments of the Lord are true and righteous altogether." With malice toward none; and charity for all; with firmness in the right as God gives us to see the right, let us strive to finish the work we are in...[and] achieve and cherish a just and lasting peace among ourselves and with all nations.

To achieve that "just and lasting peace," Lincoln intended a mild "reconstruction" of the South. He could have legitimately dealt with them all as traitors, but he thought that impractical in the extreme, and unnecessary. Instead he chose the "10 Percent Plan," by which a Southern state could rejoin the Union when 10 percent of its voters submitted a state constitution without slavery in it for approval by Congress. This of course flew in the face of the Radical legislators who had proposed the Wade-Davis Bill.

At the same time, since slavery was not abolished everywhere, Lincoln began to pressure Congress to pass legislation removing slavery from the last states that had not left the Union. But he realized that without a constitutional amendment a new Congress could restore slavery, perhaps in the entire former Confederacy. So Lincoln wanted an amendment. The essence of the Thirteenth Amendment was introduced to Congress in December 1863, passed in January 1865, and ratified by the states and officially added to the Constitution in December of that year.

Expanding the Government on the "Homefront"

Lincoln's wartime government, with the overwhelmingly Republican Congress and Senate, passed a number of measures that Whigs, and later Republicans, had desired for years. These included a transcontinental railroad (paid for by federal land subsidies), a renewal of the tariff, and the Homestead Act, which made western lands of 160 acres per person available free if the person settled on or farmed the land, or both, for five years (an earlier homestead act had charged $1.25 an acre). At the end of the five years the homesteader could get a title deed.

To ensure that "sodbusters" (as these homesteaders were called) succeeded, the Morrill Land Grant College Act was passed, bringing engineering, agricultural, and technical education to the prairie states. In 1862, Lincoln signed a bill creating the Department of Agriculture, essentially another sop to the Westerners as well. All these laws were enacted with an eye toward creating a permanent Republican majority in the Western states, a strategy that has worked up into the present. Two states were admitted to the Union during Lincoln's tenure—Nevada and West Virginia, which had seceded from Virginia after the Old Dominion joined the Confederacy.

Equally important, the wartime government—partly out of a concern for financing the war—revamped banking in the United States through the National Bank and Currency Acts of 1863–1864. Whereas previously any bank was allowed to print its own money, the Bank Acts created a new system of national banks that obtained charters from the federal government and printed U.S. banknotes, while the Currency Act taxed

★ ★ ★
A Taxing War

The first real national income tax was instituted during the Civil War, a tax of three percent of all incomes over $8,000 at the time. By the end of the war, the Income Tax Acts had produced $55 million in revenue. The taxes continued until 1872, when they were allowed to expire under Ulysses Grant. Later, the Populist movement sought to re-implement income taxes, but in 1895 the Supreme Court ruled them unconstitutional. In 1913 Progressives succeeded in adding the Sixteenth Amendment to the Constitution to allow income taxes—something we should thank them for every April 15.

state bank notes at a rate of ten percent, driving them out of circulation. Not long after the Civil War, only national bank notes circulated, so that the money supply had been centralized in the hands of the government. And, as might be expected, government grew, by degrees that would have shocked and dismayed the Founders. At the end of the war, the number of civilians working for the federal government had shot up to 195,000.

Lincoln's government had presided over a vast revolution, then, in the midst of a war. It had produced a more centralized financial system, expanded settlement in the West, emancipated over three million slaves, permanently destroyed the old planter class in the South, strengthened the Republican Party alignment of the West and the Northeast, and seen the expansion of presidential power. Lincoln ended, once and for all, the notion that a state could leave the Union; in a sense he was insisting, "We're all in this together." At the end of the war his bitterest opponents were at the extreme ends of the political spectrum: the unrepentant "Fire Eaters" in the South and the merciless Radical Republicans in the North. As the saying goes, he must have been doing something right to make such enemies.

Lincoln's assassination on April 14, 1865, ended any chance for a benign Reconstruction, inflaming the ire of Northerners who already thought Lincoln had "gone soft" on the former Confederates. One thing is certain: his successor was an infinitely less capable president than Abraham Lincoln was.

Lincoln, a President for All Seasons

There were perhaps only two or three American presidents who could have kept the Union together as Lincoln did. Probably Washington and Reagan would have succeeded. Perhaps FDR. But Lincoln had to do it first. He did not have the advantage of the history of another president who had already navigated the waters. Although he is lambasted by modern libertarians for aggrandizing power, the fact is Lincoln refrained from becoming a tyrant, which, under the circumstances, he might very well have become. While the United States did not really need government help to build the transcontinental railroads (after all, James J. Hill built the Great Northern without any government subsidies), and while most lament Lincoln's imposition of the income tax and the creation of a monopoly national bank system, these were all actions largely aimed at ensuring victory in the war. Lincoln's primary job was to save the Union. He succeeded at that brilliantly. One piece of evidence for his success is that by most measures the Southern part of the United States today is the most "patriotic" (as seen, for example, in Southerners' greater than average participation in military service). It is also to Lincoln's credit that he took the constitutional steps to see emancipation made permanent. In terms of Western expansion and growth, Lincoln merely carried on the Jefferson-Jackson tradition of moving land into the hands of the people. While he can be criticized for violating the civil rights of individuals from time to time, these instances are easily rationalized as necessities of war.

Lincoln has been labeled a "tyrant," but the accusation appears ridiculous in light of the reality that when the Radicals stood behind him after August of 1864, Lincoln the "tyrant" easily could have used the war as an excuse to postpone elections. "If the rebellion could force us to forgo, or postpone a national election, it might fairly claim to have already conquered and ruined us," he said. One shudders to think what some other presidents would have done in similar circumstances. Because of Lincoln's fidelity to the Constitution, the necessities of war changed how the powers of the president were exercised, but not the presidency itself.

CHAPTER 17

Andrew Johnson, April 15, 1865–1869

"I am sworn to uphold the Constitution as Andy Johnson understands it and interprets it."
—*Andrew Johnson*

President Johnson's Constitutional Grade: F

ndrew Johnson had the singular misfortune of following one of the two greatest presidents in American history at a turbulent time without a whit of support in either house of Congress. Under the best of circumstances, Johnson would have had a difficult time, and he almost certainly could not have gotten elected on his own. Taking office after the first presidential assassination in American history—as a Southerner to boot!—Johnson had no chance of succeeding. Instead he had countless opportunities to fail, some of which he created himself.

Born in 1808 in North Carolina, Johnson had a deprived childhood and was one of the poorest occupants of the White House. As a youth, he was apprenticed to a tailor and ran off to South Carolina at age fifteen, then on to Greenville, Tennessee. His early political career blossomed, and the future looked bright: he was alderman, mayor, state representative, U.S. congressman, governor, then finally U.S. senator before Abraham Lincoln named him to the ticket in his 1864 reelection campaign. Johnson had a reputation as a good stump speaker, was a slave-owner—which stood him

Did you know?

★ Andrew Johnson was apprenticed to a tailor but ran away at age fifteen

★ He was the only Southern senator to oppose secession and stay in his Senate seat after the Confederacy was formed

★ Johnson was one of the poorest presidents

★ He was the only president in American history to serve as a senator, become president, and then return to the Senate

★ ★ ★

Tinker, Tailor, Soldier, Spy

Johnson was easily one of the poorest men ever to hold the presidency—something he had in common with Harry Truman in 1945. Both had also been vice presidents, and both were involved in the fashion industry (in a manner of speaking). Johnson had been a tailor, and Truman ran a clothing store that went out of business in the recession of 1921.

in good stead with Southern audiences—yet never forgot his common origins and warred constantly against the "slaveocracy," the "bloated, corrupted aristocracy" of the planter elites. His unionist sentiments earned him the military governorship of Tennessee from Lincoln after the Union captured Nashville in 1862. On the night of Lincoln's assassination, Johnson himself was a target as well, but his planned assassin, George Atzerodt, got drunk and never tried to kill the vice president.

In a certain sense, Lincoln had the easy part: winning the war. Johnson had to put a divided country back together with no support from either side. The Radical Republicans disliked Johnson, a Democrat, and sought to run Reconstruction from Congress. The North didn't like him, and the South didn't trust him. Johnson had differed with Lincoln about dealing with the Rebels: in a meeting just before Lincoln's assassination, Johnson tried to persuade the president to deal harshly with traitors. And after the shooting, Johnson was furious, muttering, "They shall suffer for this. They shall suffer for this." Temperamentally, Johnson was unfit for the office. As historian Paul Johnson noted, the president had an "ungovernable temper and lost it often."

By all accounts, Johnson presided over Lincoln's funeral ceremonies with dignity. He got word that General William Tecumseh Sherman had made a deal with Confederate General Joseph Johnston to surrender troops in return for allowing the existing state Confederate government to remain in power. Johnson immediately deemed this unacceptable. He ordered Sherman to accept only unconditional surrender. "Treason is a crime," he said, "and must be punished as a crime.... It must not be excused as an unsuccessful rebellion [and] forgiven." Over time, however, Johnson softened, so that by December 25, 1868, he proclaimed, "Unconditionally, and without reservation...a full pardon and amnesty for the offence of treason against the United States...."

The struggle over Reconstruction was sectional, political in the partisan sense, and structural in that Johnson faced a battle with Congress over who would be in control. The president faced a sectional battle because the North wanted to humiliate the South, and he faced a political fight because the Radical Republicans wanted to eliminate the Democratic Party. As leading Radical Thaddeus Stevens boasted, the Radicals wanted to "insure the ascendency of the Union [that is, the Republican] party." They saw black voting rights as "punishment to traitors" in the South.

Whether or not Johnson understood the nature of this three-way battle or merely fought it as he went is not clear, but in any case it was a fight Johnson was not equipped to win. At the beginning of his presidency he hoped to accomplish Reconstruction before Congress could get involved, as it was not due back in session until December 1865. The most important pending issue was voting rights for the defeated Confederates: if the former Rebels came back as citizens in large numbers, it would be more difficult to protect the rights of the freedmen, but if strong restrictions were put on their readmission to the franchise, that could foment ongoing rebellion. Johnson promised to continue with Lincoln's 10 Percent Plan, in which a state could apply for readmission to the Union when just 10 percent of its voters had sworn an oath of allegiance to the United States, while the Radicals were pushing for a 51 percent number. Johnson's May 1865 message on Reconstruction reflected his common roots and anti-elite bias: he planned to exclude wealthy ex-Confederates from ever participating in government, and he had no intention of allowing blacks to vote. But generally Johnson's plan was "amazingly lenient," as historian Eric Foner points out. And the Radical Republicans in Congress were not willing to go along

A Book You're Not Supposed to Read

The Civil War and Reconstruction by James G. Randall (Boston: D. C. Heath and Company, 1937). In this classic, Randall sought to refute the "Tragic Era" interpretations of Reconstruction by Claude G. Bowers and similar scholars.

with it. Soon Johnson was allying with the planter elites he hated, hoping to find a center between the Radical Republicans on the one side and the unrepentant secessionists on the other.

Johnson forged ahead quickly, and Southern states formed their governments. Far from giving the newly freed blacks full civil rights, some of the newly reconstituted Southern states had implemented "Black Codes," laws that restricted the movement of the freedmen and even provided for their arrest and assignment to work gangs if they were deemed "vagrants." Many in the North believed that the black codes showed that the unrepentant South had not learned its lesson and still required federal control. But that was not even remotely possible: by November 1865, some eight hundred thousand Union soldiers had already been mustered out of the army. And in fact only a handful of *Northern* states gave free blacks the right to vote; pressure for immediate black voting rights did not exist beyond the Radical Republicans.

The South had genuinely been devastated. Some $30 million in Confederate cotton had been confiscated, and parts of Georgia and South Carolina looked like they had been struck by an earthquake. Thousands of Southerners were homeless, and bread rations handed out in Richmond alone amounted to 128,000 to some 15,000 people in April 1865 alone. Another 35,000 in Atlanta depended on the federal government for food.

The Failed Presidential Reconstruction

Johnson had a brief window to work with Congress. Initially the Radicals considered Johnson's accession to the presidency "a godsend to our cause," believing the new president would be more willing to punish the South than Lincoln had been. But when he resisted their plans they described Johnson as a "genius in depravity," and "an irresolute mule" who was "devil-bent upon the ruin of his country." Rather than getting into a war of words, Johnson looked for a more direct confrontation. In short, the president was looking for a bill to veto. When the first Civil Rights Bill and a separate bill extending the life of the Freedmen's Bureau (termed by Paul Johnson as "America's first taste of the welfare state") came up, Johnson vetoed the latter in February 1866. With a belligerent speech targeting the Radicals on Washington's birthday, in which he specifically named Senator Charles Sumner and Congressman Thaddeus Stevens, even accusing them of a plot to assassinate him, Johnson effectively destroyed any support he had among even moderate Republicans. He vetoed the Civil Rights Bill a month later. Congress overrode the veto—the first time a major piece of legislation had been overridden. Historians have not been kind to Johnson, describing his veto as a "disastrous miscalculation" (Eric Foner in *Reconstruction: America's Unfinished Revolution, 1863–1877*) and a "defining blunder" (David O. Stewart in *Impeached: The Trial of President Andrew Johnson and the Fight for Lincoln's Legacy*). But James G. Randall, one of the true traditionalists in American historiography, has pointed out that between the "nays" and those not voting, the override passed by only a thread. The Civil Rights Act contained virtually the same content as the Fourteenth Amendment, which would be passed in 1868, fundamentally reordering the way people thought of their citizenship. From that point on, one was a citizen of a state because one was first a citizen of the United States, rather than the other way around.

With his political tin ear, Johnson misjudged the reaction to his veto. Seeing that all but Mississippi and Texas had ratified the Thirteenth Amendment, most states had repudiated the Confederate debt, and all had amended their constitutions to abolish slavery, Johnson reasoned that the rebellion was over, and he made a proclamation to that extent in April 1866.

★ ★ ★

A Tale of Two Senates

The Constitution gives the U.S. House of Representatives the authority to impeach a president for "high Crimes and Misdemeanors." Those are not spelled out in the Constitution. So the House must determine whether or not a president's actions (or his failures to act) rise to the level of "high Crimes and Misdemeanors." Once it has made a decision that they do, the issue of whether those actions (or inactions) warrant impeachment is settled. The Senate has no authority whatsoever to determine whether the actions reach the "high Crimes and Misdemeanor" bar: the Senate's only charge, according to the Constitution, is simply to determine whether the president actually committed the acts in question.

Yet twice, the U.S. Senate has exceeded its authority and usurped the powers of the House in the impeachment trials before it. The "moderate" Northern senators felt sorry for Andrew Johnson, and were concerned about damage the removal of a president might do to the nation. *Johnson was obviously and clearly guilty of the articles brought against him.* Indeed he deliberately violated the law to make a point. But the Senate failed, and let an unpopular president remain in office despite his "high Crimes." Contrary to the otherwise sound judgments of Paul Johnson, this was not a "vendetta...the only political consequence" of which was "the discrediting of those who conducted it." As vengeful as the Radicals were, Johnson foolishly and deliberately broke the law, invited conviction, and was saved by the grace of the moderates.

Over 130 years later, President Bill Clinton was also impeached. Again, the House did its constitutional job, determining that he had committed violations of the law amounting to "high Crimes and Misdemeanors" and levying two articles of impeachment against him. The evidence was utterly overwhelming; even his supporters did not deny that he had done what the House accused him of doing. They argued in his defense however, that his misdeeds did not rise to the level of "high Crimes and Misdemeanors." The Senate again completely failed in its responsibilities, though for different reasons: Clinton, unlike Johnson, was popular, and he had strong support from his own party in Congress. But the crimes he had committed included perjuring himself before a federal grand jury and numerous instances of obstruction of justice. (It should be noted that the latter is the same crime that forced Richard Nixon to resign.) Senate Democrats made it absolutely clear they would not vote to convict no matter what Clinton had done. In the case of both articles, the guilty votes never got above fifty (with sixty-seven needed to convict the president and remove him from office). Thus in both presidential impeachments in American history, the Senate has failed to uphold its constitutional duty. It is ironic that in the one case where the Senate would have most certainly found a president guilty of the impeachment articles—Richard Nixon—the president resigned rather than come to trial.

In fact, the South was willing to be reasonable only so long as blacks were not to be citizens; they would be allowed to vote only if federal troops made it impossible to keep them out.

Meanwhile, to exert congressional authority over the Reconstruction process, the Radicals in Congress had created the Joint Committee on Reconstruction in December 1865. Composed of fifteen members from the House and Senate—none from the South—it gathered evidence from the military districts and concluded that rebellion still festered.

Johnson faced an insurmountable disadvantage *vis a vis* Congress: he had no mandate. He had never been elected to the presidency, he could not effectively appeal to the people, and he had no party support. The president was surprised by the insistence of former slaves that they now be given full civil rights, and more than ever he found himself tied to the planter elites. He opposed the Fourteenth Amendment, ending any chance he had of getting support from Congress. With the midterm election of 1866 looming, he hoped to build support for his National Union Party, and in August he began a Northern speaking tour, known as "the Swing around the Circle," designed to help elect candidates that he could work with to Congress. It was a disaster. Johnson was confronted by hecklers, compared himself to Jesus, and even suggested God had intervened to remove Lincoln so that he could inherit the presidency. The backlash gave the Republicans a two-thirds majority in Congress, so that future vetoes would be pointless.

On to Impeachment!

With Johnson's encouragement, Southern leaders refused to ratify the Fourteenth Amendment, infuriating the Radicals even more. In the spring of 1867, they began to enact Congressional Reconstruction by passing the Reconstruction Act, which divided the South into five military districts and guaranteed blacks the right to vote. Johnson predictably vetoed the bill, and Congress predictably overrode the veto. Since the Army now had control of Reconstruction—and Johnson was the commander in chief of the Army—the Radicals further stipulated that all orders to military commanders go through General of the Army Ulysses S. Grant. To keep Johnson from removing their favorite cabinet officials, especially Secretary of War Edwin Stanton, the Radicals passed the Tenure of Office Act. Johnson defied the law, dismissing Stanton and naming General Lorenzo Thomas to the post. He believed the Supreme Court would vindicate him by declaring the Tenure of Office Act unconstitutional.

Rumors were already circulating that the president would be impeached. Now that became reality. Johnson was charged by the House with eleven counts of "high Crimes and Misdemeanors," most specifically dealing with his violation of the Tenure of Office Act and two with denying the authority of Congress and putting the presidency "in disgrace." But the Radicals lacked a sufficient majority to convict in the Senate. When the Senate trial ended in May 1868, seven Republicans agreed to acquit Johnson, leaving the votes against the president at thirty-five—just one short of conviction. That November, Ulysses Grant was elected, and although Johnson would return to Washington, D.C., in 1875 as U.S. Senator Andrew Johnson, most historians consider his a failed presidency. He relished his impeachment battle, but his position lacked any legal or moral high ground. It was a pigheaded and politically suicidal stand. Johnson was saved only by the pity of the Moderate Republicans and their concern over the damage they might do to the office of the presidency.

Andrew Johnson, R.I.P.

There is little positive to say about Johnson, save that he was for the Union. In his effort to ally with the yeoman farmers, he ended up becoming the friend of the planters. His opposition to all aspects of civil rights reform, while understandable given his heritage and the times he lived in, was lamentable in one who aspired to lead the United States.

CHAPTER 18

Ulysses S. Grant, 1869–1877

"It was my fortune, or misfortune, to be called to the office of Chief Executive without any previous political training."

—*Ulysses S. Grant*

President Grant's Constitutional Grade: B

One might guess that Ulysses Grant's approach to government would be like his approach to warfare: "No other terms than unconditional and immediate surrender [are acceptable]." In every battle, he observed, "there comes a time when both sides consider themselves beaten, then he who continues the attack wins." "Nations," he observed, "like individuals, are punished for their transgressions." But Grant's campaign slogan was "Let us have peace." Any Americans thinking they had elected Attila the Hun suddenly found they had put Gandhi in the Oval Office. There was more to Grant than met the eye.

Born in Ohio, Grant was a West Pointer and an Army officer in the Mexican War. Like many great soldiers, he had difficulty in the civilian world. He farmed in Missouri in the 1850s, managing slaves owned by his father-in-law, and himself bought a slave in 1857. But he couldn't make it as a farmer. Forced by the Panic of 1857 to leave his farm (where he and his wife had named the house he built Hardscrabble), Grant freed his slave and began working in a leather shop. Not politically aligned, even though his

Did you know?

★ Grant never voted for a Republican before he was named to a top leadership spot in the Army

★ The *Memoirs* of Ulysses Grant is considered one of the best military memoirs of all time

★ At forty-six, Grant was the youngest president to be elected up to that time

A Book You're Not Supposed to Read

Ulysses S. Grant: A Victor Not a Butcher: The Military Genius of the Man Who Won the Civil War by Edward H. Bonekemper III (Washington, DC: Regnery, 2010).

★ ★ ★

The Last Slaveholder

Through strange fate Ulysses S. Grant, a Northerner and a Republican, was the last president to have been a slaveholder. His wife's family were slave-owners, and he bought his own slave, a thirty-five-year-old man named William Jones, from his father-in-law in 1857. When Grant had to leave farming, he desperately needed the money that a slave would bring on the market, but Grant freed William Jones. No American president after Grant had ever owned slaves.

wife's parents were Republicans, Grant gave his first presidential vote to Democrat James Buchanan on the grounds that the Republicans would provoke secession. He supported Stephen Douglas over Lincoln (but couldn't vote in Illinois).

Drawn back to the Army after secession, Grant was soon promoted to colonel, won fame at the attacks on Forts Henry and Donelson (integrating the ground troops and Union Navy on the rivers with great skill), then commanded the Army of the Tennessee at the battle of Shiloh. After initial setbacks, the Union troops pushed the Confederates out of Tennessee and into Mississippi. About that time, Grant captured the eye of Abraham Lincoln, who sent a spy to check on Grant's drinking. Word returned to Lincoln that Grant never drank while in the field, clearing the way for Lincoln to award him greater authority when the right situation arose. That was the case after Grant took Vicksburg in July 1863. First Lincoln gave him command of the Division of the Mississippi, then, in March 1864, promoted Grant to lieutenant general in command of all Union armies. Grant was the first to fully grasp the necessity of using Northern manpower and materiel to its fullest potential by attacking all the time.

Under Andrew Johnson, Grant was still commander of the Army and as such oversaw enforcement of Reconstruction and protection of the freedmen in the South. He tended to support Johnson's Reconstruction policies, believing, as Lincoln had, that Reconstruction should be carried out as quickly and painlessly as possible. Despite his claim that he only knew two songs, when he was at the White House the night after the Rebel surrender, he had asked the band to play "Dixie," which he called "one of the best tunes I ever heard." But Lincoln's assassination elicited fury from Grant: "We fought [the Rebellion] as war, now we had to fight it as assassination." He blamed himself for not going to Ford's Theater with Lincoln, thinking he could have prevented the president's death. After meeting with Johnson, Grant confided, "I felt that reconstruction had been set back, no telling how far."

Although Grant was initially hesitant to confer voting rights on blacks, by 1867 he had endorsed the concept. Phil Sheridan, assigned to the New Orleans district, had moved to desegregate streetcars and put blacks on juries with Grant's support. As the man at the top, Grant became the face of Reconstruction. After Johnson's disastrous "Swing around the Circle," chants of "Grant, Grant, Grant" began to be heard every time President Johnson showed up in public. Clearly the general would be his successor.

Grant was at his duties, in Washington, when Edwin Stanton informed him that the Republicans had nominated him for the presidency. One observer recalled the moment: "There was no shade of exaltation or agitation on his face, not a flush on his cheek, nor a flash in his eye.... I doubt whether he felt elated...." In his formal letter accepting the nomination,

A Book You're Not Supposed to Read

The Complete Personal Memoirs of Ulysses S. Grant by Ulysses S. Grant (Old Chelsea Station, NY: Cosimo Classics, 2006).

★ ★ ★

Musically Inclined?

Grant once said, "I only know two tunes. One of them is 'Yankee Doodle.' The other isn't."

A Book You're Not Supposed to Read

Grant by Jean Edward Smith (New York: Simon & Schuster, 2002).

he closed with the line he is most remembered for (other than "unconditional surrender")—"Let us have peace."

Grant was elected over New York governor Horatio Seymour in a landslide: 214–80 in the Electoral College, and the popular vote majority was delivered by the freedmen. A two-thirds Republican majority in each house rode into Washington on his coat tails. Grant had run no real campaign. He made almost no speeches, but rather "waged a calculated noncampaign as deliberate as any military action he ever commanded" in the words of Jean Edward Smith. He kept an eye on Seymour, if at a distance—by monitoring telegraphic dispatches at his home in Galena, Illinois. Johnson, in the manner of John Adams, did not attend Grant's inauguration, at which Grant called for ratification of the Fifteenth Amendment (ensuring blacks the right to vote). The new president broke with tradition by keeping his cabinet selections secret until he finally submitted them for confirmation. Among them were several non-politicians, and one appointment, of former Confederate General James Longstreet as Surveyor of Customs for the Port of New Orleans, seemed a singular attempt to heal the nation's wounds.

Despite his "unconditional surrender" moniker, Grant proved acceptable to many Democrats. Even former Rebel cavalry leader Nathan Bedford Forrest said he "cordially and heartily" welcomed the Grant presidency. His "hard money" position—he supported gold, not inflated paper money—reassured businessmen. As Henry Adams wrote, "Grant represented order."

The new president immediately hurled himself into the Reconstruction process, enforcing civil rights laws, lobbying Congress to pass the Fifteenth Amendment, and getting involved in a fight over seating black state legislators in Georgia. He added a new department to the bureaucracy, the Justice Department, and his attorneys general Ebenezer Hoar and Amos Akerman aggressively prosecuted whites who terrorized Southern blacks. He suspended habeas corpus in a section of South Carolina to crush the Ku Klux Klan. But Grant knew that such a large part of America could not be governed permanently by the military.

Grant wanted to reduce the federal government's military footprint in the South—and he thought he could afford to do so. Ratification of the Fourteenth Amendment in 1868 and of the Fifteenth in 1870 allowed many, including Grant, to think that the process of Reconstruction was working. But the U.S. Supreme Court would rule to limit the ambit of the Fourteenth Amendment in the *Slaughter-House Cases* (1873) and to limit federal power in civil rights cases in *Cruikshank* (1875). Meanwhile, the Ku Klux Klan had revived and was engaging in new rounds of terrorism. After Congress passed the Ku Klux Klan Act of 1871, Attorney General Akerman, at Grant's behest, initiated new actions and won some six hundred convictions, and Grant again suspended the writ of habeas corpus. As a result of his actions against the Klan—getting the 1871 Klan bill passed and ordering troops into the field to protect black voters and to "arrest and break up bands of disguised night marauders"—blacks would vote for the president in large numbers in the election of 1872.

Sadly, all of it was futile in the long run. State after state slid back into the control of the "Redeemers," Southern traditionalists who were intent on denying blacks their civil rights. Republican-instituted Southern state governments, which were woefully corrupt, teetered without majority support, relying entirely on the presence of troops. The states were deeply in debt, tangled in bloated bureaucracies, while corruption afflicted every level of government.

Grant, meanwhile, found himself mired in a series of scandals, and while none involved him personally, they did involve men he had appointed. One of the scandals that came closest to Grant involved his secretary Orville Babcock, who became enmeshed in "the Whiskey Ring" (exposed in 1875), which involved embezzlement of tax dollars to funnel them back to distillers, storekeepers, and even agents of the Treasury. The Ring was broken by the Treasury without Grant's knowledge; in fact he wasn't even aware of the investigation. While the president had no knowledge of the illegal activities of Babcock or others involved in the Whiskey Ring, he did, Watergate-style, try to stymie the prosecutions, firing John Henderson, the special prosecutor. (Babcock was later investigated as part of the "Safe Burglary Conspiracy," but the government lacked evidence to convict and he finished his government service as Chief Lighthouse Inspector.)

The Whiskey Ring constituted just one of many black marks against the administration's record. In 1869, for example, Grant's brother-in-law, Abel Corbin, used casual discussions with the president to determine that the U.S. government would not sell gold in the event of an emergency. Armed with that knowledge, Corbin's allies, including "Diamond Jim" Fisk and Jay Gould, in what was called "the Gold Ring," began to drive up the price of gold to corner the market. This attracted the attention of Grant, who contrary to what he had suggested to Corbin, instructed the Treasury Secretary George Boutwell to sell gold, sending the price plummeting downward. Although Fisk and Gould landed on their feet (as they had in several scams before), the incident caused some brokerage houses to fail and brought on a short recession.

The Gold Ring was only the tip of the rotting iceberg. A scandal at the New York Customs House, involving two Grant appointees who had been paid exorbitant sums for storing unclaimed goods in their warehouses, was discovered by Treasury Secretary Boutwell, who instructed another Grant appointee (and future president) Chester A. Arthur to put a stop to the excesses. On top of that, Congress, seeing the other pigs at the trough, voted itself a thirty-three percent salary increase in 1873, as well as bonuses for previous years served, all tacked onto the general appropriations bill. Passed in secret, the bill placed Grant in an impossible position: he could not veto the salary increases and bonuses or else the government would lack the money to continue—bringing on the infamous "government shutdown" often threatened in the late twentieth and twenty-first centuries.

Matters only got worse: Grant's Interior Secretary Columbus Delano had passed out contracts to John Delano, his son, and Grant's own brother, Orvil, for surveying that never took place. The secretary had to resign. Grant's Attorney General George Williams had refused to prosecute a case against the merchant house of Pratt & Boyd—as Congress learned, because of a $30,000 bribe paid to Williams, who also resigned. And yet another scandal was exposed in the Treasury Department in 1874, involving bonuses paid to civilian collectors of revenue: John Sanborn, one of these agents, had indeed collected taxes but also collected $213,000 in commissions on just $420,000 in revenue. Grant replaced Treasury Secretary William Richardson (who had replaced Boutwell), then signed a law abolishing civilian collections of government revenues.

The corruption seemed to have no end. Navy Secretary George Robeson was discovered to have received substantial "gifts" from Alexander Cattell, a grain contractor from New Jersey. Cattell did not lose his job. A postal scandal also was revealed, involving the distribution of lucrative contracts to Star Route postal contractors.

Possibly the worst scandal had actually begun in the Lincoln administration with the creation of Crédit Mobilier as a company to assist in building the Transcontinental Railroad. The Crédit Mobilier scandal involved George Francis and Thomas Durant of the Union Pacific Railroad in a scheme to overcharge the U.S. government for goods and services and benefit from stock deals. The executives of Union Pacific paid Crédit Mobilier, which they also controlled, and then Crédit Mobilier purchased Union Pacific stock at par value and sold the stock on the open market at a profit. Since the continued flow of construction contracts made Crédit Mobilier profitable, its own shares soared, and the stockholders split their winnings with Union Pacific officials, including Durant, and members of Congress who would steer tax money

★ ★ ★

Extermination, Assimilation, or Reservation?

One of Grant's major concerns was about the West, where settlers continued to press into the frontier for farming, mining, and ranching. Little attention had been paid to the Indians during the Civil War, even as atrocities such as the Sand Creek Massacre of 1864 occurred, wiping out Chief Black Kettle's Cheyenne village and killing over 150 Indians... who flew an American flag over their village.

After the Civil War, however, the frontier demanded new attention. In 1866, Chief Red Cloud sent braves to wipe out a group of wood-cutters led by Captain William Fetterman. After Red Cloud's War, the U.S. government evacuated forts along the Bozeman Trail on account of cost, and in 1868, six months before Grant took office, the government and the Sioux signed the Treaty of Fort Laramie, establishing the Sioux Reservation in the Dakota Territory. But once gold was discovered there, Cheyenne and Sioux came into conflict with gold miners and the Army moved in. A major offensive in 1876, involving three large columns to envelop the Sioux and force them back on reservations, resulted in the massacre of Lieutenant Colonel George Armstrong Custer's troops at the Battle of the Little Big Horn. Eventu-

ally, however, Generals Alfred Terry and Nelson Miles forced the Sioux to return to their reservation and ended the war.

Grant was pressured by military men such as William Tecumseh Sherman and Phil Sheridan (who is perpetually misquoted as saying, "The only good Indian is a dead Indian") to define the conflict in military terms—that is, one side wins and the other loses—which would have meant extermination for the Indians. Others, including Indian commissioner Ely Parker, sought to assimilate the Indians by turning them into farmers and "getting the Redskin into trousers." Ultimately, a middle ground—the Reservation System—was developed. It enabled Indians to live on their own (largely poor) land, but to assimilate if they chose. The Navajo in Arizona, for example, control nearly one-quarter of the state's cold and daunting northeast section. Historian Robert Trennert has termed the Reservation System the "Alternative to Extinction." Grant heroically stood against public opinion to protect the Indians, and historians have assessed Grant's policy as "remarkably progressive and humanitarian," for its time.

And today some of the tribes are not just surviving but thriving in the Reservation System. The

Reservation System protected the Indians long enough for valuable deposits, including uranium and oil, to be discovered on their lands, providing them in many cases with good income. Then in the late twentieth century large-scale capitalistic "break-outs" occurred, with the Choctaws in Mississippi starting a major business park and tribes everywhere allowed to build casinos on their land. By the 1990s, something that was utterly unheard of on an Indian reservation just fifty years earlier—"Help Wanted"—could be seen in many Indian-owned casinos. Unemployment on reservations, while still higher than in non-Indian areas, had plummeted dramatically.

toward the fraudulent project. By the time the fraud was discovered in the Grant administration, Congress had paid $94 million to the Union Pacific and $50 million to Crédit Mobilier, of which some $43 million was profit to the two companies. On top of that, the Crédit Mobilier scammers reported only half of their profits. Since, on the surface, the Union Pacific was paying legitimate bills to Crédit Mobilier, the fraud escaped examiners for years. Meanwhile the stock increases made the participants quite wealthy. The scandal finally broke in 1872 when Congressman Oakes Ames attempted to sell other members of Congress shares of Crédit Mobilier at a discounted price (which they could turn around and re-sell at the highly inflated market price). Was it any wonder that politicians who got into office by virtue of the Spoils System—by promising plummy government jobs in exchange for corralling votes—would eventually demand a payday for themselves? Grant looked bad by association, but he was not charged with any specific wrongdoing. James Garfield, who would be elected president in 1880, had received shares.

Though he was somewhat tarnished by the scandals, Grant was not seriously damaged. Running for reelection in 1872 against Horace Greeley, the newspaper editor, Grant hauled in 3.5 million votes to Greeley's 2.8 million and smashed him in the Electoral College 286–66. It was a disastrous time for Greeley, whose wife was dying and who himself died insane just three weeks after the results were announced. The landslide for the Republicans

★ ★ ★

You Can't Tell the Players without a Program

The Reconstruction Era gave us several unique and memorable names for different political groups:

• "Scalawags" were Southerners who cooperated with the Reconstruction governments. Former General James Longstreet, James Alcorn of Mississippi, and Joseph Brown of Georgia were prominent Scalawags.

• "Carpetbaggers" were Northerners who came South with their carpetbags to assist in (and in some cases profit from) Reconstruction. These were the quintessential do-gooders, and included many ex-military men, such as Milton Littlefield and Daniel Henry Cham-

berlain, as well as lawyers such as Albion Tourgee.

• "Stalwarts" were Republicans under "Boss" Roscoe Conkling, who wanted to retain the Spoils System.

• "Half-Breeds," led by Republican James Blaine, who would run for president against Democrat Grover Cleveland in 1884, were reformers who wanted to get rid of many patronage positions and institute civil service reform.

• "Mugwumps" were Republicans who crossed over to support Cleveland in 1884 in opposition to the Stalwarts.

had prevented the nation from having a second dead president in a decade. But after the election the scandals kicked into full gear. The fallout from Crédit Mobilier contributed to some extent to the Panic of 1873, but it was mostly due to the failure of the bank of bond genius Jay Cooke, which started a financial panic followed by factory closures. As in most economic crises, the president was blamed.

Reforming the Reformers

Already a group of reformers had appeared in the Republican Party who were seeking to eliminate the Spoils System as the basis for staffing many parts of the federal government. A group under the leadership of James G.

Blaine of Maine, known as the "Half-Breeds," favored the introduction of a civil service system based on merit. They were opposed by New York "Boss" Roscoe Conkling's "Stalwart" faction, who wanted to maintain the gravy train for appointees. In essence the Half-Breeds were anti-Grant, believing his administration to be guilty of corruption. Before the Half-Breeds could achieve much, though, they were pre-empted by the Democrats, whose victory in the mid-term elections of 1874 allowed them to immediately launch investigations. Meanwhile the Stalwarts found themselves opposing their own party's nominee in 1878, when Republican nominee Rutherford B. Hayes supported civil service reform.

Spoils reform constituted one major issue looming on the horizon; "the money question" was the other. The entire world had begun to suffer a slow deflation after 1865 as gold mines yielded less ore (meaning the reserves for banks such as the Bank of England and the U.S. National Bank system shrank). As their reserves fell, the Banks cut back their note issue, and the money supply shrank. In addition, the government was slowly allowing the "Greenbacks" issued in the Civil War—which had been backed only by the "faith and credit" of the United States—to drain out of the system. Then, in what became known as "the Crime of '73," the Coinage Act of 1873 demonetized silver and put the U.S. on the gold standard. Great cries went out, especially from the West and South, for money. "There is no money in Kansas," one farmer intoned. There were banks, but in the post-war period the money supply depended entirely on National Bank notes printed by the U.S. government and ultimately backed by gold.

Liberal Republicans sought to address the deflation with that time-tested vote-getter, inflation. Introducing some sixty inflation bills in 1874, Congress united behind a "Greenback" bill that would have increased the circulation of un-backed Greenbacks (which had steadily been diminishing since the Civil War to reach a level where the government could redeem the remainder in gold) by some $400 million. Grant, who knew poverty in the

Panic of 1857, who knew personally what it meant to have a business fail, nevertheless knew that inflation was fool's gold. Like strong drink, inflation would bring an immediate surge of euphoria followed by the hangover. Grant had originally intended to sign the bill, but he told his cabinet that the longer he stayed up writing his approval, the more he concluded it was a bad idea, and so he vetoed it. In so doing, Grant set the nation on a course toward "hard money" and solid finances that would culminate in the 1896 victory of William McKinley over "Cross of Gold" orator William Jennings Bryan. "I believe," Grant wrote, "it is in the power of Congress at this session to devise such legislation as will renew confidence, revive all the industries, start us on a career of prosperity to last many years, and to save the credit of the nation and the people." Over the years, Grant came to view this veto as his most important act as president.

Grant also got Congress to pass the Resumption Act, to take effect on January 1, 1879, in which the U.S. government would pay gold for Greenbacks. The Act, harking back to George Washington and Alexander Hamilton's plan to have the nation assume all the debts owed by the states, meant that under Grant the nation would live up to its debts.

Grant had achieved much. In addition to passing the Ku Klux Klan Act, preventing the extermination of the Indians by bartering a peaceful (if not perfect) compromise with them, and putting the U.S. money supply on a sound footing, he reduced the national debt by $50 million by selling gold (and by breaking the Gold Ring). And through his Secretary of State Hamilton Fish, Grant also successfully negotiated claims arising from the depredations of the CSS *Alabama*, a Confederate raiding ship that had been built in England, allowed to put to sea by the British government, and done substantial damages to Union shipping during the war. Under Grant, the United States claimed damages against Great Britain for its willingness to violate neutrality. In the 1871 Treaty of Washington, Fish and British diplomat Sir John Rose agreed to a commission of six

Americans and six English to resolve the claims as well as disputes about fishing in the Atlantic and a still-festering Oregon border claim. A final award of $15.5 million was paid by the British as a result of the negotiations at Geneva, Switzerland, and the U.S. paid England only $1.9 million for illegal Union blockades and some fishing rights. It constituted a major victory for Fish, and Grant.

Another foreign policy issue on Grant's plate was the continuing simmering situation in Cuba, where rebels were battling Spain. Grant's concern was that Britain would worm its way into the hearts and politics of the rebels and emerge with, essentially, a British base ninety miles off the shore of the U.S. Some in the administration were strident in their calls for military intervention, but Fish was cautious about involving the U.S. in a war so soon after the Civil War had ended. For the second time in fifteen years, Spain let it be known that she might entertain a proposal to purchase Cuba; but no sooner did the offer appear than it evaporated. Grant issued a statement saying that while the U.S. was willing to mediate between Spain and Cuba, it definitely would not intervene and insisting "I have not felt justified in recognizing belligerency." He made a second, similar address, quelling bubbling interventionist sentiment in Congress. Likewise, when an opportunity arose to annex the Dominican Republic, Grant and Fish scotched it, although the administration did come to an agreement to acquire rights to a naval base in Santo Domingo for fifteen years at a price of $150,000. But Congress rejected the treaty; they—and the American people—were not in the mood for foreign adventurism.

Grant was willing to consider a third term, but not immediately, and Rutherford B. Hayes was nominated. Grant, as the president and the top Republican in office, had to both deftly negotiate the too-close-to-call Hayes-Tilden election and reassure the country that the government of the United States was not crumbling while the results were sorted out in the aftermath of the hotly contested election. Grant would uphold democracy over party

★ ★ ★
Smoking Will Kill You

In 1884, eight years after he left the presidency, Grant was diagnosed with throat cancer—a disease for which, at the time, no cure existed. He had smoked cigars most of his adult life. But smoking was not even known to be a cancer risk during Grant's lifetime—the Surgeon General's warning would not appear until more than eighty years later.

Having lost his military pension when he became president, Grant had written several articles for *Century Magazine*, for which he received $500 each, then a considerable sum. That magazine's editor, Robert Underwood, suggested that the well-received articles could be the basis for Grant's memoirs. Grant saw the opportunity to leave his wife, Julia, enough money to be comfortable, and began work immediately. Following his diagnosis, he gave his last public speech to ten thousand Civil War veterans in Ocean Grove, New Jersey. When Congress learned of the former president's condition they restored him to the rank of general of the Army, which entitled him to full retirement pay.

Although his health faded steadily, Grant persevered to complete his work, assisted by his son and by Adam Badeau, who had been one of his staff officers. In his final weeks battling cancer and writing furiously, Grant displayed the same great talent and determination he had once shown as a general.

When Mark Twain read Grant's contract proposal from *Century Magazine*, he said it was what "they would have offered to any unknown Comanche Indian." So Twain, through his own firm, offered Grant the seventy-five percent royalty that was standard in the age. Grant said he didn't want to make money if the publisher didn't make any. Twain observed, "This was just like General Grant....It was absolutely impossible for him to entertain for a moment any proposition which might prosper him at the risk of any other man." Eventually Julia was paid almost a half-million dollars for a work that was hailed by no less than Twain as "a literary masterpiece." The project would have made Grant rich, but he died of the cancer before he saw the money. Military historian Mark Perry, the author of *Grant and Twain: The Story of a Friendship That Changed America* (New York: Random House, 2004), has called the *Memoirs* "the most significant work of American non-fiction." *The Personal Memoirs of Ulysses S. Grant* are widely considered some of the finest military memoirs ever, on a plane with Julius Caesar's *Gallic Wars*.

regardless of the cost: "Any outbreak [of violence] would have been suddenly and summarily stopped. If Tilden was declared elected, I intended to hand him over the reins, and see him peacefully installed. I should have treated him as cordially as I did Hayes, for the question of the Presidency was neither personal nor political, but national." When the matter was finally settled in Hayes's favor, Grant stayed for the Inauguration.

He and Julia embarked on a two-and-a-half-year world tour and were greeted as "the Emancipator" in England by thousands of laborers. Emperors shook his hand (Grant was often the first commoner ever to have such an honor). When he returned home, he tried to gain another term as president. But he had missed his moment (a not uncommon flaw in political plans) and his popularity had already peaked. When that run failed, he joined his son in a Wall Street firm that ended up being defrauded by a con man named Ferdinand Ward, and once again, Grant faced poverty. "I don't see how I can ever trust any human being again," he said.

Grant's Constitutionalism

Ulysses Grant had to juggle three sensitive and difficult issues while president: Reconstruction, corruption and the Spoils System, and the end of cheap money. To have resolved even one would have been impressive; two, nearly miraculous. And that's what Grant achieved: he did the best that could be done with Reconstruction as frontier troubles and the Panic of 1873 distracted the public's mind from the South and its problems. His twin triumphs in the Resumption Act and ending inflation were victories of the highest order. And he also kept America from foreign entanglements and adventurism.

That he did not end the Spoils System is understandable, and not just because so many of his crooked subordinates were involved in it. The fact is that the Republican Party as a whole was not yet ready to call a halt to

★ ★ ★
What If?

Grant was a very good president. However, with Grant there is an intriguing "what if" scenario: What if Ulysses S. Grant had been as good a president as he was a general?

the system that had been put in place by Democrat Martin Van Buren half a century earlier and that had only grown in power ever since. For a president whose closest advisors were almost all enmeshed in corruption, Grant's two terms were a roaring success, for he achieved what he did in spite of his appointees and supposed friends. Yet it was beyond his power—or that of any president—to make good on his campaign slogan, "Let us have peace."

CHAPTER 19

Rutherford B. Hayes, 1877–1881

"Let every man, every corporation, and especially let every village, town, and city, every county and State, get out of debt and keep out of debt. It is the debtor that is ruined by hard times."
—*Rutherford B. Hayes*

President Hayes's Constitutional Grade: B+

You have to give Rutherford B. Hayes credit for trying. He vetoed numerous examples of congressional overreach, but he had little of the support that might have enabled him to show what he could really accomplish. He also had the bad luck of being elected in the most seriously contested election since the "Corrupt Bargain" election of 1824, and the first in American history when the winner in the Electoral College was outpolled in the popular vote by the loser. As we shall see, however, that popular vote total was under a cloud of suspicion and controversy, and must be taken with a grain of salt.

Hayes, born in Delaware, Ohio, went to Harvard and practiced law in Ohio, then fought in the Civil War in the Shenandoah campaign, becoming a major general. Even before the war was over he was elected to Congress, where he voted for the Republican Reconstruction acts. In 1867 he was elected governor of Ohio in an extremely close election—a harbinger of things to come. Reelected, Hayes led the Ohio effort to ratify the Fifteenth Amendment, then thought he had retired from politics in 1872. However,

Did you know?

★ Hayes and his family spent an hour in prayer every morning before he began his presidential duties

★ Hayes was elected in what was up to that point the closest election in American history; in electoral votes, it was the closest ever

★ Hayes was one of the first to call for giving American Indians full citizenship

Awaiting the Verdict of History

"I am not liked as a President by the politicians in office, in the press, or in Congress. But I am content to abide the judgment—the sober second thought—of the people."

—Rutherford B. Hayes

in 1876, he was encouraged to run for president, with the backing of influential Ohio Senator John Sherman. Nevertheless, he was opposed by the powerful Republican politician James G. Blaine of Maine. Blaine could not collect enough votes to win, and as delegates drifted away from him, they ended up in Hayes's lap. In the general election, Hayes ran against Samuel Tilden, the governor of New York. Unfortunately for Hayes, Tilden was much like him—a hard-money man who favored civil service reform. Moreover, Hayes had to run against the legacy of corruption left by Ulysses Grant and the lingering effects of the Panic of 1873.

Still, Hayes had the Civil War and Reconstruction on his side; when necessary, the Republicans could still "Wave the Bloody Shirt." Tilden won New York, Connecticut, New Jersey, and the South—with the exception of three protested southern states, Louisiana, South Carolina, and Florida. All three had Reconstruction governments that, lacking the support of whites, teetered on the brink of collapse. There was also a single Oregon elector who was up for grabs—the replacement for an elector there who had been disqualified. The result was that Hayes was twenty electoral votes short of winning, while Tilden was only one vote away. It was the Democrats who had disqualified the Oregon elector, but they agreed to lump his case in with the other disputed delegates (which proved a mistake).

In accordance with the Constitution, the disputed election landed in the lap of the House of Representatives, which created an electoral commission to settle the disputed ballots. The committee was in theory to be balanced: five members of the Senate, five of the House, and five from the

Supreme Court, including seven Republicans, seven Democrats, and one genuinely nonpartisan member—Justice David Davis. But Davis immediately resigned because of his election to the Senate from Illinois and was replaced by Joseph Bradley, a Republican. There was no doubt which way the commission would find. In each case, on an eight to seven vote, the disputed ballots all went in favor of Hayes.

Democrats threatened to filibuster the proceedings, and the South threatened to erupt in a renewed civil war, although already negotiators from Southern states were discussing options with Hayes's representatives. Arthur Colyar, a Memphis lawyer, had suggested Southerners would accept Hayes if certain conditions were met, chief among which were federal support for a transcontinental railroad with its terminus in New Orleans and the removal of federal troops from the Southern states. Hayes told his campaign manager that he would be generous when it came to internal improvements.

A Book You're Not Supposed to Read

From Hayes to McKinley: National Party Politics, 1877–1896 by H. Wayne Morgan (Syracuse, NY: Syracuse University Press, 1969). This should be paired with the somewhat drier book, Paul Kleppner's *The Cross of Culture: A Social Analysis of Midwestern Politics, 1850–1900* (New York: Free Press, 1970), which pinpoints a narrow group of religious voters in the Midwest who, Morgan argues, controlled all the elections during this era. When that group swung to McKinley in 1896 the Republicans gained a dominance that would be unbroken until 1932 except for Woodrow Wilson, who got into office only because his opposition was split between the Republicans under William Howard Taft and the Bull Moose Party under erstwhile Republican Theodore Roosevelt.

On March 2, 1877, the vote count ended with Hayes winning 185–184. Tilden withdrew. The "Compromise of 1877" gave Hayes the presidency—at the cost of the end of Reconstruction. The Republican president-elect had agreed to remove federal troops from the South, and also to appoint a Southern Democrat to his cabinet. Most but not all historians think that Hayes would have won a fair election, taking not only the contested states of Florida, Louisiana, and South Carolina, but

Balancing the Ticket All on His Own

"I am a radical in thought (and principle) and a conservative in method (and conduct)."

—Rutherford B. Hayes

also possibly Mississippi, where blacks had been intimidated from voting by threats of violence.

There were eerie similarities between the razor-thin election of 1877 and the contest of 2000, when George W. Bush narrowly defeated Al Gore Jr. In both cases, Florida was a key to the election (Bush by one count only having a 536 vote margin of victory in that state). In both cases, questions of states' rights arose (in 2000, the issue of when votes are certified by the secretary of State). Both struggles involved civil rights (for blacks in 1877, and for a fair count of votes in 2000, when Gore wanted to recount only certain counties favorable to him as opposed to all Florida counties, which likely would have yielded a bigger margin for Bush). Both times the candidate with the popular majority lost—although both were tainted "majorities." With Tilden, there is no question that blacks were denied the right to vote, and with Bush, the so-called "early call" of Florida—and thus, seemingly, of the election—likely caused many voters across the nation to give up and not vote. (One Democrat strategist thought the "early call" of Florida might have cost Bush fifteen thousand votes in the Florida Panhandle and up to one million votes nationally). In both cases the loser, after some maneuvering and legal posturing, departed from the political landscape (Tilden to Europe and Gore to his environmental pursuits). But the post-election results were quite different: in 1877, having received what they bargained for, the Southern Democrats bided their time until the "Redeemer" governments were again fully in control after federal troops left. But in 2000, the Democrats began an eight-year assault on Bush as "selected, not elected," and—aside from a two-month long rally after 9/11—mercilessly attacked Bush on all fronts, offering him not a smidgen of cooperation.

Hayes impressed everyone with his inaugural address. "There have been few inaugural addresses," wrote *Harper's Weekly*, "superior to that of President Hayes in mingled wisdom, force, and moderation in statement." Two of the new president's most influential appointees—for different reasons—were Carl Schurz in the Interior Department and David Key as postmaster general. Key, of Tennessee, was a Southerner whose appointment fulfilled Hayes's promise to the Democrats. Schurz was entrusted with taking over Indian policy from the Army, thereby saving the plains Indians from destruction. And he also proved to be a capable writer who helped shape the narrative of the Gilded Age. Hayes named Lincoln's secretary, John Hay, as secretary of State, where he proved able. Opposed to the Spoils System, Hayes was beset by a horde of office-seekers. He named black abolitionist editor Frederick Douglass marshal of the District of Columbia.

Meeting the main condition of the Compromise of 1877, withdrawing federal troops from the South, would prove trickier. If he did it too abruptly, he risked the enmity of the congressional Republicans. So first the president sought assurances from Southern leaders, such as South Carolina Governor Wade Hampton, that they would protect the rights of the freedmen. Of course such assurances were given, but the promises broken the moment troops departed. Reconstruction ended in South Carolina on April 10, 1877, and troops were taken from Louisiana's statehouse just over a week later. "Within three days," the *New York Evening Post* predicted, the "Southern question will disappear from federal politics." It may have disappeared for a time, but the issue was far from resolved, and the nation would battle over civil rights for blacks for the next ninety years.

A Book You're Not Supposed to Read

Reunion and Reaction: The Compromise of 1877 and the End of Reconstruction by C. Vann Woodward (New York: Oxford University Press, 1991).

As Hayes slowly attempted to reform the patronage system, he confronted the thorny problem of the New York Custom House, whose collector, Chester A. Arthur, was part of Boss Roscoe Conkling's machine. Arthur was an able man, but associated with the wrong element, and Hayes tasked Hay with heading a commission to look into the New York Custom House. Hay's group reported back that the position should be de-politicized and removed from the hands of Conkling's machine. Hayes sent a letter to all federal officials that no Treasury officer should in any way engage in caucuses, conventions, or even express his views on political questions. Schurz, in the Interior Department, applied Hayes's dictum scrupulously.

His Fraudulency

Before much else could be done, Hayes suffered several blows. Tilden re-emerged to claim the election had been stolen (leading Democrats to refer to Hayes as "His Fraudulency"), then a number of railroad strikes escalated to the point that riots occurred in Chicago, St. Louis, Baltimore, and other transportation hubs. The West Virginia governor called for federal help against the strikers, and Hayes sent in troops first there, then in Maryland and Pennsylvania. Although he understood the strikers' concerns, Hayes thought they had no right to interfere with the nation's commerce in a way that disrupted the lives of millions of people.

As peace returned, so too did Hayes's efforts at spoils reform. This time he took on Conkling directly, demanding the resignations of Arthur and other Conkling men. Eventually, Hayes would remove Arthur when Congress was not in session to oppose him, under the Tenure in Office Act. Boss Roscoe fought back in the New York Republican Convention by calling for a plank in the party's platform that would entitle job-holders to their positions. Hayes allies were defeated in several state elections when Stalwarts were placed in party positions.

These battles were soon made even murkier by the silver issue. As we have seen, international deflation had set in since the Civil War. But silver continued to be mined generously, compared with gold. Pressure mounted on Hayes to inflate the currency by coining more silver and having the government purchase it at a fixed price of 16:1 (sixteen silver dollars for a gold dollar) when in fact the value of silver had dropped—it now took seventeen silver dollars in the market to purchase a gold dollar. This scheme was what economists call a "rent," a special regulation or law that benefits a particular group (in this case, debtors and silver miners). Hayes specifically opposed the Bland-Allison Act of 1878, which would require the government to purchase additional silver, but Congress overrode his objections. Now Hayes was detested not only by the spoilsmen but also by the silverites, and they were not necessarily overlapping groups. Plus, former Radical Republicans disliked his appeasement of the South. In other words, he was rapidly stripping himself of allies.

Hayes's sound money policy proved wise. In January 1879, implementing the Resumption Act from the Grant administration, the Treasury began paying out gold for Greenbacks. There was no rush on the market; only $130,000 of the outstanding $346 million Greenbacks were presented for gold. While that would not end the silver issue—indeed, it would linger until the passage and repeal of the infamous Sherman Silver Purchase Act of 1890—the "money question" subsided temporarily.

Mexico had begun to deteriorate, however. Porfirio Diaz had taken power and chaos had enveloped the northern border of Mexico, where roving bands of marauders repeatedly crossed into the United States. Hayes sent General Edward Ord to police the region, giving him authority to pursue the bandidos into Mexico. The Mexican government responded, secured the border, and in early 1878 the United States recognized the Diaz government. The administration also negotiated a territorial dispute between Argentina and Paraguay, so successfully that Paraguay named a department of that nation after Hayes ("Presidente Hayes").

In his last two years, Hayes continued to battle congressional attempts to end any federal support for black civil rights in the South. Congress tried to prohibit military interference in state elections—Hayes vetoed the bill—then tried to repeal parts of the Enforcement Acts (protecting blacks' rights as citizens)—and Hayes also vetoed that. Congress then, through a judicial appropriations bill, tried to defund compensation for federal officials at election time, prompting yet another successful Hayes veto. Over the next year, he would issue several more vetoes of similar bills, all sustained. But the constant battles left Hayes pining for retirement.

His last two years also saw new Indian troubles, despite Schurz's careful work. Problems with the Ute Indians were dealt with, and Hayes advocated greater education of Indians and eventual U.S. citizenship. Hayes also encountered new challenges with a backlash against immigration on account of the Chinese who had come to build the Transcontinental Railroad. At first they provided a source of cheap labor without taxing the schools or hospitals. But soon their families arrived and coastal states began to enact legislation limiting the number of Chinese who could come into the country. Hayes vetoed an act to limit Chinese immigration in 1878, but could not do anything about a California law a year later that gave the state government the right to decide who could reside in the state. Instead, Hayes obtained a new treaty with China that would allow the U.S. to limit immigration from that nation. (In 1882, President Chester Arthur would sign the Chinese Exclusion Act.)

By the time the election rolled around, Hayes was ready to leave, and he supported John Sherman as his successor. But Sherman failed to muster the votes and a more acceptable nominee, James A. Garfield was selected. However, to balance the ticket, a Stalwart was needed, and Chester A. Arthur, whom Hayes had removed from his New York Custom House job, was tapped. Hayes had no personal beef with Arthur, who was in fact a capable man with a good record. Once Garfield was elected, Hayes worked closely with him to ensure a smooth transfer of power.

Hayes's Legacy

For a man who inherited the office under such a cloud, and during whose tenure in office political squabbles made it difficult to muster overwhelming support for anything, Hayes had a respectable measure of success. He used his constitutional powers to continue civil rights protections in the South as far as possible; his appointment of Schurz advanced Indian policy as much as was feasible; and his foreign policy was solid if not splashy. Hayes's stance on hard money proved sound. His tough line with Mexico was laudable. It is hard to imagine anyone in his circumstances accomplishing more.

CHAPTER 20

James A. Garfield, March 1881–September 19, 1881

"The President is the last person in the world to know what the people really want or think."
—*James A. Garfield*

President Garfield's Constitutional Grade: N/A

While James A. Garfield may not have had the shortest tenure as president, he nevertheless was barely settled in the office when he was assassinated by Charles Guiteau, a fanatical disaffected job-seeker. In death, Garfield achieved what he might not have had he served out his term: passage of the Pendleton Act to reform the civil service in the United States.

Garfield, an Ohioan like Hayes, was born in a log cabin and grew up in the northwestern part of the state, and like Johnson and Grant, he experienced poverty. By his teen years he was working on boats on Ohio's canals before a school teacher saw his potential and arranged for him to get an education. Garfield became a professor of ancient languages and literature at Hiram College, then the school's president at age twenty-five, then a Republican state senator before joining the Union Army and becoming a major general at age thirty-one. The following year he was elected to the U.S. House of Representatives and emerged as a leading Republican in

Did you know?

★ James Garfield was the last president born in a log cabin

★ He was nominated for president on the thirty-sixth ballot at the 1880 Republican Convention

★ Garfield didn't die until more than two months after he was shot

Striking a Fine Balance

"I am trying to do two things: dare to be a radical and not a fool, which is a matter of no small difficulty."

"The Law of my life [is] never to ask for an office."

"The truth will make you free—but first it will make you miserable."

—James Garfield

Congress. He had been an abolitionist before the war, and afterward he was a hard-money man.

Garfield thought money—more than his congressional pay—should come with political positions, and as a member of the powerful Appropriations Committee he accepted fees and kickbacks for directing work to certain contractors. He associated with Oakes Ames, the representative at the center of the Crédit Mobilier scandal. Garfield accepted—but never actually took possession of—stock for greasing the wheels for the deeply corrupt company, which had just come under federal investigation. In short, Garfield personally epitomized the struggle over patronage and spoils. He tried to stay out of the battle between the Half-Breeds (the reformers under James Blaine) and the Stalwarts (those followers of Roscoe Conkling who wanted to maintain the spoils system).

Garfield was not supposed to draw any votes at the 1880 Republican Convention; in fact John Sherman, a fellow Ohioan, asked Garfield to give his nominating speech. Yet neither Sherman nor Ulysses Grant nor Blaine had a commanding majority in the early votes, and some thirty-three ballots taken over two days resulted in little change. Finally, on the thirty-fourth ballot, Garfield began to gather some support. Then, by the thirty-sixth ballot, the supporters of Grant and Sherman—seeing the hopelessness of their position—went over to Garfield. He said that getting the nomination "unsought and unexpected like this will be the crowning gratification of my life." Given how long he had to live, that prediction wasn't far off.

Like most other politicians of his era, Garfield stayed home during the campaign, only once traveling to New York City. Facing Civil War hero

Winfield Scott Hancock in the general election, he won a solid victory in the Electoral College (214–155) but only a tiny majority in the popular vote (the margin was 9,464 out of 9 million votes cast). He "assum[ed] the office with a kind of dread," and left Ohio for Washington, D.C., with feelings similar to those with which he had left for the Civil War.

He immediately found himself at odds with Conkling, having made his first appointments to the reformers. On the other hand he did eventually name two Stalwarts to his cabinet (one of them Abraham Lincoln's son Robert Todd Lincoln, appointed as secretary of War). Then again he appointed a Conkling enemy to the New York Custom House, a key political plum. He even maneuvered Conkling and his ally Thomas Pratt, a New York state senator, into resigning their positions—in the belief that the legislature would immediately return them to office. That proved a miscalculation on their part, and so Garfield had won a crucial victory over his most significant foes.

He intended to increase trade with Latin America and to enhance relations with countries in the southern hemisphere. To that end, he authorized Blaine to set up a Pan-American Conference in 1882. He also wished to review the Clayton-Bulwer Treaty so as to allow the United States to build a canal through the Panama region, independent of the British. And he charged Navy Secretary William Hunt with an investigation of the Navy, with an eye toward building up America's naval power.

Garfield also put into motion reforms in the Post Office, which had suffered a scandal involving kickbacks on inflated contracts for delivery of the mail on the Western "Star Routes." He appointed Frederick Douglass as the recorder of deeds in Washington, D.C., and made several other appointments of African Americans.

Lucretia Garfield, James's wife, had contracted malaria in May of 1881 and gone to New Jersey to convalesce, leaving Garfield alone in the White House. Energized by her return in June, and encouraged by the defeat of

★ ★ ★

The Medical Evidence

A debate continues to the present about Garfield's medical treatment. Some critics maintain that with today's medical practices, the bullet would have been found and Garfield might have been up and about in weeks. Others are not so sure. They point to the fact that serious infection was not Garfield's only problem: the bullet likely damaged internal organs and spread bone chips around. To compound his unhealthy situation, Garfield lost his appetite. At least one doctor claims starvation played a part in his demise.

Conkling, Garfield planned a speaking tour in New England. On July 2, the president was talking with Blaine in the Baltimore train station in preparation for beginning his trip when Charles Guiteau, a lunatic who saw himself as breaking the logjam in Washington, shot Garfield twice. One shot caused a minor arm wound, but the other a serious wound to the back.

In fact, Guiteau had already met with Garfield once about a job and the president had referred him to Blaine, in whose office he became a regular. Blaine had brushed him off, seeing him as clearly incompetent, but Guiteau thought he was being summarily turned down because he was a Stalwart. He had fantasized about killing Garfield and believed that allowing Vice President Chester Arthur to become president would end all struggles within the Republican Party. After shooting the president, Guiteau freely announced, "I did it. I will go to jail for it. I am a Stalwart and Arthur will be President."

Garfield got immediate medical attention. That was the good news. The bad news was that that attention consisted of doctors not yet versed in Joseph Lister's sterilizing techniques, probing the wound with their unsterilized fingers to find the bullet. They could not. Even Alexander Graham Bell, who examined him with a new (but still primitive) metal detector, could not locate the bullet. From July to September Garfield's recovery ebbed and flowed. At times it looked like he would pull through—he was relocated to a seaside mansion near Elberon, New Jersey, where he developed pneumonia and heart pains. On September 19, 1881, James A. Garfield died, the second president in less than twenty years to be felled by an assassin. Guiteau had his wish: Chester Arthur was president. But Guiteau was executed.

The Verdict of History

Like William Henry Harrison, James Garfield was in office too short a time for his presidency to earn a grade. Although he generally favored reform, his concern with appeasing all the warring factions might well have kept him from achieving much in that regard. The naval buildup he contemplated would eventually begin in earnest with Benjamin Harrison. But a final positive assessment of Garfield can only be based on the most generous reading of his stated intentions—and even those were often contradictory.

CHAPTER 21

Chester A. Arthur, September 19, 1881–1885

"I may be president of the United States, but my private life is nobody's damned business."
—*Chester A. Arthur*

President Arthur's Constitutional Grade: B

It is perhaps unsurprising that Chester A. Arthur—a man permanently, if somewhat unfairly, associated with spoils and patronage—was with Boss Roscoe Conkling when a telegram arrived to announce that James Garfield had been shot. They both thought Garfield would not survive the night, and there was worse news to come: Arthur learned that the assassin had mentioned his own elevation to the presidency as the motivation for his heinous act. The vice president went to Washington briefly and then, as Garfield struggled to recover, went back to New York—looking "devastated" according to eyewitnesses. Arthur immediately became an object of sympathy, perhaps as much as the dying president. He was widely seen as not up for the job. The *New York Times* called him "about the last man who would be considered eligible" for the presidency, intoning that "no holder of that office has ever made it so plainly subordinate to his self-interest as a politician and narrowness as a partisan." *Harper's* noted that future nominating conventions would likely take the vice presidential position more seriously.

Did you know?

★ Until he became vice president, Chester Arthur had virtually no experience in national politics

★ Arthur did not move into the White House for three months, claiming the previous occupants had left it a mess

★ One job-seeker walked into President Arthur's office at the White House, put his feet up on the desk, and called him "Chet"

A Book You're Not Supposed to Read

The Presidencies of James A. Garfield and Chester A. Arthur by Justus Doenecke (Lawrence, KS: University of Kansas Press, 1981).

Arthur arrived in Washington on September 21 to begin what one biographer described as a "brief and joyless" transition. There was a different feel, however, from the mood after the assassination of Lincoln. The nation did not believe that they had lost a giant. And the fact that Garfield had lingered for months had allowed the nation more time to prepare.

Arthur was certainly well versed in politics, in fundraising, and in administration. His successful service as quartermaster in the Union Army was no small achievement, and no taint of corruption had attached to him in that job. The New York Custom House was another story, with the Republican Boss Conkling sponsoring him for the remunerative job of collector there, and Arthur strong-arming Custom House employees to make "voluntary" contributions to the Republicans. As we have seen, when Rutherford B. Hayes won the presidency and began a systematic reform of the civil service, he targeted Arthur's position (and Conkling's power). First, in 1877, Hayes submitted the name of Theodore Roosevelt Sr. (father of the future president) for the position to the Senate, but it rejected the nomination. Then, the next year, Hayes flat out removed Arthur, and the Senate reluctantly approved Roosevelt. A loyal soldier, Arthur continued to raise money for Republicans in New York until he was added as a "Stalwart" to balance reformer James Garfield on the national ticket.

As Arthur biographer Zachary Karabell has noted, "No one knew what direction the Arthur administration would take, not even Arthur himself." In fact, Arthur's presidency—like that of Hayes not long before him—was a case of a man known as a partisan hack doing his best to fashion a nonpartisan presidency. Contrary to expectations, Arthur did not cater to Conkling and the Stalwarts. Blaine resigned and, with Conkling already ousted by the New York party, Arthur found the two most prominent personalities who could oppose him—or seek to control him—out of the picture. Even so, the patronage demands by then were nearly impossible to support. Arthur spent three days a week simply conducting interviews for government jobs.

In his Inaugural, Arthur gave a brief review of the nation's status—the United States had grown to a population of thirty million, and while still paying off the Civil War debt, was taking in more in revenue than it paid out. Then he suggested that Congress establish a civil service exam—which would effectively end the spoils system. Instead of being a political reward, government jobs would now be doled out on the basis of merit. That was an astonishing proposal for a politician as closely identified with patronage and spoils as Arthur was.

The new president undertook a thorough redecoration of the White House ("I will not live in that house," he had said, pointing out that it had become shabby under the care of its recent occupants.) He brought in Louis Tiffany to oversee the renovation, and the decorator—who had not yet become famous for his lamps—revamped the White House in high style, putting in, among other things, a fifty-foot-tall glass screen. Not until Theodore Roosevelt forty years later did another occupant substantially renovate the executive mansion.

Arthur's appointees were unremarkable, save for William Chandler, who replaced William Hunt at the Navy Department. Both men were dedicated to expanding the size and quality of the U.S. Navy, which had fallen into obsolescence after the Civil War. (There was even a joke in the British play *The Canterville Ghost* in which the ghost replies to a character who claims that America had no ruins or curiosities, "You have your Navy and your manners.")

On the reform of the civil service, Arthur worked with Democratic Senator George Pendleton, who devised a plan to select government employees

★ ★ ★

How "Reform" Serves the Reformers

The Pendleton Act was supposed to cure the corruption of presidents giving jobs to cronies. They certainly were doing that. This "reform" bill, however, constituted just one more example of how the public should always be concerned when a politician wants to "reform" anything. Usually he or she is the one benefitting from the reform.

That was the case with the Pendleton Civil Service Act. It certainly was unfair that able, well-meaning federal employees got canned just because someone of a different party—or even a different faction of their own party—came into office. No doubt there were outrages in both Democrat and Republican administrations. But the abuses were contained, the harms minimal, and the costs to American government negligible. Some have viewed the Pendleton Act as a democratic measure that opened up bureaucratic offices to everyone. Its fundamental assumption, however—that "reform" could achieve perfection in this world—became a key component of the new Progressive agenda. Usually, these "reforms" had similar results—the "reformers" ended up with more power.

After Pendleton, special interest groups had more influence than ever and presidential candidates less discretion than ever. There is no doubt that the pressure on presidents to deal with hundreds of job-seekers was getting to be an impossible burden. No one *personally* knows two thousand people they can trust—let alone, is capable of evaluating their skills for a particular post. But once federal hiring was no longer the responsibility of one man, the presidents lost their control over the nation's budgets along with their ability to grant patronage plums.

In the spoils system, there was necessarily a political competition between the two parties to give away jobs to political allies who had made themselves useful in the election. But with the end of the spoils system, it was not just the federal bureaucracy up for grabs, but the whole economy. Candidate A would promise a program that would provide, say, New York with a thousand jobs, so that Candidate B was forced to promise a program that would provide two thousand. Such a giveaway mentality was on full display in the Democratic primary debates in 2016 between Hillary Clinton and Bernie Sanders, where each outdid the other in promising the creation of jobs by the federal government.

on merit. The Pendleton bill passed in 1882 and the first civil service rules were established a year later.

Over the long haul, the end of the spoils system greatly benefitted the presidents. It had become utterly impossible to conduct business for at least the first six months in office while attending to job-seekers. And the Garfield assassination showed that it was becoming potentially dangerous to choose one candidate over another. But the Pendleton Act did not solve the larger problem of the growth of government as a result of election promises. Quite the contrary. Once presidents could no longer hand out a few hundred specific jobs, elections hinged on making promises to much larger, more generic bodies that soon became known as "interest groups." Indeed, Pendleton acted like a booster rocket to the expansion of government, even though at first it only applied to about ten percent of federal jobs. It marked a fundamental transformation in how candidates appealed for votes. No one cared about a few hundred postmaster jobs across the country any longer, when a candidate could make a speech in, say, Savannah, Georgia, promising a new naval base, and the sounds of the cash registers could be heard before the office-seeker left the stage. Martin Van Buren's system not only failed to prevent a Civil War, but left a permanent flaw in the American political system. After 1883, federal candidates at all levels had to promise economic benefits (that is, jobs) to larger and larger "special interests."

When it came to government finance, Arthur opposed the excise taxes left over from the Civil War, and named a commission to review the nation's tariffs. That commission, though it was dominated by the usually protectionist Republicans, called for reducing tariffs by a fifth or a quarter, but the House of Representatives wasn't willing to go below a 10 percent protective tariff, then further negotiations with the Senate chopped the reduction to a mere 1.4 percent. At the same time, Congress passed a $19 million rivers and harbors act, which Arthur vetoed, insisting the funds were "not for the common defense or general welfare, and...do not promote commerce among the states." Although Congress overrode his veto, Arthur had made a principled stand.

In foreign affairs, Arthur found Congress deaf to his calls to expand trade with Santo Domingo, the Kingdom of Hawaii, and other nations in the Western hemisphere. He signed the Immigration Act of 1882, which placed a $.50 tax on all immigrants and excluded anyone who might need public assistance. The president had already reluctantly signed the Chinese Exclusion Act earlier that same year. The nation had allowed unrestricted Chinese immigration since the 1860s, largely to build the railroads, but in 1879, after the Panic of 1873 had led to widespread unemployment, Congress tried to stop Chinese immigration with the Chinese Exclusion Act, vetoed by Rutherford B. Hayes. A similar bill with a twenty-year immigration ban came before Arthur, and he vetoed it too. Finally, a compromise bill, putting a ten-year ban on Chinese immigration, passed in 1882 and Arthur signed that, knowing that if he didn't Congress could override his veto.

The president began to notice health problems and was diagnosed with Bright's disease, a kidney disorder that affects the body's ability to process foods, leading to buildups of toxins. At the time there was no cure, and sooner or later it would be debilitating. Bright's brings on extreme fatigue, but sick or well, Arthur was well known for working short hours. He found the White House depressing, had few friends in Congress, and presided over a badly divided party. Worse, the Republicans took a beating in the 1882 mid-term elections, in which Democrats gained a 2:1 majority in the House (though the GOP held the Senate). Some blamed Arthur for his party's condition.

A, B, C, D, Can You Build a Ship for Me?

Still, despite the Democrats' opposition, Arthur's Navy Secretary William Chandler managed to get the "ABCD" ships (the so-called "Protected Cruisers," named the *Atlanta, Boston, Chicago,* and *Dolphin*) funded. Those ships would not finally enter service until 1889, but the tide had turned toward rebuilding the navy. Soon another president, Benjamin Harrison, would reinvigorate many naval construction programs.

Following in the footsteps of Hayes, Arthur favored an allotment system for individual Indians and an end to the Reservation System. On the advice of his Interior secretary, Henry Teller, he opened up the Crow Creek Reservation in the Dakotas to white settlement, giving settlers title to many Indian lands. (Grover Cleveland, Arthur's successor, would revoke these titles in a few months.)

Although he considered a run for reelection in 1884, Arthur faced not only his health problems but also the factionalism within the Republican Party itself. Arthur made a token effort, but lost to James Blaine, who in turn lost to the Democrat, Grover Cleveland. After stepping down in 1885, Arthur returned to New York City and died the following year. Had he won the nomination and the presidency again, Arthur would have left America with a legacy of two dead presidents in five years, and three in fifteen.

Chester Arthur's Solid Term

It might be said of Arthur that he did a great deal with little, and that he accomplished a lot in a short time. Beginning the rebuilding of the U.S. Navy was alone an important achievement. The Pendleton Act was a blow to the heart of the spoils system—though, as we have seen, the paradoxical long-term result would be the growth of government. In any case, the spoils beast was more than a shortened single term could handle; it would take a determined Grover Cleveland to make serious inroads into government growth and abuse.

CHAPTER 22

Grover Cleveland, 1885–1889, 1893–1897

"In the scheme of our national government, the presidency is preeminently the people's office."
—*Grover Cleveland*

President Cleveland's Constitutional Grade: B+

Easily the most underappreciated president of the nineteenth century, and one of the top five presidents of all time (behind only Washington, Lincoln, Reagan, and Calvin Coolidge), Grover Cleveland was the first president born in New Jersey. His family did not stay there long, moving to New York when Cleveland was four. (He is often mistakenly said to be from New York.) Cleveland studied law and was admitted to the New York bar in 1859.

Cleveland gained a reputation as an excellent lawyer and was elected sheriff of Erie County as a Democrat. He did not hesitate to hang murderers himself. He agreed to run for mayor of Buffalo after insisting that some of the corrupt career politicians be removed. As mayor, Cleveland got his first taste of fighting corruption and spoils when the Common Council gave a street-cleaning contract to the highest bidder (their friends) rather than the lowest. Cleveland exposed the graft and made the council take the lowest bid. This attracted the attention of the state Democrat Party members, who ran Cleveland for governor in 1882. As governor he stood firm against a

Did you know?

★ Grover Cleveland was the first Democrat elected president after the Civil War

★ He was the only president whose wedding took place in the White House

★ Vetoing a farm relief bill, President Cleveland suggested that Congress take up a collection for the farmers out of their own pockets

★ He remains the only president to have lost his reelection bid but then returned to the presidency in a subsequent election

A Book You're Not Supposed to Read

Grover Cleveland: A Study in Character by Alyn Brodsky (New York: Truman Talley Books, 2000).

railroad rate reduction aimed at railroad tycoon Jay Gould, who, for a change, had acted entirely within the law, raising rates to make the railroad profitable. Cleveland's veto of the rate reduction was upheld.

When the Republicans nominated James Blaine to replace the ailing Chester Arthur, the Democrats gravitated to Samuel Tilden, who declined to run. Cleveland won the support of the "Mugwumps," reform-minded Republicans who opposed Blaine. (Carl Schurz, who had been a valuable friend to the Indians as Interior secretary in the Hayes administration, was a Mugwump.) And Cleveland had all the right enemies—especially Tammany Hall, the epicenter of corruption in New York that was now in decline after its heyday under Boss Tweed. Ultimately, even the Tammany Hall spoilsmen decided they were better off with a Democrat than with Blaine.

During the campaign, Cleveland faced the charge that he had had an illegitimate child with Maria Halpin. Charles Dana, of the *New York Sun*, referred to Cleveland as a "coarse debaucher." Cleveland had engaged in an affair with Halpin, as had his business partner Oscar Folsom. There was no proving the paternity of the child, but Cleveland, as the only bachelor among any of the men who could have fathered the child, assumed responsibility and was subject to chants of "Ma, Ma, where's my Pa?" Cleveland's hiring of a substitute to fight in his place in the Civil War—he would be the only president to have done so—soon became an issue as well.

It was a sign of the times—the "Gilded Age"—that such character deficiencies could be ignored by the electorate. Only a handful of elected presidents up to this point had not served in the military: the two Adamses, who had both been involved in diplomacy during wartime, Jefferson, who

★ ★ ★

Gimme That Old Time Religion

Grover Cleveland, like many other presidents, has been wrongly described as a deist. He was nothing of the sort. Cleveland believed in a simple Christianity, in reaction against the "higher critical" movement of the day. "The Bible is good enough for me: just the old book under which I was brought up," he said. Moreover, on the subject of the United States and its religion, he sounded more like John Adams than Thomas Jefferson:

> [The United States] would not be in existence and it could not hope to live if it were not Christian in every fiber. That is what has made [America] and what will save it in all its perils. Whenever we have departed from this conception of life and thought,

nationality has suffered, character has declined, and difficulties have increased. While slavery remained, we could not hope to fully work out Christian ideals, and whenever we overlook the fact that "righteousness exalteth a nation" we pay the penalty.

Cleveland, a staunch Presbyterian, believed in fellowship across denominations and wanted to reunite the northern and southern wings of the Presbyterian church, which had split because of the Civil War. Although he believed people of any religion should be able to come to America, he predicted that "we shall assimilate them to our religion by demonstrating—as Christianity at its best estate has always done—its superiority and power."

was serving as governor during the Revolution, Martin Van Buren, and Andrew Johnson. Only Jefferson had ever been accused of an extra-marital affair. But Cleveland survived both charges, as well as campaign attacks denouncing the Democrats as the party of "Rum, Romanism, and Rebellion" (that is, booze, the Catholic Church, and the Confederacy). Cleveland won the Electoral College 219–182 by taking a very slim popular vote majority and closely winning four swing states (he carried New York by only 1200 votes). He was the first Democratic president elected since James Buchanan, before the Civil War.

An Article You're Not Supposed to Read

"Grover Cleveland: The Veto President" by Burton Folsom Jr., *The Freeman* (August 2004): 34–35.

Once in office, Cleveland faced the same thing his predecessors had grappled with—the crushing burden of dealing with political office-seekers. Despite the Pendleton Act, he still had to fill 126,000 jobs through presidential appointment. At the same time, the government was still small enough that he greeted people in his office on a regular basis and ran the White House with a staff of a dozen. Some of his friends were denied jobs because he didn't want it to seem that New York was favored. His cabinet appointees included William Whitney, a solid attorney, as Navy secretary, and Thomas Bayard of Delaware as the secretary of State.

It can be argued that Grover Cleveland was the first president, ever, to confront the growing size of government and try to control it. Aside from the civil service, the largest growth sector in the federal government was military pensions, supported by the Grand Army of the Republic, which acted as a military lobbying organization. The Grand Army was a powerful four-hundred-thousand-member-group that sought to ensure that every widow, orphan, and dependent parent of a soldier received assistance. While the number of such cases should have steadily decreased after the war as veterans and their widows died off, Cleveland found that they had increased by five hundred percent. Cleveland signed more assistance bills than he vetoed, but he set himself to stop abuses.

He cut the number of pensioners, but carefully reviewed every case personally. He found ridiculous cases—men who had sustained injuries *after* the war and a widow whose husband fell off a ladder in 1881. The GAR, once the voice of the Union Army, even toyed with the notion of allowing *Confederate* soldiers to get pensions. Senator Henry Blair of New

Hampshire introduced a bill to provide a pension to any veteran disabled for any reason, including old age!

Cleveland vetoed the Blair bill. "I have considered the pension list of the republic a roll of honor," he said, and there was little honor in what Blair proposed. Indeed, Cleveland found his voice with the veto pen, vetoing 414 bills in his first term alone. "Though the people support the government," he observed, "the government should not support the people."

A Sinking Ship?

"The ship of democracy, which has weathered all storms, may sink through the mutiny of those on board."

—Grover Cleveland

On the race issue, Cleveland supported the new constitutional rights for freedmen, but he was a segregationist, believing blacks were still behind whites as a result of their period in bondage. He became acquaintances with the abolitionist black editor Frederick Douglass and invited him to the White House on several occasions. Cleveland extended every courtesy to Douglass and his wife, to the consternation of many whites present. "This manly defiance," Douglass noted, "of a malignant and time-honored prejudice, won my respect for the courage of Mr. Cleveland." Douglass noted that in the election he had worked to defeat Cleveland, who kept Douglass in office as the District of Columbia's Recorder of Deeds despite "fierce and bitter reproaches" from other Democrats.

A president given to close reading of the law and the Constitution, Cleveland defied Congress on the Tenure of Office Act when he removed the U.S. Attorney from Alabama's southern district—a Republican named George Duskin—and replaced him with Democrat John Burnett. When the Senate demanded documents from the attorney general on both men, Cleveland had him hand over documents on Duskin but not Burnett, insisting that the 1867 Tenure of Office Act had been superseded in 1869 by a law amending it. The Senate censured the attorney general, but Duskin was out and Burnett was in.

★ ★ ★
Love Is in the Air

As the administrator of the estate of his deceased law partner, Oscar Folsom, Cleveland came to know Folsom's widow and his daughter, Frances. By the time he was in office, Frances had grown up to be a desirable young woman, and Cleveland proposed in 1885. The two were married in the Blue Room of the White House in 1886 in a ceremony in which Captain John Philip Sousa led the Marine Band in playing the wedding march. Frances became the youngest first lady in history and only the second to have graduated from college.

The Union Label

Labor unrest drew Cleveland's attention in 1885 when the Knights of Labor launched a series of nation-wide strikes and engaged in violence against railroads. Although Cleveland set up a board to review the circumstances, little was done. Then came the Haymarket Riot. In May of 1886, anarchists led a protest against the McCormick Harvesting Machine Company at Haymarket Square in Chicago, and a bomb was thrown into the ranks of policemen, killing several. Organizers were rounded up and tried, and four of them were hanged for their role in the bombing. In 1887 these concerns would contribute to the passage of the Interstate Commerce Act, which Cleveland signed.

Perhaps Cleveland's most memorable statement on limited government came in 1887 when Congress passed the Texas Seed Bill to extend relief to drought-ridden Texas farmers. This legislation would have provided $10,000 directly to farmers to purchase new seed. But Cleveland vetoed it, citing the Constitution in rejecting it: "I can find no warrant for such appropriation in the Constitution; and I do not believe that the power and duty of the General Government ought to be extended to the relief of individual suffering...." He urged Congress to take up a collection, in which the wealthy members could have easily raised the money. Congress declined to do so.

Despite a number of successes, Cleveland lost his bid for reelection to Benjamin Harrison, the grandson of former president William Henry Harrison. Cleveland's first election had been close, and his reelection bid turned on the state of New York, where Cleveland had engaged in personal squabbles with David Hill, New York's governor. The president had not supported his reelection, and Hill got his revenge by denying Cleveland support in the presidential election. The president lost New York by fourteen thousand votes, and although Cleveland won the overall popular vote, he lost the Electoral College 233–168. He

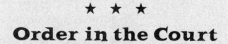

★ ★ ★
Order in the Court
Cleveland appointed two strict constitutionalists to the Supreme Court, Lucius Lamar and Melville Fuller.

was out, and had no plans to return. But as Mrs. Cleveland prepared to leave the White House, she instructed the staff to take care of things, for she planned to return in four years. Cleveland himself, however, made no such predictions.

In the interregnum under Harrison, Congress passed the high, protectionist McKinley Tariff, which caused prices to rise. (During the campaign, the Democrat Cleveland had argued for lowering tariffs, while the Republican Harrison favored higher ones.) The addition of several Western states enabled the powerful "free silver" lobby, which had not been satisfied by the Bland-Allison Act of 1878, to push through the Sherman Silver Purchase Act in 1890. Easily one of the worst pieces of legislation in American history, the Silver Purchase Act required the government to purchase and mint 4.5 million ounces of silver a month (twice what Bland-Allison had required), and it fixed the price of the ratio of silver to gold at 16 ½ to 1, which was half a dollar higher than the actual market price of 17 to 1, though not as high as the 16 to 1 price demanded by the silverites. Indeed, the "free silver" movement in the defining 1896 election would campaign on a slogan that today would seem utterly incomprehensible—not to mention, completely un-motivating—"Free and Unlimited Coinage of Silver at 16 to 1." Technically the silver was purchased with paper money, but that money was immediately convertible into gold or silver—except that silver was over-valued and gold, under-valued. So a speculator could exchange 16.5 silver dollars for a gold dollar, and then sell the gold dollar at the market price for seventeen silver dollars, making a tidy profit—then repeat the transaction. As foreign speculators began to exchange silver for gold, American gold flowed out of the country as cheaper silver flowed in. It was a classic dramatization of Gresham's Law: "Bad Money Drives Out Good."

By 1892, Harrison, now saddled with a listing economy, ran for reelection. Cleveland was persuaded to run again, and this time David Hill supported him. Both Cleveland and Harrison found themselves confronting a powerful third party candidate, James Weaver, an Iowa attorney who ran as a Populist, favoring radical inflation and outright government ownership of the railroads. Both labor unrest and Populist appeal were intensifying, with hotspots of labor violence including the Homestead Strike at the Carnegie steel works in Homestead, Pennsylvania, the Coeur d'Alene, Idaho, silver mine seizure—which Harrison sent troops to put down—and the Buffalo railroad strikes—which also required federal troops. Harrison became the object of labor criticism during these outbreaks.

Hard Money

Cleveland was no ordinary Democrat. He was a "hard money" man, meaning he backed the gold standard, something that was usually associated with the Republicans. With Weaver splitting inflationist votes off from the Republicans, Cleveland regained the presidency with 277 electoral votes to Harrison's 145, a margin of victory larger than his loss four years earlier. (Cleveland again out-polled Harrison in the popular vote, though this time Weaver siphoned off one million votes.) Cleveland thus became the first (and, to this day, only) president to lose an election, then return to the presidency.

Thanks to the Sherman Silver Purchase Act, banks were already in a weakened state, with their gold reserves flowing out of the country. Railroad stock prices started to fall in early February, and by the time Cleveland took office in March, a full panic was under way. With the arbitragers working overtime to take advantage of the Sherman overvaluation of silver, the government's gold stocks fell as well, dropping to half what Cleveland had had during his first term. Some urged Cleveland to call a special session of Congress to repeal the Sherman Act, but before he could do that, he saw a doctor about a painful spot in his mouth. Tests proved he had a tumor in his mouth, but news that the president was being operated on might further exacerbate the economic crisis.

Cleveland opted for a secret operation on the *Oneida*, the yacht belonging to a friend. Part of Cleveland's left jaw was removed and replaced by a prosthesis so life-like few noticed he had it. The surgery took place on June 30, and Cleveland was back in public on July 5. But a follow-up examination showed more tissue needed to be removed. Once again, Cleveland recovered quickly, and the public did not find out about the secret surgery until 1917.

Meanwhile the economy had continued to sink. While Cleveland was not opposed to having silver coins in circulation, he insisted the U.S. remain on the gold standard. He called Congress into a special session in August to repeal the Sherman Silver Purchase Act. Even the repeal, however, did not fully solve the problem, as the damage was deep. Once confidence in American dollars had been shaken, foreign investors continued to convert paper money into gold, which fled the country. Banker J. P. Morgan visited Cleveland and proposed a solution: he and a group of other bankers would sell the government 3.5 million ounces of gold (worth $65.1 million) at a discount of about $.80 an ounce, and receive government bonds totaling $62.3 million in return. The bonds would pay four percent interest and be convertible over time into gold or silver at the government's discretion. Once the U.S. gold reserve was restored to $100 million, confidence in the U.S. dollar was restored.

But the crisis that had been brought on by the Sherman Act didn't stop the cries from Populist groups to inflate the currency. In 1894, Jacob Coxey led an "army" from Massillon, Ohio, on a march to Washington, D.C., but the protest came to nothing. Coxey and a few others were arrested for trespassing and then sent home. To address some of the economic concerns of ordinary people, however, Congress enacted the Wilson-Gorman Tariff, which in its initial form lowered rates on many goods and eliminated tariffs entirely on some. To offset lost revenue from tariffs, Congress included an income tax. (As we have seen, Congress had enacted an income tax during the Civil War—at the instigation of Salmon Chase, Lincoln's secretary of the Treasury—but it had expired in 1872.) But in negotiations over the bill in Congress, the lower rates were bumped back up and Cleveland finally had to accept a bill that achieved little.

The economy was still sluggish, and labor unrest continued with the Pullman Railroad Car strike of 1894, a national strike that caused further economic disruption. Attorney General Richard Olney got a federal injunction against the strikers in July, and when workers attacked a U.S. marshal and his deputies near Chicago, Cleveland sent in the Army and declared martial law in Chicago. Cleveland had stood for public safety, but at a cost with voters who identified with the unions. He saw a taint of socialism and even communism on the unions. "Communism is a hateful thing," he observed, "and a menace to the peace and organized government."

In 1890, during the Harrison interregnum, Congress had passed the Sherman Antitrust Act prohibiting any business combination "in restraint of trade." During Cleveland's second term the Supreme Court began to rule on the Sherman Act. (Cleveland would name two more justices to the court in his second term, including Edward White of Louisiana and Rufus Peckham of New York.) In the *E. C. Knight* case, the American Sugar Refining Company was charged with violating Sherman when it gained control of the E. C. Knight Company, which gave American Sugar control of ninety-eight percent of the nation's sugar refining. In 1895 the Court ruled 8–1 in favor of the sugar company.

The problem with "antitrust" legislation is that monopolies in America have seldom survived if government doesn't assist them. And often, even near-total control of an industry has not translated into public harms. For example, when John D. Rockefeller's Standard Oil Company controlled over eighty percent of the petroleum refining capacity in the United States, the price of its main product, kerosene, continued

A Book You're Not Supposed to Read

Grover Cleveland: The Last Conservative Democratic President by Jeffrey K. Smith (Scotts Valley, CA: CreateSpace, 2016).

to plummet. A hundred years later, as the Justice Department was forcing a settlement to punish Microsoft for "bundling," consumers expressed overwhelming satisfaction in surveys about Microsoft and its pricing.

The Cleveland Court was also active elsewhere. In 1895 it struck down the income tax from the Wilson-Gorman compromise as a violation of the Constitution's "no direct tax" clause. Finally, in one of the worst rulings in Supreme Court history, the Court handed down a decision in the *Plessy v. Ferguson* case, arising from a black man sitting in a train seat reserved for whites, that established the "separate but equal" standard of racial discrimination.

With the ascent of the "Free Silver" advocate William Jennings Bryan in the Democratic Party in 1896, and with Cleveland set to observe the two-term tradition that had been established by George Washington, Grover Cleveland prepared to do something no other president had ever done—step down a second time. The Democrats had been taken over by their silverite wing, and the Republicans nominated William McKinley of Ohio. The popular vote difference was about half a million, and the Electoral College margin was similar to the margin in Cleveland's elections (271 for McKinley to 176 for Bryan). But historians have viewed McKinley's victory as a major turning point—a "realigning election" in that a large swath of the Midwest would vote reliably Republican for decades, save for Woodrow Wilson's reelection in 1916 (and even then Minnesota, Iowa, Illinois, Wisconsin, and Indiana

A Book You're Not Supposed to Read

The Forgotten Conservative: Rediscovering Grover Cleveland by John Pafford (Washington, DC: Regnery History, 2013).

would hold true to the Republicans), giving the Republicans a virtual lock on the presidency.

Cleveland's Legacy

As Grover Cleveland left office, he bore the moniker "the veto president," but he has also been termed "the forgotten conservative." "Some day I will be better remembered," Grover Cleveland predicted, and in recent decades he has been proven right. His presidential stock has risen substantially. Several new biographies have portrayed him as an unyielding constitutionalist and a man of courage and common sense. When he needed to, he swallowed his pride and took assistance from the "moneyed men." When he could, he slashed the pension programs without doing harm to the good intent behind them. "What is the use of being elected or reelected," he asked, "unless you stand for something?"

CHAPTER 23

Benjamin Harrison, 1889–1893

"We Americans have no commission from God to police the world."
—Benjamin Harrison

President Harrison's Constitutional Grade: C

Benjamin Harrison joined Thomas Jefferson and Andrew Jackson as a candidate who lost an election, only to return and win on another try. He also was one of the U.S. Navy's best friends. Like other Army veterans, such as Theodore Roosevelt and later Ronald Reagan, he would have an important impact on America's sea power.

The grandson of the first president to die in office, Harrison was born in Ohio and graduated from Miami University in Oxford, Ohio, then moved to Indiana, where he practiced law before the Civil War broke out. Breveted a general, after the war he returned to legal practice in Indiana, then failed twice to become its governor, then failed in his attempt to become the U.S. senator from Indiana. Finally, in 1881, he won a Senate seat and came to be a Blaine-ite, supporting James G. Blaine's bid for the presidency in 1884. But Blaine lost to the Democrat Cleveland, and four years later, after several ballots in which Blaine failed to secure the nomination, Harrison was named by the Republicans. He had his grandfather's name, but still he lost the popular vote to Cleveland—but won the Electoral College 233–168.

Did you know?

★ Benjamin Harrison was known as the "Centennial President" because he took office one hundred years after George Washington

★ Harrison was the second member of the second family to hold the presidency more than once, following in the footsteps of John Quincy Adams

★ Harrison refused to shake hands, believing it unhygienic

★ ★ ★

Touch Me Not!

Harrison would not shake hands and even thought that the practice had played a part in his grandfather's death. Viewed as a cold man—his nicknames were "the refrigerator" and "the human iceberg"—Harrison was not known for showing his feelings.

Harrison did reward Blaine, his old mentor, by naming him secretary of State, but he deliberately postponed Blaine's nomination until most of the rest of the cabinet was set, so as to avoid Blaine's tinkering with the choices. Having campaigned on ending the spoils system, Harrison nevertheless dutifully spent much of his time handing out jobs, but not necessarily based on political loyalty. As much as anything, Harrison appointed people because of their membership in the Presbyterian Church.

The failure to cut taxes after the Civil War meant that federal revenues exceeded expenditures, and Harrison saw a budget surplus as something of a sin, to be quickly extinguished. But with the Dependent and Disability Pension Act of 1890, pensions threatened to swamp the federal budget. Under Pension Bureau Commissioner James Tanner, Harrison saw pension payouts reach $135 million. The president became convinced that he had erred in appointing Tanner. Harrison asked for Tanner's resignation and received it, only to appoint Green Raum, who was soon charged with receiving kickbacks in return for hustling pension cases through the system. Raum got the benefit of a favorable congressional investigation and stayed in office. But the massive pot of money that was the pension system still constituted a major source of temptation for those administering it.

In 1890 protectionist Republican Ways and Means chairman (and future president) William McKinley introduced a tariff bill containing some of the highest rates in U.S. history. Harrison, fearing a trade war, attempted to persuade Congress to include a reciprocity clause, so that the U.S. would lower its rates when another nation lowered its rates on American goods. Even with reciprocity, the McKinley Tariff put in place some of the most protectionist tariffs ever, and continued the flow of money into the U.S.

treasury. Already both Harrison and the "Billion Dollar Congress" were being accused of wasting the huge surplus.

When it came to the silver issue, Harrison tried to walk the middle of the road. He supported John Sherman's disastrous Sherman Silver Purchase Act, which required the government purchase essentially all the available silver but pay $16.50 in silver for an ounce of gold, which was less than the market price of $17.00, but more than the $16.00 that the "free silver" movement wanted. The predictable result was economic chaos, as speculators and arbitragers exchanged the over-valued silver for gold and destabilized the banks. But Harrison would not be the one to suffer for the horrible legislation—that would be his successor, Grover Cleveland. Harrison also has to be held accountable for signing the Sherman Antitrust Act—allowing unprecedented federal government interference in the economy—which had even longer-term consequences.

On civil rights, Harrison's heart was in the right place but he could not persuade the Senate to pass the Federal Elections Bill of 1890. He had always opposed slavery and, as much as possible in the late 1800s, fought for civil rights. He recommended to Congress both education and legal protection for "the colored people [who] have, from a stand-point of ignorance and poverty, which is our shame, not theirs, made remarkable advances." He supported the Blair Bill, which would have given federal aid to public schools, mainly in the South. But it became entangled in concerns over aid to Catholic schools and died. But the Lodge Bill, which allowed federal circuit courts to appoint federal supervisors at local congressional elections, passed.

Harrison's Legacy

Harrison said that a president could not act as a crusader, but in fact he saw everything through evangelical eyes. And on his watch, two of the worst pieces of legislation in American history—the Sherman Silver Purchase Act and the Sherman Antitrust Act—were passed. He should have vetoed both.

CHAPTER 24

William McKinley, 1897–September 14, 1901

"I have never been in doubt since I was old enough to think intelligently that I would someday be made president."
—*William McKinley*

President McKinley's Constitutional Grade: B+

The historical consensus (not always to be trusted) is that William McKinley's election marked a turning point in American politics. The period from 1865 to 1896 had been an era of extremely close elections in which one state (often New York) held the balance. As we have seen, one historian has even suggested that a handful of counties in the rural Midwest regularly selected the victor. McKinley's was a "watershed" election in that he ushered in an era in which the GOP won every national election for the next twenty-six years with the exception of a split ticket in 1912, followed by Woodrow Wilson's reelection. (Had Theodore Roosevelt and William Howard Taft not divided the Republican vote, it's highly likely Wilson never would have been elected at all.)

William McKinley, or "Major" McKinley as people often knew him, was the last American president to have served in the Civil War. Eight presidents were born in Ohio, although not all were "from" that state when elected (such as Ulysses Grant). But McKinley was right in the middle of a string

Did you know?

★ McKinley heroically drove supply rations to men under a hail of fire at the battle of Antietam

★ He defended a group of miners who had fought with strike-breakers *pro bono*, winning the acquittal of all but one

★ McKinley lost $100,000 in a business deal, but supporters established a fund to pay the notes off and when he tried to repay the contributors, no one would give him the list

A Book You're Not Supposed to Read

The Triumph of William McKinley: Why the Election of 1896 Still Matters by Karl Rove (New York: Simon & Schuster, 2016).

of Ohio presidents that included two of the next four, William Howard Taft and Warren G. Harding.

Stern and unsmiling, McKinley practiced law after the Army and was elected to Congress in 1876. His area of expertise was the tariff, so much so that in 1890 the McKinley Tariff bore his name and cost him an election. Installed as Ohio's governor, he worked closely with Mark Hanna—one of the foremost political managers in American history. Aided by the Panic of 1893, McKinley got the Republican nomination, then beat William Jennings Bryan (in the first of several attempts Bryan made at the presidency) to take the 1896 election.

Bryan had absorbed the Populist dogma of "free silver" and saw the gold standard as a crushing burden on ordinary people. But many ordinary people, and certainly most businessmen, knew that inflation was the epitome of wealth destruction. The growth of American industry and manufacturing after 1865 had given millions of Americans jobs and created tens of thousands of new business owners, none of whom wanted to see their assets and income shrunk through inflation. While farmers and miners stood to benefit directly from "free silver," they were an electoral minority and largely concentrated in a few Southern and Western states.

McKinley knew that Bryan, who was engaging in a national "whistle-stop" tour, was a notoriously good speaker. When Hanna suggested to McKinley he might want to do his own tour, McKinley retorted, "I might just as well set up a trapeze on my front lawn and compete with some professional athlete as go out speaking against Bryan. I have to *think* when I speak." Instead, the Major ran a "front porch campaign" from Canton, Ohio.

He was available to the public every day except Sunday, and railroads devised special rates to haul all the visitors to Canton. But McKinley did not speak "off the cuff"; as he said, he thought about what he said, tailoring talks to each specific delegation. He won a majority of the popular vote, beating Bryan by a half million votes and winning the Electoral College 271–176. In his Inaugural, McKinley restated his commitment to a protective tariff and announced, "We want no wars of conquest. We must avoid the temptation of territorial aggression."

A Book You're Not Supposed to Read

William McKinley and His America by H. Wayne Morgan (Kent, OH: Kent State University Press, 2003).

McKinley would greet the new century as president and see breathtaking breakthroughs in invention and technology. His inauguration was the first ever filmed, telephones became common during his time, and American cities were quickly transforming from gas lighting to electricity. Outside of farms, Americans had seen real gains in their income over the second half of the 1800s, and tinkering with the structure that had made that possible did not appeal to the new president. Most of all, McKinley had common sense.

The new president named John Sherman as secretary of State, and Sherman was immediately put to work with the bubbling revolution in Cuba, where revolutionaries were seeking independence from Spain. Like many Spanish possessions, Cuba had strained under the yoke of colonialism. Americans had a natural sympathy with the Cubans, and the presence of Spanish General Valeriano Weyler, "the Butcher," stoked those sympathies. Of course, America had sought Cuba as its own territory going back before the Civil War. McKinley tried negotiating with Spain, which was not about to give its colony independence. When riots broke out in Havana, McKinley sent the battleship *Maine* there to serve as a warning to leave American lives and property alone. The ship was in Havana harbor for some time before an explosion on February 15 sank it, killing 266. Both pro-rebel and pro-Spanish writers blamed the other side, but McKinley hesitated to jump to conclusions. He ordered an inquiry, which returned a verdict in March that concluded a mine had blown up the ship. (A subsequent investigation, by Admiral Hyman Rickover in the 1970s, concluded it was likely an internal explosion unrelated to a mine). After more negotiations with Spain, which the Spanish considered "demands," McKinley asked Congress for its direction and Congress responded with a declaration of war on April 20, with the attached Teller Amendment, in which the U.S. repudiated the possibility of retaining Cuba as a territory.

An Empire? No Thanks

Thanks to Undersecretary of the Navy Theodore Roosevelt Jr., the Asiatic Squadron under Commodore George Dewey had already been deployed to Hong Kong, in the expectation that a Spanish-American War would mean assisting the Filipinos in their own revolt against Spain. When McKinley learned of the order he did not cancel it, and on May 1 Dewey's ships smashed the Spanish at Manila Bay without loss of a single American life. The Philippines de facto became an American protectorate. By June, more troops arrived to force Spain entirely out of the Philippines. By then, the presence of British and German fleets had convinced McKinley that simply liberating the islands was not an option—that that would only mean turning them over to another power. While Cuba would be released to independence, therefore, the Philippines were kept as an American territory until World War II.

Soon thereafter, American forces in Cuba opened the back door to the Spanish fleet at Kettle Hill and San Juan Hill, forcing the Spanish to sail out and do battle. In the resulting Battle of Santiago de Cuba, the Spanish sought to escape but ran into the American battle fleet with its superior guns. In an hour, five-sixths of the Spanish fleet was out of action. The battle not only firmly established the United States as the central force in the Western Hemisphere, but virtually ended Spain's tenure as a world naval power.

The United States also won Puerto Rico in the war. In the same year, 1898, thanks to the efforts of both Benjamin Harrison and Grover Cleveland, the U.S. acquired Hawaii through annexation. ("We need Hawaii just as much and a good deal more than we did California," the president noted. "It is Manifest Destiny.") Finally, the U.S. claimed the uninhabited (but strategically important) Wake Island. In the course of a "splendid little war" that lasted only three months and saw only 345 battle deaths (over two thousand died of disease, prompting Doctor Walter Reed to tackle the malaria epidemic in Cuba) McKinley had expanded American territory—by only a few islands, but in terms of geographic reach, the United States now had key bases all over the Caribbean and the Pacific. These important coaling stations later proved essential in "projecting power" during World War II. McKinley said, "In the time of darkest defeat, victory may be the nearest," but it is hard to imagine any time in the Spanish-American War when he could have thought defeat even a remote possibility.

America's new-found influence was amplified by Secretary of State John Hay who, seeking to rein in European imperialism in China during the Boxer Rebellion there, delivered an Open Door

Divine Guidance

William McKinley had expressed concern about acquiring foreign territories, but after the Spanish fleet was defeated in Manila Bay, he sought help from the Lord: "I am not ashamed to tell you...that I went down on my knees and prayed Almighty God for light and guidance that one night. And one night later it came to me this way.... There was nothing left for us to do but to take them all and to educate the Filipinos and uplift and civilize and Christianize them, and by God's grace do the very best we could by them, as our fellow men for whom Christ also died." Interestingly, as historian Paul Johnson noted, over eighty percent of them were already Roman Catholics. Nevertheless, while it came somewhat late, the United States eventually did make good on its pledge to liberate the Philippines. And, still later, when the Filipinos wanted the U.S. to abandon its naval base at Moro Bay, America complied with that request as well. As the last American ships pulled out, a Filipino held a hand-written sign: "Yanqui go home...and take me with you!"

Note in 1899, asking the Europeans to stay in their own spheres of interest in China and not to discriminate against other foreigners. He followed it up with a second Note in 1900 in which he urged the Europeans and the Japanese to observe "Chinese territorial and administrative integrity." When all agreed, McKinley had yet another major foreign policy victory, preserving American interests in China while looking like China's protector. The Sino-American alliance would last through World War II.

The Philippines, however, did not stay quite so pacified. Emilio Aguinaldo, a Filipino revolutionary, quickly saw the hopelessness of taking on American forces. So in one of the first instances of foreigners seeking to affect an American election for their own interests, Aguinaldo stated that his intention was to inflict as many casualties as possible with his revolutionary forces so as to persuade the American people to throw McKinley out at the next election. Aguinaldo's insurrection failed, but soon thereafter resistance in Mindanao and other areas of the Philippines drew in more American troops. American forces under governors Leonard Wood and John J. Pershing (who established the "Philippine Scouts") were brutal in combat with the Muslim Moros, even, as some writers claimed, throwing pigs in the graves of Moro soldiers, thereby extinguishing their hope of entering paradise. By that time, however, McKinley himself was long dead.

McKinley "always had a way of handling men so that they thought his ideas were their own," recalled Elihu Root, his secretary of War. The Major was ambitious and not above manipulating people. He was one of the first to dispatch his cabinet secretaries and staff to regularly meet with the press and in fact, far more than any of his predecessors, McKinley saw the news as a tool to be controlled. He realized that the media of the day had itself undergone a major change. Just as Lincoln was the "telegraph president," Franklin Roosevelt would be the "radio president," and Ronald Reagan would be the "television president," McKinley was the "newspaper president." As one historian has noted, "he spoon-fed the press his version of events, and the newspapers (with a few notable exceptions, such as the sensationalistic New York yellow press) grew dependent on the handouts and even acquiesced when he later censored bad news from the war in the Philippines." (Of course, censoring war news didn't end with McKinley and soon would be viewed as a part of the constitutional duty of presidents to "protect and defend" the nation). For a time, McKinley even banned the "yellow press" from the White House.

A Wise President

"That's all a man can hope for during his lifetime—to set an example—and when he is dead, to be an inspiration for history."

"The free man cannot be long an ignorant man."

"Our differences are policies; our agreements, principles."

—William McKinley

Under McKinley the proponents of high tariffs in Congress succeeded in passing the Dingley Tariff, including reciprocity agreements that proved difficult to understand and interpret, let alone enforce. The president followed through on his intent to put the United States solely on the gold standard with the Gold Standard Act of 1900 (he used a gold pen to sign the bill). When it came to race relations, McKinley faced the reality that Reconstruction was steadily being rolled back. He named a few blacks to federal posts, such as former Senator Blanche Bruce, and visited the Tuskegee Institute, where he met with Booker T. Washington, but increasingly a president could do little to change attitudes. Most recent historians have been sympathetic to McKinley on this issue, especially in comparison with the outright racist Woodrow Wilson.

Vice President Garret Hobart died in 1899, so when it came time for McKinley to run for reelection, he needed a new running mate. His initial choice was Elihu Root, but Root was so good at the War Department that McKinley thought better of removing him. Instead, he named Theodore Roosevelt, who was then New York governor—partly to keep Roosevelt under wraps, in campaign manager Mark Hanna's Machiavellian world.

New York political boss Senator Thomas Platt wanted Roosevelt out of the state. The ambitious Roosevelt was glad to have a place on the ticket, expecting that the vice presidency would elevate him to the top office. He had no idea the ascent would come so soon.

The campaign of 1900 featured a rematch with Democrat nominee William Jennings Bryan, and again Bryan failed to catch on with his "free silver" message. Again, McKinley stayed home, but this time he sent out Roosevelt to speak on his behalf. McKinley's slogan, "A Full Dinner Pail," seemed to confirm that America had reached new heights of prosperity. Bryan carried the South, but only four other states and was beaten soundly, even losing his home state of Nebraska. McKinley won the Electoral College 292–155, expanding the Republican edge, and this time beat Bryan by nearly a million votes.

McKinley took a victory lap, planning to visit the Pan-American Exposition in Buffalo only a few months after his second inauguration. But the first lady took ill, and he postponed the trip until September.

The world had changed, and heads of state were routinely being assassinated. Between 1898 and 1913, there would be forty political figures assassinated, including six prime ministers and four kings. America had already witnessed two presidents murdered in office in the previous forty years. Yet security around McKinley was still relatively relaxed, compared to modern times. In Buffalo, the president first spoke before fifty thousand people; then, the following day, as McKinley greeted people at the Temple of Music, anarchist Leon Czolgosz, concealing his gun in a handkerchief, shot McKinley twice.

Like Garfield, McKinley did not die immediately. As with Garfield, the problem was that the doctors could not locate a bullet. But unlike in Garfield's assassination, the doctors did not attempt to employ new technology (Alexander Graham Bell had used an early metal detector to try to locate the bullet in Garfield's body in 1881, but an X-ray machine actually on

Exposition grounds was not used in McKinley's case). Like Garfield, though, McKinley was dying of internal injuries and infection that the doctors could not stop. McKinley died on September 14 in Buffalo. He had not made it back to Washington. Theodore Roosevelt, who rushed back from a camping trip, arrived in Buffalo for the oath of office, and Czolgosz was arrested, tried, and then executed on October 29, 1901. It was swift justice indeed.

A Book You're Not Supposed to Read

A Patriot's History of the Modern World, vol. 1: From America's Exceptional Ascent to the Atomic Bomb: 1898–1945 by Larry Schweikart and Dave Dougherty (New York: Sentinel, 2012).

Grading McKinley

McKinley left a vastly larger America than he inherited, not so much in actual physical space occupied, but in influence and world power. He had come in on the tail of a depression, but when he died the United States was prosperous. He had done nothing to defy the Constitution, and much (with a little maneuvering) to uphold it. To most he symbolized the continued expansion of the American economy and prosperity, and while there were concerns about the dominance of the "Trusts" and the "monied men" (which McKinley's successor would address, to a fault), there was no doubt that those same "monied men" had created vast economic development that, for the most part, even the poorest had begun to experience. It is hard to imagine that, had McKinley lived through another term, his existing legacy could have been enhanced.

CHAPTER 25

Theodore Roosevelt Jr., September 19, 1901–1909

"In any moment of decision, the best thing you can do is the right thing, the next best thing is the wrong thing, and the worst thing you can do is nothing."
—Theodore Roosevelt Jr.

President Roosevelt's Constitutional Grade: C–

It is fitting that the four presidents whose faces are on Mount Rushmore are all included in this volume, and that Theodore Roosevelt is one of them. Despite only serving for seven years, Roosevelt (or "TR," as he was often called) had as much influence on the American presidency—and the American character in general—as anyone other than Washington or Lincoln.

A blustery personality who entered a room like an out-of-control bowling ball, Roosevelt attracted attention wherever he went. Bram Stoker, the author of *Dracula*, wrote of TR, "Must be President some day. A man you can't cajole, can't frighten, can't buy." New York assemblyman Newton Curtis called him "a brilliant madman, born a century too soon." His accentuated speech ("Mistaaaahhh Speeee-kaaaar" and "Aieeeee" for "I"), his rich education, his broad personal experience all made him attractive to ordinary Americans. He was much more popular than William McKinley, who was certainly not unpopular at all. Theodore Roosevelt was iconic in every way. He resigned a powerful (and safe) government position as assistant secretary of the Navy

Did you know?

★ Theodore Roosevelt, aged forty-two, became the youngest president in American history when William McKinley was shot

★ In 1882 Roosevelt had published a book, *The Naval War of 1812*

★ Roosevelt is the only president in American history to have received both the Nobel Prize and a Medal of Honor

A Book You're Not Supposed to Read

The Rise of Theodore Roosevelt by Edmund Morris (New York: Random House Trade Paperbacks, 2001).

to lead a volunteer cavalry unit in the Spanish-American War. He stood counter to the "consensus" of the scientists of his day to side with Dr. William Gorgas and Dr. Walter Reed and defeat malaria in Panama, then build the Canal. He was the only U.S. president ever to win both a Medal of Honor (for "acts of bravery" and "extraordinary heroism" in the Spanish-American War) and a Nobel Peace Prize (for negotiating an end to the Russo-Japanese War). It has often been noted that he was a contradictory character: as president this rugged individualist did more than most of his predecessors to expand the role of government and alter its nature.

Historian Edmund Morris aptly captures TR's incredible life and adventures prior to becoming president. His experiences in everything except business made him capable of becoming a great leader. As a Progressive, Roosevelt believed that humans could achieve perfection in this life through a process of "reform." That principle dominated the Progressive movement and was applied to all the government agencies when Roosevelt became president. One of the first areas he addressed was public health, urging Congress to pass the Pure Food and Drug Act and the Meat Inspection Act (both in 1906). Roosevelt signed the two bills on the same day. There had indeed been abuses in the meat industry—highlighted in Upton Sinclair's book *The Jungle*—with producers selling tainted meats. (Sinclair wanted to start a socialist revolution, which never occurred.) But one of the first products assaulted under the Pure Food and Drug Act was the carbonated beverage Coca-Cola, which was asserted to have cocaine in it. During a high-profile trial, when it was shown there was no cocaine in "Coke," the government clumsily tried to reverse course and accuse Coke of false advertising. (Bizarrely, under the Bureau of Chemistry in 1902, Dr. Harvey Wiley had recruited men to eat meals dosed with outrageous levels of preservatives, such as borax, benzoate, and formaldehyde. This trick soon backfired when the public became concerned that "the Poison Squad" amounted to the government using human beings as lab rats.)

The Trustbuster

Roosevelt acquired the nickname "Trust-buster" after his Justice Department began stringent application of the Sherman Antitrust Act, filing some forty actions against companies. One of the most famous, the *Northern Securities Co. vs. the United States*, involved a number of railroads that had formed a combination, triggering a government claim that Northern Securities was "in restraint of trade." The Court ruled in favor of the government, even though Northern Securities had not actually been proven to have caused any damage to customers. (McKinley had refused to bring a case.) The Court found that even the *chance* that Northern Securities might be in restraint of trade in the future was sufficient to find it guilty of violating antitrust legislation. Railroad tycoon James J. Hill had to dissolve the holding company. An even larger antitrust case brought by the Roosevelt administration, the Standard Oil breakup, was not adjudicated until 1911, after Roosevelt had left office, but again the Supreme Court ruled for the government and against business.

These cases, and his dealings with various industry officials, showed Roosevelt's blind spot: having never run a business (his cattle ranches were

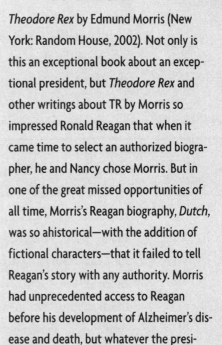

A Book You're Not Supposed to Read

Theodore Rex by Edmund Morris (New York: Random House, 2002). Not only is this an exceptional book about an exceptional president, but *Theodore Rex* and other writings about TR by Morris so impressed Ronald Reagan that when it came time to select an authorized biographer, he and Nancy chose Morris. But in one of the great missed opportunities of all time, Morris's Reagan biography, *Dutch*, was so ahistorical—with the addition of fictional characters—that it failed to tell Reagan's story with any authority. Morris had unprecedented access to Reagan before his development of Alzheimer's disease and death, but whatever the president told him is forever lost.

hardly under his operational hand), TR never understood the difficulties of making a profit. It was a serious weakness that exacerbated his Progressive tendencies.

Roosevelt was a contradiction in terms. A self-made man, he nevertheless threw the power of government onto the side of the employee in labor struggles. Roosevelt convinced the parties to end the Coal Strike of 1902, for example, through a commission citing a "square deal for every man." But the mine owners agreed to settle only after the president had called them "wooden-headed," accused them of "arrogant stupidity," and threatened to send in ten thousand troops to operate the mines. When told it would be unconstitutional to do so, he said, "To Hell with the Constitution when the people want coal." He managed to get away with assaults on business by balancing his rhetoric with attacks on labor radicalism. TR invoked the Sherman Act some twenty-five times during his administration and created a new cabinet-level department, Commerce and Labor, whose main job was to investigate any violations of the laws regulating interstate commerce. "We do not wish to destroy corporations," he reassured business leaders, but "we do wish to make them subserve the public good"—as defined by TR. Even more disconcerting was that Roosevelt's comment suggested that businesses did *not* serve the public good by paying taxes, furnishing jobs, and making products everyone needed. He lambasted the "tyranny of mere wealth," but, in 1904, when he needed Republican Party support in his reelection campaign, he hastily repaired relationships with financier J. P. Morgan and other business leaders.

In 1904, facing two opponents—Democrat Alton B. Parker and the socialist Eugene V. Debs—Roosevelt won fifty-six percent of the vote and a commanding 336–140 Electoral College victory. It was another chapter in the continued Republican dominance of the White House. Even before he was inaugurated, Roosevelt announced that he would not seek another term, in

★ ★ ★

Pana-mania

Ever since the French—under Ferdinand De Lesseps, the builder of the Suez Canal—had failed to dig a canal across Panama, the British and the Americans had their eyes on the land. At the time, Panama was a territory of Colombia. An alternate route, through Nicaragua, was prone to earthquakes, so Roosevelt favored the Panama route, despite the fact that Colombia owned it. A rebellion in Panama was conveniently assisted by an American gunboat that arrived on the scene to ward off Colombian vessels that might have stopped the revolution. A canal treaty was signed hastily in New York by Secretary of State John Hay and a "representative" of Panama, a Frenchman named Philippe-Jean Bunau-Varilla. Bunau-Varilla had provided money to the rebels for years, but he had not gone back to Panama. In the treaty, the United States guaranteed the freedom of Panama (with Colombia in mind), and the U.S. got the right to build a canal and operate it as a monopoly (as well as all of the shares of the French canal company). The resulting Canal Zone would be American sovereign territory. However, once built, the Panama Canal was to be free to all. America paid $10 million immediately and $250,000 per year. When Roosevelt was challenged about his authority to support the Panamanian revolution, in typical fashion he said, "I took Panama and left Congress to debate *me*." TR backed Drs. Walter Reed and William Gorgas, who had a new theory of how malaria was spread, over the "consensus" of scientists at the time. The result was that eradication of the mosquito began, and within a year the Canal Zone was relatively free of malaria.

keeping with Washington's two-term precedent (even though TR hadn't served a full first term).

Roosevelt was famous for his saying "Speak softly and carry a big stick," and he used that principle to great effect in Latin America and the Caribbean. With his "Roosevelt Corollary" to the Monroe Doctrine, he asserted not only that Europeans should stay out of the New World but that the United States would assume responsibility as the region's policeman. Often TR got away with intimidation because he did it so darn cleverly. But he also believed in having—and, if necessary, using—a big Navy to back him up, and the Canal was key to that.

Roosevelt is also known for his efforts to create national parks, something that came out of his hunting background. In 1905 he appointed the first professional forester, Gifford Pinchot, to head the newly created U.S. Forest Service with an eye toward "conservation" and "reclamation." Roosevelt jumped on the Newlands Reclamation Act bandwagon in 1902. That law applied a portion of public lands receipts to dam construction and other water projects—in essence taxing some farmers who lived in areas with heavier rainfall to support others who did not. But TR was no "environmentalist whacko," as Rush Limbaugh would term some of the members of the environmental movement today. Roosevelt's first principle was, as Pinchot phrased it, "development, the use of natural resources now existing on this continent for the benefit of the people who live here now"—an astounding contrast with the modern environmentalists' position.

But Roosevelt got greedy. He attempted to set aside two hundred million acres of public land as national forests, but was eventually backed down by angry farmers (although he still carved out sixteen million acres for the government).

Roosevelt had Booker T. Washington to the White House for dinner, but the interracial dinner so shocked many Americans that TR never had him back again. In August 1906, black troops in Brownsville, Texas, were accused of going on a shooting spree after mistreatment by locals. Officers reported that all the men had been in their quarters. Still, 167 members of black units were questioned after evidence of spent cartridges was produced. None of the men would testify against another. Roosevelt, after reading the Army inspector general's report, ordered the 167 soldiers dishonorably discharged. (Later 14 were reinstated into the Army.) Under pressure from civil rights groups in 1972, a new investigation concluded the cartridges were planted, and a bill was passed requiring the Defense Department to re-investigate the matter. The Army found the accused men innocent, and President Richard Nixon pardoned them.

★ ★ ★
Buying Bison

One of the little-known facts in American history is that while both Indians and, later, white hunters nearly exterminated the buffalo, it was white ranchers and philanthropists who saved the bison. Several ranchers, including legendary cattleman Charles Goodnight, bought and bred animals, usually for their meat. Goodnight created a herd that eventually numbered seven hundred bison. When Yellowstone National Park started its bison herds in 1902, the government got its animals from the private sector.

When it came time for TR to honor his pledge not to run again, he did. His handpicked successor was William Howard Taft, whom Roosevelt labeled a "Genuine Progressive." Taft beat perennial loser William Jennings Bryan in the general election, and TR thought he had achieved, in essence, a third term. Events would soon prove him wrong.

Who Was Teddy Roosevelt?

Was Roosevelt an American hero or a big-government villain? A peacemaker or a warmonger? A conservationist or a land grabber? He was probably all of the above. Despite his penchant for exercising government authority, often on the fringe of the letter of the Constitution and frequently in violation of its spirit, Roosevelt was a man almost anyone would be

Books You're Not Supposed to Read

Both *The Ecological Indian* by Shepard Krech III (New York: Norton, 1999) and *The Destruction of the Bison: An Environmental History, 1750–1920* by Andrew Isenberg (Cambridge: Cambridge University Press, 2001) show that the Indians were rapidly exterminating the bison herds before whites arrived, and that whites merely accelerated the process until individual white cattlemen, ranchers, and philanthropists began to save the buffalo.

drawn to. His magnetic personality, his can-do optimism, and above all his great love for America can cause one to minimize the damage his presidency did to economic freedoms in America. TR's trustbusting set disturbing precedents, especially the ruling that a company could be guilty of restricting trade before it had ever acted. He slowly shifted the clout of the government from the side of business to that of the unions—not so much by supporting the latter as by intimidating the former. Yet his foreign policy was always America First, and the Panama Canal offsets a few of his constitutional debits.

CHAPTER 26

William Howard Taft, 1909–1913

"Politics, when I am in it, makes me sick."
—*William Howard Taft*

President Taft's Constitutional Grade: C–

Under the best of circumstances, following Teddy Roosevelt was probably going to be a losing proposition. Who was Michael Jordan's replacement in Chicago? You get the point. It didn't help that Taft was unorthodox in a number of ways. "I do not believe in the divinity of Christ," he stated. He also said, "I love judges, and I love courts." (Indeed, he once noted that "Presidents come and go, but the Supreme Court goes on forever.") Even then, those were not winning opinions.

When Roosevelt became president, he wanted Taft on the Supreme Court, but Taft refused, saying his work as governor of the Philippines was not done. Later, when Secretary of War Elihu Root announced he would retire, TR asked Taft to take the position. Again, Taft turned the president down, saying he'd rather return to his law practice, but Roosevelt finally convinced him to take the position. Since the Panama Canal construction fell under the jurisdiction of the War Department, Taft visited Panama before Roosevelt did, in 1904, and eventually replaced chief engineer John Stevens with a man named William Goethals.

Did you know?

★ William Howard Taft, the heaviest U.S. president, tipped the scales at over 300 pounds and once got stuck in the White House bathtub

★ William Howard Taft started the tradition of throwing out the first pitch of baseball season

★ Socialist Eugene V. Debs got nearly a million votes in the 1912 race against Taft, Teddy Roosevelt, and Woodrow Wilson

Taft's girth—he weighed three hundred pounds—became a point of humor for people both in and out of the administration. When he got sick as governor of the Philippines, he cabled Secretary of War Elihu Root to let him know that he had ridden a horse to the mountain resort to recover. Root's reply: "How is the horse?"

By the end of Roosevelt's second term, TR had come to regret his pledge to step down, but honored it. Although Taft was the natural successor, once again he didn't want the job. He left Roosevelt's cabinet in 1907, creating distance between him and the president. After repeated efforts to draft him, Taft relented. His opponent in the general election was William Jennings Bryan, who was running for the third time in four electoral cycles. By then, Bryan actually claimed to be running on Roosevelt's issues and on an anti-big-business platform. Roosevelt was still popular, but the Panic of 1907 had done some damage to the public's confidence in the government and the financial system, and banking reform was in the air. Ultimately, while Taft won with a Roosevelt-esque Electoral College margin of 321–162, the popular vote for the Republican candidate slipped back to a margin of about a million.

President Taft called Congress into special session to deal with the tariff, which by then had become a national pain in the neck. Since the government had stopped making the lion's share of its revenue off land sales, tariffs had become its major source of revenue. But there was a price. First of all, consumers ended up footing the bill in the form of higher prices. Second, there were always ongoing negotiations with foreign countries over "reciprocity," meaning "you lower yours, I'll lower mine." Third, because each congressional delegation had its own interests to protect, the squabbling over which rates to raise and how much was consuming much of Congress's time. By the time all the logrolling was done, rates had gone up on almost everything.

As a Progressive, Taft wanted to lower the tariff and offset the revenues with income taxes—which were still (until the adoption of the Sixteenth

Amendment) unconstitutional. But Taft also had another problem: two of the most prominent leaders in Congress, Speaker Joseph Cannon in the House and Senator Nelson Aldrich of Rhode Island, were pro-tariff men who represented industrial interests. Cannon derided "this babble for reform." And Taft did not wish to get his hands dirty by attempting to shepherd legislation through Congress. His job, he thought, was merely to sign bills or veto them. So it was up to the "Insurgents" in Congress, a group of Progressives in the House, to push the tax reform that the president wanted. They put forth a bill lowering the tariffs on over eight hundred items and introducing a federal inheritance tax (another Progressive goal). Taft approved, but kept his hands off, and the tariffs were revised significantly upward in the Senate—with some rates even higher than when the entire process had started. When Taft got what was called the Payne-Aldrich Tariff, he signed it and even praised it in public. Insurgents and Progressives were incensed.

Taft was equally unsuccessful in diplomatic affairs in China, where he tried to restrain the British, French, and others who were expanding their "spheres of influence." Lacking TR's personality and aura of power, Taft was simply ignored. In the Caribbean, he helped create a new government in Nicaragua but in 1910 had

★ ★ ★

The Most Powerful Man in America

Arguably President William Howard Taft was not the most powerful man in America (let alone the world). That would be Speaker of the House Joe Cannon. Generally considered the most powerful Speaker ever, eclipsing even Henry Clay, Cannon wielded an iron fist. His absolute control eventually inspired Progressives to revolt in 1910. By that time he no longer had the clout he had had even two years earlier—when he controlled all debate and committee selections—but he still was formidable. The Speaker was forced out in a lengthy process when Nebraska Congressman George Norris corralled forty-two "Insurgent" Republicans to ally with his 149 Democrats to remove him. Initially many of the Speaker's own allies were absent, and he sent the sergeant-at-arms to track them down while his subordinates kept up the House version of a filibuster, a "point of order" debate. But even when all his cronies were produced, he still could not block the resolution stripping him of his powers—at which point he resigned.

A Book You're Not Supposed to Read

The William Howard Taft Presidency by Lewis Gould (Lawrence, KS: University of Kansas Press, 2009).

to send in troops to keep it afloat. American forces remained in that country for twenty years.

Perhaps the final nail in Taft's rather large coffin was the Ballinger-Pinchot controversy. This involved a battle between Richard Ballinger, Taft's Interior secretary, and Gifford Pinchot, the Forest Service chief who was a holdover from Roosevelt's administration. Ballinger countermanded orders from TR that would have set aside a million acres of land for forests rather than development. Pinchot objected, and made an enemy of Taft. When a report surfaced that Ballinger was transferring the lands to his industrialist friends, Pinchot picked up on it. The controversy landed in Taft's lap, and he sided with Ballinger. The affair became public and Pinchot tried to make a martyr of himself by provoking Taft into firing him—which he did. The incident lost Taft more Progressive support.

Roosevelt had gone abroad, but kept up with the news and felt betrayed by Taft, who, he thought, had "completely twisted around the policies I advocated and acted upon." U.S. Steel's acquisition of the Tennessee Coal Company had been quietly approved by Roosevelt and had gone ahead with assurances that the government wouldn't interfere. But Taft saw the acquisition as a violation of the anti-trust law and filed a suit, in essence taking a shot at TR. This, as much as anything, brought Roosevelt out of retirement to run again. By then, Taft was convinced he would lose anyway.

When Roosevelt couldn't get the Republican nomination in 1912, he formed his own third party and ran against Republican nominee Taft, Democrat nominee Woodrow Wilson, and Socialist Eugene Debs. TR's Progressive Party, popularly known as the "Bull Moose Party"—Roosevelt had said he felt "fit as a bull moose"—split the vote, ensuring the election of

Woodrow Wilson, a man even more "Progressive" than either TR or Taft. Taft won only 8 electoral votes from two states in an embarrassing loss. Roosevelt got 88 electoral votes, but was crushed by Wilson's 435. But in the popular vote, Roosevelt and Taft together netted 7.5 million to Wilson's 6.2 million (with almost a million votes going to the socialist Eugene V. Debs). "Politics make me sick," Taft told his family. It was easy to see why. He was later appointed by President Warren Harding as chief justice of the U.S. Supreme Court. Always a jurist at heart, Taft never understood the hurly burly of politics, in which appeals to the public and to congressional allies can be far more powerful than even the written word.

A Book You're Not Supposed to Read

The Politically Incorrect Guide® to the Presidents from Wilson to Obama by Steven F. Hayward (Washington, DC: Regnery, 2012).

Taft's Legacy

Ideology aside, the presidency of William Howard Taft is a cautionary tale: if a president wants to have influence in policy, he must get his hands dirty and involve himself with Congress. Taft continued the quasi-constitutional pummeling of "big business," failed internationally, and had a legacy of next to nothing. That will get you unelected in a hurry.

CONCLUSION

The First Twenty-Six

merica's first twenty-six presidents established a magnificent
foundation for the United States.*

It did not come easily, or without considerable bloodshed. But by 1912
the first twenty-six had instituted a functional and effective government,
paid off the nation's debts, ensured "domestic tranquility" by squelching
rebellions, and honored the electoral process by ensuring fair and honest
elections. They had slapped down foreign pirates who threatened American
lives, dispatched the British a second time, taken the American West
from a seemingly superior enemy, and won a foreign war. Confronted with
problems for which there were no peaceful solutions—slavery and the
Indians—the first twenty-six presidents made considerable errors, but
ended up in the right place. And their errors were not of malice or ill-
intent, but rather of a desire to postpone initiating the turmoil, conflict,

---

* William Howard Taft was the twenty-seventh president, but only the twenty-
sixth man to hold the office, because Grover Cleveland counts as both the
twenty-second and the twenty-fourth.

and suffering that they all knew would ensue. With great reluctance, they had forced America to confront the reality behind the claim in the Declaration that "All men are created equal," then pushed as hard as was practical under the circumstances to see that it stuck.

Their judicial appointees had put in place a legal system that encouraged land ownership, business development, and job creation; that rewarded invention and innovation; that celebrated genius; and that honored contracts. While not all the government officials named by the first twenty-six were brilliant—in fact some were barely functional—the overall record of such diplomats as James Monroe, John Quincy Adams, James Buchanan, and John Hay in settling disputes, solidifying boundaries, and eliminating potential sources of conflicts that could have led to war was impressive. In dealing with Congress, the earliest presidents, in particular, held to the Whig notion of allowing the legislature to shape the laws; only in the event of the Civil War did a president substantially depart from that principle. Even then, Lincoln repeatedly urged Congress to act on matters he could have reserved for himself.

Without question, much of the credit for the record of the first twenty-six goes to George Washington, who understood he would be their model. All of them followed his example in stepping down after two terms. Most considered the presidency a burden and celebrated the day they left.

Most of the first seventeen (up to the time of the Civil War) had owned a slave at one time or another, and the overwhelming majority of the twenty-six had served in the military. As time went by, more of them came from ordinary backgrounds and some had even known hardship and poverty. As the nation over which they presided grew, the demands on the office expanded, to the point that merely selecting staff to fill the various federal agencies itself became a problem that required a solution.

Five of them died in office; three were assassinated. Yet in their deaths, the Republic was strengthened all the more, for, thanks especially to the example of John Tyler, the business of government continued seamlessly. One president came within a vote of being removed from office, but he was not, and no president either stepped down or was removed (except by natural death or an assassin's bullet) in the first 130 years of the Republic.

Again and again they turned the levers of power over to parties they fundamentally disagreed with or to men they personally could not stand. Yet the Republic carried on. Virtually every one was called vicious names, slandered, lied about, but though there was a brief flirtation with stifling criticism under John Adams, no one was ever permanently incarcerated or personally pilloried for opposition to the head of state. Newspapers printed outrageous cartoons of each, but no papers were burned. Writers even called for the death of some—but no guillotines were erected.

While the constitutional scope of what was admissible definitely expanded, virtually every president up until 1913 considered what the document said, and thought regularly about how his own actions measured up against the Constitution. Whether the issue was the power of big business or the threat of violent mobs, the first twenty-six sought to act for the "public good," not in pursuit of some nebulous "hope and change." While some of the first twenty-six were weaker than others (and still others scarcely had a chance to show what they could do), they all took the office seriously, their responsibilities as a sacred trust, and their election by the people of this great land as the highest honor of their lives.

Selected Bibliography

Allen, William B., editor and compiler. *George Washington: A Collection*. Indianapolis, IN: Liberty Fund, 1988.

Atack, Jeremy, and Peter Passell. *A New Economic View of American History: From Colonial Times to 1940*, 2nd ed. New York: W. W. Norton & Co., 1994.

Beard, Charles. *The Rise of American Civilization*. New York: Macmillan, 1930.

Best, James D. *Tempest at Dawn*. Tucson, AZ: Wheatmark, 2010.

Bonekemper, Edward H., III. *Ulysses S. Grant: A Victor Not a Butcher: The Military Genius of the Man Who Won the Civil War*. Washington, DC: Regnery, 2010.

Brinkley, Alan, and Davis Dyer, eds. *The American Presidency*. Boston: Houghton Mifflin, 2004.

Brodsky, Alyn. *Grover Cleveland: A Study in Character*. New York: St. Martin's Press, 2000.

Brown, Richard H. "The Missouri Crisis, Slavery, and the Politics of Jacksonianism," in Stanley N. Kurtz and Stanley I. Kutler, eds., *New Perspectives on the American Past, vol. 1, 1607–1877*, 241–55. Boston: Little, Brown, 1969.

Callow, Alexander. *The Tweed Ring*. New York: Oxford University Press, 1979.

Calomiris, Charles and Stephen H. Haber. *Fragile by Design: The Political Origins of Banking Crises and Scarce Credit*. Princeton: Princeton University Press, 2014.

Chase, James Stanton. "Jacksonian Democracy and the Rise of the Nominating Convention," *Mid-America* 45 (1963): 229–49.

Chernow, Ron. *Alexander Hamilton*. New York: Penguin, 2004.

Chitwood, Oliver Perry. *John Tyler, Champion of the Old South*. New York: Appleton-Century, 1939.

Craven, Avery. *The Coming of the Civil War*. Chicago: University of Chicago Press, 2nd ed., 1957.

Current, Richard N. *The Lincoln Nobody Knows*. New York: Lawrence Erlbaum, 1963.

Dangerfield, George. *The Era of Good Feelings*. Detroit: Ivan R. Dee, 1989.

DiGregorio, William A. *The Complete Book of U.S. Presidents*, 7th ed. Fort Lee, NJ: Barricade Books, 2009.

Doenecke, Justus. *The Presidencies of James A. Garfield and Chester A. Arthur*. Lawrence, KS: University of Kansas Press, 1981.

Eisenhower, John S. D. *Zachary Taylor*. The American Presidents Series, the Twelfth President. New York: Times Books, 2008.

Ellis, Joseph J. *American Sphinx: The Character of Thomas Jefferson*. New York: Vintage, 1998.

Fitzhugh, George. *Cannibals All! Or, Slaves without Masters*. Richmond, VA: A. Morris, 1857.

Flexner, James Thomas. *George Washington, Anguish and Farewell (1793–1799)*. Boston: Little, Brown and Company, 1972.

———. *Washington: The Indispensable Man*. Boston: Back Bay, 1994.

Folsom, Burton, Jr. "Grover Cleveland: The Veto President," *The Freeman* (August 2004): 34–35.

Freehling, William W. *Prelude to Civil War: The Nullification Crisis in South Carolina, 1816–1836*. New York: Oxford, 1992.

Gould, Lewis. *The William Howard Taft Presidency*. Lawrence, KS: University of Kansas, 2009.

Graff, Henry F. *Grover Cleveland*. New York: Henry Holt, 2002.

Grant, Ulysses S. *The Complete Personal Memoirs of Ulysses S. Grant*. Old Chelsea Station, NY: Cosimo Classics, 2006.

Hammond, Bray. *Banks and Politics in America from the Revolution to the Civil War*. New York: Princeton University Press, 1957.

Hayward, Steven F. *The Politically Incorrect Guide® to the Presidents from Wilson to Obama*. Washington, DC: Regnery, 2012.

Heidler, David S., and Jeanne T. Heidler, *Washington's Circle: The Creation of the President*. New York: Random House, 2015.

Hickey, Donald J. *The War of 1812: The Forgotten Conflict*. Bicentennial Edition. Champaign, IL: University of Illinois Press, 2012.

Higgs, Robert. *Crisis and Leviathan: Critical Episodes in the Growth of American Government*. 25th anniversary edition. Chicago: Independent Institute, 2013.

Holt, Michael F. *The Political Crisis of the 1850s*. Boston: W. W. Norton, 1983.

Hummel, Jeffrey R. *Emancipating Slaves, Enslaving Free Men: A History of the American Civil War*. 2nd ed. Chicago: Open Court Publishers, 2013.

Hurst, James Willard. *Law and the Conditions of Freedom in the Nineteenth Century United States*. Madison, WI: University of Wisconsin Press, 1964.

Huston, James L. *Calculating the Value of the Union: Slavery, Property Rights, and the Economic Origins of the Civil War*. Chapel Hill, NC: University of North Carolina Press, 2003.

Jaffa, Harry V. *Crisis of the House Divided: An Interpretation of the Issues in the Lincoln-Douglas Debates*. 50th anniversary edition. Chicago: University of Chicago Press, 2009.

John, Richard R. *Spreading the News: The American Postal System from Franklin to Morse*. Cambridge: Harvard University Press, 1998.

Johnson, Paul. *A History of the American People*. New York: HarperCollins, 1997.

Jortner, Adam. *The Gods of Prophetstown: The Battle of Tippecanoe and the Holy War for the American Frontier*. New York: Oxford University Press, 2011.

Karabell, Zachary. *Chester Alan Arthur*. The American Presidents Series. New York: Times, 2004.

Kenyon, Cecelia. "Alexander Hamilton: Rousseau of the Right," *Political Science Quarterly* 75 (June 1958): 161–78.

Ketcham, Ralph. *James Madison: A Biography*. Charlottesville, VA: University of Virginia Press, 2000.

Kleppner, Paul. *The Cross of Culture: A Social Analysis of Midwestern Politics, 1850–1900*. New York: Free Press, 1970.

Kuypers, Jim A. *Partisan Journalism: A History of Media Bias in the United States*. Lanham, MD: Rowman & Littlefield, 2014.

Lillback, Peter, and Jerry Newcombe. *George Washington's Sacred Fire*. King of Prussia, PA: Providence Forum Press, 2006.

Marriott, Michel. "Verdict In: 12th President Was Not Assassinated," *New York Times*, June 27, 2011.

Marshall, Lynn. "The Strange Stillbirth of the Whig Party," *American Historical Review* 72 (January 1967): 445–69.

McCormick, Richard P. "New Perspectives on Jacksonian Politics," *American Historical Review* 65 (1960): 288–301.

McCullough, David. *John Adams*. New York: Touchstone, 2002.

———. *The Path between the Seas: The Creation of the Panama Canal, 1870–1914*. New York: Simon & Schuster, 1978.

McWhiney, Grady, and Perry D. Jamieson. *Attack and Die: Civil War Tactics and the Southern Heritage*. University of Alabama, 1984.

Morgan, H. Wayne. *From Hayes to McKinley: National Party Politics, 1877–1896*. Syracuse, NY: Syracuse University Press, 1969.

———. *William McKinley and His America*. Kent, OH: Kent State University, 2003.

Morris, Edmund. *The Rise of Theodore Roosevelt*. New York: Random House Trade Paperbacks, 2001.

———. *Theodore Rex*. New York: Random House, 2002.

Neustadt, Richard. *Presidential Power: The Politics of Leadership from FDR to Carter*. New York: Wiley, 1979.

Nevins, Allan. *Ordeal of the Union: Fruits of Manifest Destiny, 1847–1852*. New York: Scribner's, 1947.

Nichols, Roy F. *Franklin Pierce*. Newton, CT: American Political Biography, 1931.

Oates, Stephen B. *With Malice Toward None: A Life of Abraham Lincoln*. New York: Harper Perennial, 2011.

Pafford, John. *The Forgotten Conservative: Rediscovering Grover Cleveland*. Washington, DC: Regnery, 2013.

Parton, James. *Life of Andrew Jackson*. 3 vols. London: Forgotten Books, 2015.

Potter, David. *The Impending Crisis: 1848–1861*. Completed by Don E. Fehrenbacher. New York: Harper Perennial, 2011.

Randall, James G. *The Civil War and Reconstruction*. Boston: D. C. Heath and Company, 1937.

Remini, Robert V. *The Life of Andrew Jackson*. New York: Harper Perennial, 2010.

———. *Martin Van Buren and the Making of the Democratic Party*. New York: Columbia University Press, 1959.

Rove, Karl. *The Triumph of William McKinley: Why the Election of 1896 Still Matters*. New York: Simon & Schuster, 2016.

Ruddy, Daniel. *Theodore the Great: Conservative Crusader*. Washington, DC: Regnery, 2016.

Schlesinger, Arthur, Jr. *The Age of Jackson*. Boston: Little, Brown and Company, 1945.

Schweikart, Larry. *America's Victories: Why the U.S. Wins Wars and Will Win the War on Terror*. Point Pleasant, NJ: Knox Press, 2015.

———. "Jacksonian Ideology, Currency Control, and 'Central Banking': A Reappraisal," *Historian* 51 (November 1988): 78–102.

———. *Seven Events that Made America America*. New York: Sentinel, 2010.

———, and Dave Dougherty. *A Patriot's History of the Modern World, vol. I: From America's Exceptional Ascent to the Atomic Bomb: 1898–1945*. New York: Sentinel, 2012.

———, Dave Dougherty, and Michael Allen. *A Patriot's History Reader: Essential Documents for Every American*. New York: Sentinel, 2011.

———, and Michael Allen. *A Patriot's History of the United States: From Columbus's Great Discovery to America's Age of Entitlement*. 10th Anniversary Edition. New York: Sentinel, 2014.

Sellers, Charles Grier. "Andrew Jackson vs. the Historians," *Mississippi Valley Historical Review* 44 (March 1958): 615–34.

Smith, Hamilton. "The Interpretation of the Arsenic Content of Human Hair," *Journal of the Forensic Science Society*, vol. 4, summarized in Sten Forshufvud and Ben Weider, *Assassination at St. Helena*. Vancouver, Canada: Mitchell Press, 1978.

Smith, Jean Edward. *Grant*. New York: Simon and Schuster, 2001.

Smith, Jeffrey K. *Grover Cleveland: The Last Conservative Democratic President*. Scotts Valley, CA: CreateSpace, 2016.

Smith, Justin H. *The Annexation of Texas*. New York: Baker and Taylor, 1911.

Temin, Peter. *The Jacksonian Economy*. Boston: Norton, 1969.

Tennert, Robert. *Alternative to Extinction: Federal Indian Policy and the Beginnings of the Reservation System, 1846–51*. Temple University, 1975.

Timberlake, Richard H. *The Origins of Central Banking*. New York: Harvard, 1978.

Trefousse, Hans L. *Rutherford B. Hayes*. New York: Times Books, 2002.

Wheelan, Joseph. *Jefferson's War: America's First War on Terror, 1801–1805*. New York: Carroll & Graf, 2003.

White, Leonard D. *The Jeffersonians: A Study in Administrative History, 1801–1829*. New York: Macmillan, 1951.

Woodward, C. Vann. *Reunion and Reaction: The Compromise of 1877 and the End of Reconstruction*. New York: Oxford University Press, 1991.

Unger, Harlow Giles. *The Last Founding Father: James Monroe and a Nation's Call to Greatness*. Philadelphia: Da Capo Press, 2009.

Unger, Irwin. *These United States: The Questions of Our Past*. Concise Edition, 4 vols. Upper Saddle River, NJ: Prentice Hall, 2002.

Zinn, Howard. *A People's History of the United States*. New York: Harper Perennial Modern Classics, 2015.

Index

Index